De Gaulle's Foreign Policy

1944-1946

De Gaulle's Foreign Policy 1944-1946

A. W. DePorte

Harvard University Press
Cambridge, Massachusetts
1968

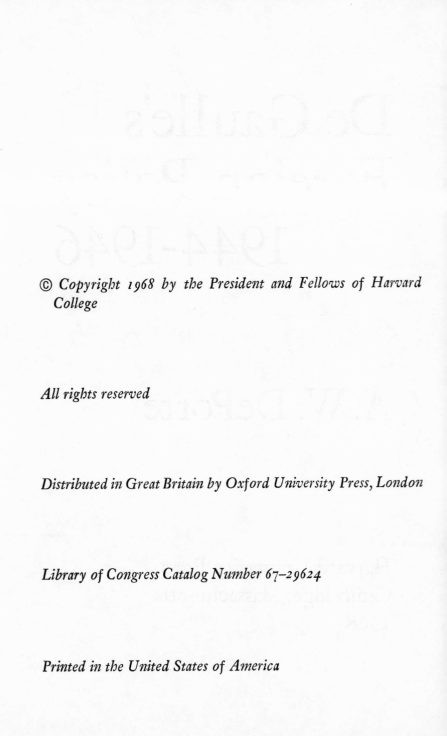

To E.M.S.

PREFACE

The least known period of Charles de Gaulle's political career is that of his rule of liberated France from August, 1944, until his resignation from the presidency of the provisional government of the French Republic on January 20, 1946. De Gaulle's writings prior to 1940 have been closely studied because they are intrinsically interesting and because they throw light on his later career. His wartime role as the leader of Free France—his "heroic period"—is increasingly well documented, not least by his brilliantly written war memoirs. His activities between 1947 and 1953 as the leader of the Rally of the French People have been the subject of a considerable literature, and of course de Gaulle's rule of France since 1958 continues to be dealt with in a flood of commentary and analysis. Relatively little study, however, has been given to the seventeen months in 1944–1946 when de Gaulle spoke, not for a refugee organization subsisting largely on the largesse of its great allies, but as the leader of an enfeebled but nevertheless independent state which aspired in all its acts to establish its security and regain its status as a Great Power.

Perhaps the relative neglect of this year and a half arises from the fact that it is, from a dramatic point of view, an anticlimax to de Gaulle's reappearance in liberated France as the head of its government. The last nine months of the Second World War and the nine months that followed it were hard for de Gaulle and for France. He achieved much but seemingly also failed of much, and his memoirs trail away as if the period held little interest for him. The surface mood is one of deepening sadness, ending with the bleak Sunday in January when he resigned from office and began an exile from power that was to last for over twelve years.

The events of 1945, however, are of great interest in themselves, and France, though it was not a first rank participant in them, was nevertheless deeply involved. Beyond this, de Gaulle's postwar rule can also profitably be studied for what it tells us of the origins of the foreign policy of the Fourth Republic—and the Fifth. As I hope to show, many lines of French foreign policy laid down by de Gaulle in 1944–1945 provided the foundations for the policies of his successors of the Fourth Republic. But our main interest today in this first period of Gaullist rule is obviously tied to our interest in the second. Indeed, I cannot but speculate—even though de Gaulle's second exercise of power may still be far from its end—whether its pattern may not resemble that of the first: a striving, almost heroic on the personal level, after goals that finally cannot be attained, and an ending in disappointment but not without some legacy to those that come after. However this may be, there is enough success in the earlier period to remind us—and it is sometimes overlooked—that de Gaulle is really a miracle man of politics. This is the man who brought France from where it was in June, 1940, to where it was in 1945, and who returned from the political graveyard in 1958 after an absence of twelve years. He is clearly a man with reason to believe he can accomplish tasks that others think grossly unrealistic, although this does not mean that he has been or will finally be proven right in this belief.

De Gaulle is widely thought of as an enigma or a sphinx, all-knowing and all-seeing, and his worst blunders are explained away by some as arising from plans too subtle to be appreciated by the vulgar eye. He, indeed, has purposely cultivated an air of mystery, deliberation beyond the normal, and omniscience. In fact, his purposes are in most cases nearer the surface than those of some other contemporary statesmen who have not sought—or do not enjoy—his theatrical success. It is also true, however, that de Gaulle's tactics can sometimes be uncommonly devious, although not necessarily disproportionately to the problem (as, for example, in the case of the Algerian conflict). At any rate he is treated by friends and opponents as a man apart, whose words and acts receive a sometimes undeserved amount of scrutiny, to the point that they have become the subject of a new pseudo-science, Elyseeology. The word and the idea may be absurd, but they are a tribute to the man and are evidence of the interest in his policy.

This book undertakes to examine de Gaulle's conduct of French foreign policy in the 1944–1946 period, presenting the story in its own terms, although underlining developments that seem to cast particular light on the policies of the Fourth and the Fifth Republic. It presents at least one advantage in that it deals with de Gaulle's actions as well as his words—a distinction that is always valuable in considering his policy. The first chapter outlines French foreign policy between 1918 and 1940. While this is an appropriate introduction to the main body of the work, I should like it to be read also as an attempt to place de Gaulle himself within a certain tradition of French diplomacy. Much has been made of his nationalism, and many have compared him to Richelieu, Louis XIV, and Napoleon I, among others. I think it is pertinent to note that in fact the roots of his policy—if not of his mystique or his basic political attitudes—are rather more recent than the careers of these figures. Need we look much farther afield than Raymond Poincaré and Louis Barthou to find de Gaulle's predecessors? What I hope will be clear from the first chapter is that these men had very few active followers in the France of the late 1930's, and the tradition in foreign policy that they represent has tended to be overlooked since 1940. Between those in France who accepted dependence on Germany and those who accepted dependence on Great Britain, those who refused any dependence at all were a remarkably small minority. The point is of further interest because of de Gaulle's still obsessive fear of depending on allies. It is well to remember that his experience of the problem did not begin with his much advertised wartime difficulties but is rooted in what he saw in France during the long agony of the 1930's.

Chapter II reviews de Gaulle's wartime experience. Besides providing an outline of the essential facts, it underlines his wartime preoccupation not only with the actual liberation of France but with the full restoration of its territories (in Europe and overseas) *and* its status as a Great Power. This chapter deals with the long quarrel between the Free French and the western Allies, or, more particularly, between de Gaulle and Roosevelt. This has been discussed at length in several books, and I have tried, while presenting the Free French approach to these problems, to avoid going too deeply into judgments on their merits, which are probably more subtle than is sometimes thought.[1] Personalities no doubt entered into this quarrel, but its root was simply a basic divergence between de Gaulle and Roosevelt on the present and future *status* of France. For de Gaulle the defeat of 1940 was a temporary event, in no way depriving France of her inherent prerogatives as a Great Power; that is, in no way changing her *nature*. For Roosevelt, France had been eliminated for an indefinite period from among the powers with the means to influence events in a major way and therefore with the right to do so.

Roosevelt's judgment of the matter—from his wartime point of view—was not absurd, though it might be described as brutal or realistic depending on one's preference. He has been severely criticized, however, for his drawn-out refusal to accept de Gaulle as the spokesman for France, his attempts to deal with other

French leaders, his belief that de Gaulle could not achieve or hold power by democratic means in postwar France, and his hardly disguised unwillingness to see the prewar French colonial empire restored. Certainly it seems that Roosevelt held back from recognizing de Gaulle's position for too long. No doubt, also, he was misinformed on the extent of de Gaulle's support among the French resistance groups and therefore radically underestimated the general's ability to establish his authority in France after the liberation. But, we should remember, had Roosevelt lived another nine months he would have seen de Gaulle deprived of organized political support and driven from office. Perhaps Roosevelt erred most basically in his somewhat strange inability to grasp the historic significance of de Gaulle's gesture in saying NO to the defeat of France. Roosevelt himself was sensitive to the grand gesture; why de Gaulle's left him cold is still something of a puzzle.

Roosevelt's reluctance to see the French Empire restored was sometimes expressed in an offhand or even breezy manner. But was de Gaulle's attempt in 1945 to impose France's will on Syria and Lebanon by force a precedent for which his successors of the Fourth Republic—who followed his example for the most part—had reason to thank him? In this instance, Roosevelt's insight into the implications of the war for the colonial empires of the world was far clearer than de Gaulle's. (It is, of course, one of the ironies of de Gaulle's career, and of history, that he himself was to return to power in 1958 because his successors were unable to deal with these very problems; he then had to complete the liquidation of the French Empire after 1958.)

The remaining chapters of the book are grouped, partly chronologically and partly topically, in a way that should require no further explanation. The inclusion of a certain amount

of material dealing with French domestic affairs is warranted by
the fact that de Gaulle's actions, including his foreign policy,
never took place in a vacuum. During the war his relations with
the underground resistance within France were critical for his
eventual success, and after the liberation his freedom of action,
even in foreign affairs, was conditioned to some extent by the
political groups represented in his government.

The point is not labored in the text, but one can hardly consider the main events and attitudes of French foreign policy
during this period—the Franco-Soviet pact, the distrust of allies
and their "blocs," the attempts to organize groupings in-between
those blocs, the suggestions of a Western European entity of
some kind in which Germany, or part of it, could find a place,
and, above all, the constant thrust for Great Power status—
without thinking also of Gaullist France today. We cannot fail
to be struck by de Gaulle's many setbacks in the earlier period,
but also by the fact that French status, his most basic objective,
which was not achieved during his own tenure of office, was
won by his successors. The last meeting of the Big Three without France was at Moscow in December, 1945—until (further
irony!) the same Big Three met in the same city in July, 1963,
to sign a nuclear test ban treaty from which de Gaulle excluded
himself. But de Gaulle's second act is not yet played out; we
shall reserve judgment on his successes and failures. Perhaps this
book will turn out to be the first of two. In that case the simi-
larities and contrasts between the Gaullist policy of 1945 and
that of the Fifth Republic would be clearer. In any case, the
story of 1945 deserves telling for its intrinsic interest and significance.

A brief comment is in order on the problem of sources. Official papers of the French government, with the exception of
those published by de Gaulle in his memoirs and a scattering of

others, are unavailable. The reader will observe, in addition, that documentation from any quarter on such matters as the London session of the Council of Foreign Ministers (September, 1945) and the politics of the German occupation in the latter part of 1945, is quite defective. Further publications in the *Foreign Relations of the United States* series should help to fill some of these gaps in the relatively near future. These problems, however, are among the servitudes—and not the only ones—of writing contemporary history.

Most of the work on this book was completed before I became an employee of the United States Department of State. All judgments and conclusions in it are entirely my own.

A. W. DePorte

Washington, D.C.
July 1, 1967

ACKNOWLEDGEMENTS

The author would like to thank General Charles de Gaulle, President of the French Republic, for permission to quote from the J. B. Lippincott edition of his *The Army of the Future*. He would also like to thank the following publishers for permission to quote material copyrighted by them: Librairie Plon, *Mémoires de Guerre*, by Charles de Gaulle; *Foreign Affairs*, "The Permanent Bases of French Foreign Policy," by Jules Cambon; and *Le Monde*.

CONTENTS

De Gaulle's
Foreign Policy

1944-1946

CHAPTER I

INTRODUCTION: THE DECAY OF FRENCH FOREIGN POLICY

In January, 1930, there appeared in *Foreign Affairs* an essay by Jules Cambon, the veteran French diplomat, on "The Permanent Bases of French Foreign Policy."[1] In this summary and rationalization of contemporary French policy, Cambon argued that despite apparent change and diversity, the history, and particularly the foreign policy, of nations are obedient to certain laws. "Revolutions," he wrote, "do not work any definite change; the institutions which a people set up are only the expression of its ideas at a certain moment, and they do not modify its position with regard to other nations. The relations of a government with foreign governments may be affected, but not the necessities imposed upon it by its geographical position, its need to live, its history. That is what we call its traditions. . . . The geographical position of a nation, indeed, is the principal factor conditioning its foreign policy—the principal reason why it must have a foreign policy at all."

The "insular" policies of Great Britain and the United States, Cambon held, are to be traced to their geographical situations, whereas France, behind her open northern and eastern frontiers, has been obliged to rely on military power in her eternal quest for security. The traditional policy of France was inaugurated in the sixteenth century by Francis I who, menaced on every side by the Habsburg dominions, sought security for France by creating equilibrium in Europe; that is, by forming alliances with distant powers, such as Turkey, and with the weaker princes. This "classical policy" was occasionally abandoned by the French; but the adventures of Louis XIV and the aggressions of Napoleon I, who did not think in terms of purely French interests, were mere episodes standing out from the traditional defensive quest for security. Henry IV, Sully, Richelieu, Mazarin, Vergennes, Talleyrand, the ministers of the Third Republic—all sought to achieve French security by alliances with the smaller states of Europe against the states that successively tried to win hegemony. Despite occasional aberrations of dynastic or ideological imperialisms, Cambon argued, "the tradition of our policy was something altogether different; it cared only for France; it was essentially conservative, circumspect, deliberate." This traditional policy of France had never been as manifest as in the period after 1918: "M. Briand . . . has found his inspiration in the same order of ideas that governed apostles of the balance of power. Political methods change, but the objectives remain the same. In essence, the traditional aims of France, the aims which she has today, center about the quest for security. And what is that but the maintenance of peace?"

For those who believed that the new order of things at Geneva outdated the traditional diplomacy of the balance of power, he added, "it would be a mistake to take this view. There are groups, cabals and oppositions inside the League of Nations, and though political action may take new forms, at heart it is the same. National aspirations are the expression of national interests, and these, as I have said, persist through the ages because human nature does not change." Thus France, even in the day of the new diplomacy, and speaking a new vocabulary, continued to pursue the aims she had sought with few exceptions since the sixteenth century: "Security! The term involves more indeed than the maintenance of a people's homeland, or even of their territories beyond the seas. It also means the maintenance of the world's respect for them, the maintenance of their economic interests, everything, in a word, which goes to make up the grandeur, the life itself, of the nation." In short, the goal of classical French policy had been defined to mean not only the physical inviolability of the frontiers and the integrity of the Empire, but also the maintenance of her "grandeur"— her status as a Great Power.

Divesting this analysis of its claim to embody the eternal principles of French foreign policy and considering it as a generalized expression of traditional or "classical" thought on foreign policy since 1870, the following principles appear as the fixed bases of that policy:

1. The goal of policy is the maintenance of French security, which includes both the physical integrity of the territory and the maintenance of France's international position—of her Great Power status.

2. The basic methods of policy are military strength and alliance with other states equally threatened by the powers that challenged the status quo, of which France, after 1919, was the foremost defender.

3. To these ends, new forms, such as the League of Nations, could be utilized, but without ever losing sight of the basic power realities of international politics.

During the two decades between the wars, however, French foreign policy retreated from these principles. This was manifest not only in the work of most of the foreign ministers after 1933, but also, in varying degrees, in that of the two diplomats who, almost without interruption, represented the continuity of policy at the Quai d'Orsay between 1920 and 1940: Philippe Berthelot and Alexis Léger, the successive secretaries-general.

When Philippe Berthelot became secretary-general of the Foreign Ministry in September, 1920, the central problem of French diplomacy was the preservation for France of the security created for her by the victory and the peace settlements.[2] But the alliance which, as the diplomats knew well, had brought France victory in the war was in full dissolution by 1920. Revolutionary Russia had been removed from the councils of the Great Powers; the United States had rejected the treaty of alliance with France for which France had abandoned her demand for permanent detachment of the Rhineland from Germany; and, as a consequence of the American action, Great Britain had been released from her contingent and parallel engagement. The grand alliance of the war was replaced by French alliances with the small states of central Europe: Poland, Czechoslovakia, Rumania, and Yugoslavia. The exchange was a poor one for France. But as partial compensation for this loss of major allies, France enjoyed two advantages unknown in 1914. The first was the League of Nations, which, however tenuous and imperfect, was a potentially valuable instrument for the preservation of the status quo in the name of the abstract principles of peace and general security, and also a link to Britain and other states. The second novel element in Europe, and the most significant for the French position, was the forced and artificial reduction of German power by the Treaty of Versailles. Disarmed, heavily indebted by reparations, and with the Rhineland occupied and demilitarized, Germany was reduced to a level of power which it seemed possible for France and her small allies to equilibrate. As long as the demilitarization of the Rhineland was maintained, any German attack on her eastern neighbors could be followed by the incursion of the French army across the demilitarized zone into the heart of Germany—provided, of course, that the French army retained its offensive mobility and that French policy retained the will to act. For French diplomacy, it seemed, security had at last been won and had only to be preserved.

Berthelot apparently tried to bridge the old and the new diplomacy; that is, to adjust to the league and "diplomacy of conference" without sacrificing the traditional elements of French security, including military strength, guarantees, and alliances. Somewhat skeptical of the league and a believer in the alliance system as being more nearly in accord with the nature of man, he was the strongest advocate of Eastern European ties. Yet he believed also that Germany could not be indefinitely coerced, and, above all, he opposed any policy which might endanger the British entente—the beginning of a dependence which was to mark French foreign policy deeply in the 1930's.

Berthelot's views did not coincide with those of Raymond Poincaré, who dominated French policy in the first half of the 1920's and who favored the pursuit of an independent French policy and strict enforcement of the Treaty of Versailles, even over British opposition. Accordingly, Berthelot was ejected from office in 1922. The Ruhr invasion of 1923, however, which was the summit of Poincaré's independent policy, not only ended in a check to that policy but had a far more important long-term result. Because of the psychological reaction to this disappointment, little serious thought was given in France thereafter to the occupation of German territory in defense of the Versailles settlement. The unpopularity of the Ruhr episode partly contributed to the defeat of Poincaré in the elections of 1924, and, as a result, Aristide Briand presently replaced him at the Quai. Although the 1924 coalition of the left was soon destroyed by financial crisis, and Poincaré returned to power to "save the franc," there was no return to his foreign policy. Briand remained practically the permanent minister of foreign affairs. The country, it has been said, demanded Poincaré's economics and Briand's foreign policy, and though the views of the former were unchanged, he could not dispense with the latter.

With the failure of the policy of coercion of Germany, Berthelot returned to his post of secretary-general in 1925, working this time with a minister inclined to implement Berthelot's analysis of the European situation. Although ties continued to be forged with Germany's eastern neighbors, the Locarno agreements of October 1925 embodied the new turn in French policy. To Germany, Locarno meant a return to the European family, entrance as a Great Power into the League of Nations, and a guarantee against future French invasion in enforcement of the treaty; to Britain, it meant a guarantee by her of France's frontier against Germany, and a general normalization of European relations; to France, Locarno solidified the British entente insofar as it provided a guarantee of her eastern frontier and, presumably, of the demilitarized Rhineland. But, on the other hand, it closed the door to future unilateral invasions of Germany in defense of the treaty; it placed France on the same level as Germany in the operation of the new guarantees; and, despite the inclusion of Franco-Polish and Franco-Czechoslovak alliances in the overall Locarno settlement, it divided Eastern from Western Europe in the degree to which the security of each area was guaranteed. Britain firmly declined to undertake any commitments in Eastern Europe beyond those involved in league membership, and France, to win the British guarantee of the Rhine frontier, in a sense agreed to follow the British lead in the event of a German attack in Eastern Europe.

Every alliance involves some limitation on the freedom of action of the parties, even when they are Great Powers, but

there was implicit in the Locarno accords a fundamental surrender of France's freedom of action and leadership into the
hands of Great Britain. The French might have hoped to balance this dependence by eastern alliances, but the eastern states
were weak and divided among themselves, and, above all, the
development of French military strategy in the late 1920's was
increasingly at variance with the alliance policy. The alliance
system relied for its effectiveness on the thrust of a mobile
French army across the demilitarized Rhineland in the event of
a German attack in the east. But by 1930 the long internal
political struggle over the nature and role of the army had been
resolved—with the concurrence of both right and left—in favor
of the "Maginot line system," that is, of a defensive, garrison
army. Although the French general staff favored the eastern
alliances, its strategic concept increasingly reduced their value.[3]

Thus implemented, the elements of French policy fell increasingly short of maintaining the guarantees of security seemingly
won in 1919. Berthelot himself was increasingly aware of this
and concealed his growing pessimism by taking refuge in the
routine of the Quai. The sense of drift and despair, so manifest
in French politics and diplomacy in the late 1930's, had already
laid hold of the first generation of postwar statesmen, perhaps
as early as 1925. Berthelot was one of the first of those diplomats who saw the basic insecurity of the French position but
who felt powerless to remedy it.

Alexis Léger, who succeeded Berthelot as Secretary-General
of the Foreign Ministry in 1932, had been Briand's *chef de
cabinet* for seven years and considered himself the heir to
Briand's policies.[4] Briand had maintained France's eastern ties,
conciliated the Weimar Republic, remained on close terms with
Britain, and through the Kellogg-Briand Pact, flimsy as it was,
forged at least a tenuous link with the United States and other

nations not otherwise connected to the French security system. This was the triple concentric circle of French policy: direct alliances with Germany's neighbors, the wider system of the League of Nations, and the worldwide bonds of the Pact of Paris. At the same time, the idea of European union was developed to provide a firmer basis for Franco-German conciliation and European peace.

But while Léger had supported Berthelot and Briand in their limited conciliation of Weimar, the threat to French security as guaranteed in the Versailles settlement was so evident in the rise of Hitler that the problem facing those adhering to the traditional analysis of French security was, after 1933, entirely one of containment; that is, in Léger's words, "to concentrate exclusively upon assembling all forces necessary for the exercise of collective action in prevention." Yet, though the advent of Hitler might have been expected to reconcile the friends and enemies of conciliating the Weimar Republic in France—the liberal supporters of the Briand-Berthelot policy and the traditional nationalists of the right—in fact the revolution in Germany increasingly involved French foreign policy in domestic ideological struggles and undermined the traditional security policy which these new conditions demanded. Although a partisan of collective security and resistance to Germany, Léger was to serve under a series of foreign ministers who, either from motives based in domestic policies or from simple lack of vision or will, lost sight of the traditional principles of French security and allowed the material guarantees of that security, won in 1919, to be lost in the pursuit of personal and extemporized policies.

The Four Power Pact of 1933, which inaugurated the period, belied postwar French policy by attempting to establish a Great Power directorate of European affairs. By including Germany and Italy, both of which favored treaty revision, and Britain, which did not oppose it, the pact isolated France from her small status quo allies, aroused their suspicions of her policy, and drove the most important of them, Poland, into a bilateral entente with Germany. The domestic disorder which led to the formation of the national government of Gaston Doumergue in February, 1934, marked the renewal of the political schism in France which was soon to haunt all effective foreign policy; but it also brought to the Quai the only foreign minister with whom Léger was able to develop his policies. Louis Barthou, a nationalist of the old school and a friend and disciple of Poincaré, made Léger's project for an "eastern Locarno" his own. This project was intended to bring the Soviet Union into the French security system. In other ways as well Barthou pursued a policy of integral resistance to German encroachments.

Barthou's assassination in October, 1934, left the Quai to Pierre Laval and, from his maladroit and unprepared visit to Rome early in 1935 through the long ambiguity of the Ethiopian crisis and the scuttling of the league, Laval's tenure was nothing less than disastrous to the traditional French system. The Franco-Soviet alliance, sole remnant of the "eastern Locarno," was signed on May 2, 1935, but remained without substance for lack of staff conversations and ancillary agreements with Poland and Rumania. Meanwhile, Italy was alienated by the farce of sanctions, the league undermined by their failure, and France's eastern allies given clear warning by Laval's flirtations with Germany and Italy that they could not rely on the guarantee of their security by Paris.

Emboldened by the disarray of the status quo powers, Germany reoccupied the Rhineland on March 7, 1936. Léger and his colleagues at the Quai particularly wished to preserve this last tangible guarantee of French security, and Léger believed that Great Britain would honor her Locarno commitment if France took the initiative of resistance. But Flandin, the foreign minister, excluded him from the conversations with the British government in London, and Léger returned to Paris convinced that war was now inevitable, at Germany's convenience—a war which would no longer involve only a police action on a limited scale, as was possible before March 7, but general mobilization and heavy sacrifice. To Léger, this conference at London, rather than Munich, marked the ruin of the French security system, for Germany was now free of the artificial restraints imposed upon her by the Treaty of Versailles. By remilitarizing the Rhineland, Germany had deprived France of the last guarantee of her own immediate territorial security and of that ultimate security which depended on her unimpeded access across the Rhineland to the heart of Germany in the event of a German attack on Poland or Czechoslovakia.

The virtual inability of France after 1936 to bring immediate relief to her eastern allies and the doubt, in view of British reluctance, whether she would even attempt to do so, in effect destroyed the possibility, small as it was, that Europe might be able to find a precarious equilibrium among four power units— Britain-France, Germany, the eastern states, and the U.S.S.R.— of whom the first and third, as status quo states, might have been able, at least for a time, to form a defensive alliance with either of the other two against whichever of them most threatened the peace at a given moment. The simplification of the power structure after 1936 into one of three units, of which only one was a defender of the status quo, meant that long-term stability was practically impossible, and that, for the short term, France could balance the growing power of Germany only by an understanding with the Soviet Union.

The French right, however, though the traditional defender of nationalist resistance to Germany, feared the implications of the Franco-Soviet pact, since it seemed to legitimatize the French Communist Party and to foreshadow a war with Germany which would assume the form of an anti-Fascist crusade. The loss of Italy as a "safe" ally during 1935 and the advent of the Popular Front to power in May, 1936, which implied some influence on French policy by the U.S.S.R. through the Communist Party, alienated the right even further from support of the measures required by French security. The Blum government itself was highly cautious in its foreign policy and increasingly dependent on Britain, and the Spanish Civil War called forth only the non-intervention policy, tailored to British wishes. More than once during this period Léger had wished to resign, but he always stayed on, carrying out policies of which he disapproved and hoping to restrain his ministers. By 1938 the General Staff still clung to the eastern allies, without making any attempt to develop a military policy which would give substance to those alliances, and the diplomats, working from hand to mouth, neither dared to abandon the eastern alliances, lest they admit that France no longer considered herself a Great Power, nor to perfect them by an accord with the Soviet Union. Foreign Minister Georges Bonnet, while seeking a way out, restated the old formulas as the Czech crisis approached, and willingly followed the British lead to Munich.

In the eleven months of peace following the Czech crisis, some of the *Munichois* in France frankly elaborated the theory that France should jettison her eastern commitments and fall back upon her own resources and her empire—an open abdication of her Great Power status in Europe. Yet when Britain at last reversed her policy and gave a guarantee to Poland on March 31, 1939, France, having followed her through appeasement, now followed her toward resistance. But the negotiations with the Soviet Union, more indispensable than ever to the success of a policy of resistance, were pursued through the spring and summer in a desultory manner, and Léger himself discounted the possibility of a Russo-German agreement. The Ribbentrop-Molotov pact of August 23 took from the western allies any real hope of victory over Germany, yet the attack on Poland left them no choice other than resistance or total bankruptcy. They chose the former, but the slow and reluctant drift from semi-peace to semi-war lacked the sudden and dramatic sweep which had bred the *Union Sacrée* of 1914. Internal division and dissension continued during the *drôle de guerre* of 1939–1940, and in the spring Léger himself fell a victim to the intrigues which surrounded the Reynaud government. The end of the diplomatic career of one whom the Germans were said to have named the "last defender of the last French victory" was followed within a few weeks by the end of the Third Republic itself.

An essential point of departure for any study of the decline of France from the strong position of 1919 to the debacle of 1940 is the fact that, after the colossal manpower losses of the First World War, the French were perhaps more war-weary than any other nation and more determined than any other to avoid a repetition of these losses—the more so as victory seemed to have assured security. Politicians knew that they could find favor with their constituents by avoiding war, and were confirmed in this belief by the unpopularity of the Ruhr adventure of 1923–1924 and the political reverse suffered by its champion, Poincaré, as a consequence. After 1924, an occupation of German territory in defense of the Versailles settlement was never again seriously in question. In addition, the military staff, generalizing on the conditions of the war, fixed their strategy in terms of a permanent "trench," the Maginot line, behind which France would hold off the enemy with a minimum of losses until the resources of her maritime allies could be brought to bear, as in 1917–1918. Such a strategy, however, was at variance with the policy of eastern alliances promoted by the military as well as by the diplomatic authorities, which implied that mobile French units would be able to sweep across the demilitarized Rhineland into the heart of Germany in the event of a German attack on Poland or Czechoslovakia. But the dominant states of mind—determination to avoid war and to minimize losses if it came—prevailed over this analysis and put military policy sharply at odds with diplomatic.

The conservatism of the policies of the military staff and their obsession with the methods of the war of 1914–1918 have often been cited in connection with the French defeat of 1940. But many diplomats and politicians were no less the prisoners of the concepts of the First World War than most of the military. These men were convinced that victory had been won only because of the French alliances; they were therefore inclined to put an overwhelming importance on her postwar alliances and, above all, on the entente with Great Britain, which in their eyes assumed an unquestioned importance because of the doubtful quality of the eastern alliances. Their analysis, valid for 1914 and the war itself, was less so for the postwar period, when the artificial reduction of German power by the peace settlement made the Versailles guarantees, rather than alliances, the core of French security. But this infatuation with the British entente led French policymakers, as early as Locarno, to abandon France's independence of judgment and action in return for the British guarantee against a German attack. The Briand-Berthelot policy of conciliating the Weimar Republic pleased the British and was perhaps worth trying, though, as Berthelot seems to have realized, it provided no permanent solution to the German problem. But when conciliation should have been replaced by resistance, after 1933, the French diplomats followed

Britain in successive abandonments of the guarantees provided France by the Versailles settlement, and the more they abandoned, the more they clung to Great Britain. Thus, even those who saw the German menace in its true proportions were unable to respond to it as was required; for example, in the decisive instance of the Rhineland crisis of 1936, or by an agreement with the U.S.S.R. for which neither Britain nor French opinion was prepared.

While French policy had thus practically abandoned the nation's Great Power status in return for British protection—which was both uncertain and inadequate to the menace—French opinion, rather than uniting before the growing danger, was increasingly divided on ideological lines. In addition to the practically universal abhorrence of war and the blind reliance placed by many on the Maginot line—prompted, perhaps, by fear of alternative policies—many on the right, though traditionally anti-German, now feared their internal enemies more than the enemies of France. The more extreme of these were prepared by 1939 to accept German hegemony in Europe in the hope that France might find some place, even as a subordinate, in the New Order. Others attempted to conceal France's abdication in Eastern Europe by theorizing on the development and self-containment of the empire.

Although some were ready to abandon the traditional French policy, including resistance to Germany and the search for physical security, many others clung to security on the narrowest and most inadequate basis and sacrificed all real guarantees to the British entente, which could not give security but which had the great advantage of relieving France of the burden of making the decision for war. Thus, not only by her retreat from Eastern Europe but by her increasing acceptance of British leadership, France plainly signified her reluctance, or inability, to play the independent role of a Great Power. Both those who would surrender to Germany and many of those who wished to resist were agreed that France could not play her former independent and leading role. As D. W. Brogan has said, comparing the French state of mind in 1939 with that in 1914: ". . . what was changed was the disappearance of the old French unity around the idea of the powerful and independent role of France as a great Power."[5]

CHAPTER II

FREE FRANCE AND THE RESISTANCE

Charles de Gaulle

The French defeat of 1940 seemed to confirm the policy of those who had already proclaimed that the future of France lay within the German New Order. By throwing the defenders of the Third Republic into disarray, it allowed the enemies of the regime, as so often in French history, to utilize national disaster for factional advantage by establishing themselves in power. The National Revolution of Vichy convinced many Frenchmen in the first shocked months after the armistice that the country had deserved defeat because of its social and political iniquities and must seek redemption in contrition and discipline. Only eighty votes were cast in the National Assembly on July 10 against the law granting full powers to Marshal Pétain, and it was many months before there was any widespread movement within France to resist the German occupant or his Vichy allies. A small number, however, had left France before the surrender and, despite the magnitude of the defeat and the precarious position of the British, refused from the first to accept either Vichy or the armistice, blindly placing their faith in an Allied victory when there seemed little reason indeed to hope for it.[1] Most important among these was General

Charles de Gaulle who, on June 18, 1940, first raised the banner
of Free France.

De Gaulle had made something of a name for himself in the
1930's by his appeals for a mechanized army, and he had worked
with Paul Reynaud in unsuccessful efforts to secure its adoption
by parliament and the military staffs. Long before June, 1940,
he had evolved the clear-cut concepts of the place of France in
the world and of French foreign policy that are basic to any
appraisal of his work as the leader of Free France and of the
Provisional French Government that assumed power in the
summer of 1944. The dominant element of de Gaulle's political
psychology is his almost mystic patriotism and his conception
of the unique role of France in the world:

> All my life I have had a certain idea of France. Feel-
> ing has inspired me as well as reason. What is emotional
> in me readily imagines France, like the princess in the
> fairy tales or the madonna of the frescoes, consecrated
> to an eminent and exceptional destiny. I have the in-
> stinctive impression that Providence has created her for
> perfect successes or model misfortunes. If it nevertheless
> happens that mediocrity marks her acts and gestures, I
> have the feeling that it is an absurd anomaly, attribut-
> able to the faults of the French but not to the genius of
> the country. Further, the positive side of my mind con-
> vinces me that France is really herself only in the first
> rank; that only great enterprises can compensate for the
> ferments of dispersion which her people carry in them-
> selves; that our country, such as it is, among the others,
> such as they are, must under threat of mortal danger
> aim high and hold firm. In short, to me France cannot
> be France without grandeur.[2]

For de Gaulle, as for Cambon, the security, the very existence of France as such cannot be distinguished from her grandeur. Even if nominally independent, a France reduced below the first rank of a Great Power would cease to be France.

De Gaulle's analysis of the international position of France, as expressed in his important prewar book, *Vers l'Armée de Métier*, is based—again like Cambon's—on the geographical realities of the nation:

> As looking at a portrait suggests the impression of the subject's destiny to the observer, so the map of France tells our own fortune. The body of the country has in its centre a citadel, a forbidding mass of age-old mountains, flanked by the table-lands of Provence, Limousin, and Burgundy; and, all around, vast slopes, for the most part difficult of access to anyone attacking them from the outside and split by the gorges of the Saône, the Rhone and the Garonne, barred by the walls of the Jura Alps and the Pyrenees or else plunging in the distance into the English Channel, the Atlantic, or the Mediterranean; but in the Northeast, there is a terrible breach between the essential basins of the Seine and of the Loire and German territory. The Rhine, which nature meant the Gauls to have as their boundary and their protection, has hardly touched France before it leaves her and lays her open to attack.
>
> This breach in the ramparts is the age-old weakness of the country. Through it, Roman Gaul saw the Barbarians hurl themselves upon her wealth. It was there that the Monarchy struggled to resist the pressure of the Holy Roman Empire. There, Louis XIV defended his power against the combined forces of Europe. The

Revolution all but came to grief there. Napoleon suc-
cumbed there. In 1870, disaster and shame advanced
along the same road. In this fatal passage-way we recently buried one-third of our young men. Quite apart
from war crises, with what a heavy load has the possession of this weak frontier burdened France!

How many projects have proved abortive, how many
hopes have been shattered, how many enterprises
brought to nothing, all for want of a good hedge around
the estate! The command of the sea has been lost, our
expansion has been mortgaged, we have made alliances
for which we pay too dearly, we have to submit to ex-
tortion and have been forced to abandon positions, and
the people themselves, ceaselessly obsessed by the same
threat, are in a constant state of uneasiness, division and
irritation.

Besides, this chronic danger becomes greater as time
goes on. For Paris to be where she is no doubt mattered
little to a Carolingian. People living under the Capets
took a more serious view of the situation. Under the
Valois, they thought of little else. Under the Bourbons
it became intolerable. Nineteenth-century France endured its crushing slavery. Think of it during the Great
War! What will it be like tomorrow? There are but a
hundred and twenty-five miles between Paris and the
frontier, six days' march, three hours by motor-car, an
hour by aeroplane. A single reverse at the sources of the
Oise, and the Louvre is within gun range. . . .

The policy of a state, said Napoleon, is decided by its
geography. France has, through the centuries, sought
by diplomacy the protection which nature has denied
her. Others have been able to concentrate on the dom-

ination of the seas, the exploitation of distant lands and of free outlets, the uniting of a scattered race; but what haunts us most is the safety of our own hexagonal territory. All the schemes prepared and treaties concluded by France during the past thousand years have had as their object the establishment of a political system which should prevent our enemies from molesting us. . . .[3]

These paragraphs clearly amplify and elaborate the thought of Cambon, who not only said, "The geographical position of a nation, indeed, is the principal factor conditioning its foreign policy—the principal reason why it must have a foreign policy at all," but who also emphasized the conservative character of French policy—always in search of the security denied it by geography. In this, as in his emphasis on France's essential status as a Great Power, de Gaulle shares the traditional analysis of Poincaré, Cambon, and Barthou.

To what extent did de Gaulle accept the attempts made to adopt this basic analysis to postwar realities? He recognized that France after 1919 was destined to protect the status quo, and because he repudiated the purely defensive Maginot line strategy, he agreed with the diplomats in rejecting a policy of French isolation. He looked, however, with a rather sceptical eye on international organization and treaty-signing as substitutes for effective guarantees of French security:

It is true that France, disappointed by the old political system, is seeking, in a new international order of things, the security she used to find in her traditional methods of procedure. The dream of France is, preeminently, that of an organized world, where the strictness of the law, the moderateness of desires and the ubiquity of the police would guarantee peace for all and allow everyone to live his own life. Tired as we are of adventures, well provided for in land and factories, overloaded with colonies, our interests become confused with this hope. . . . A thousand practical or noble reasons make France to-day the Penelope of international work. From this comes the network of pacts, protocols, and general acts which she is trying to weave around the world. . . .

Meanwhile, time passes and it does not seem as though all these efforts have helped to make France more secure. No doubt, by taking advantage of the credit conferred on our idealism through victory, and of the personal tact of our statesmen, helped by a certain Anglo-Saxon piety, it has at times been able to give the statue an appearance of life. But, first and foremost, there is nothing legal nor efficacious to oppose to violence.[4]

Therefore, as a soldier whose political wisdom is imbued with military caution—"Justice which does not bear a sword beside its scales soon falls into ridicule"—de Gaulle sees the ultimate security of France in her armed forces.[5]

Gaping wide open, exposing her defenceless body to blows, deprived of all respite and all refuge, where, then, can our country find her latent protection except in arms? The sword is not only the last argument in her quarrels; it is also the only thing that makes up for her weakness. Everything that is ill-adapted in her territory, absurd in her political system, infirm in her character has, in the last resort, nothing to offset it but the warlike arts, the skill of her troops, the sufferings of her soldiers.[6]

From these passages it is clear that, in general, de Gaulle's political vocabulary is that of realism. He views the multiplicity of international organizations and treaties as the thinnest of coverings for the permanent national interests, expressed in force and violence, which lie eternally beneath. His concepts of foreign policy in the 1930's were those of the traditional French nationalists and were not greatly affected by the application made of those concepts by the postwar officials of the Quai d'Orsay. He accepted the status quo position of France after 1919 and looked for security in alliances and in a highly efficient and organized military force, relying on quality in default of quantity. Above all, in his insistence on French independence and greatness, de Gaulle stood apart not only from those who would accept a secondary position within a German New Order or who attempted to describe French surrender in Europe as "imperial retreat," but also from the diplomats and politicians who, while willing to resist Germany, sacrificed French initiative and leadership to the British alliance. His nationalism and his dedication to the idea of French independence in greatness are less the concepts of Berthelot or Léger than of Clemenceau and Poincaré—and few Frenchmen indeed, whether appeasers or resisters, still held to this position by 1939.

On the basis of these ideas, it is not difficult to understand the role which de Gaulle in 1940 assigned to himself and his movement. The whole rationale of the Free French movement lies in his conviction that, although France could be physically liberated by a British or Allied victory, she could regain her true independence, that is, her status as a Great Power, only by playing a significant and above all an autonomous role in the war. To those who thought that the overseas French could best serve in the British forces, or that the Free French organization itself could be a British auxiliary, de Gaulle firmly insisted that the important object was to bring back into the war not a group of Frenchmen but France herself.[7] In speech after speech during the war, de Gaulle reiterated that French might must be present at the victory, which must also be a French victory.[8]

The discrepancy between the means available to de Gaulle in June 1940 and the enormity of the task which he set himself was not lost on him: "I seemed to myself, alone and deprived of everything, like a man at the edge of an ocean across which he intended to swim!"[9] But while he himself may have felt a challenge similar to that which he believed Churchill was experiencing at the same moment, he had no illusions about the difficulty of the undertaking or the means necessary to achieve success.[10] A policy of large claims conducted in the antechambers of the more powerful, with borrowed strength, was not conducive to respect or success and required, in de Gaulle's view, all the singleness of purpose, the rigidity and inflexibility with which he was taxed by his Allies. If his proud nationalism and military antecedents fitted him by character for such a role, there seems little doubt that it was consciously cultivated as a necessity of his position:

It is by acting as the inflexible champion of the nation and the state that it would be possible for me to gain the consent and even the enthusiasm of the French and the respect and consideration of foreigners. The people who throughout the drama were shocked by this intransigence did not want to see that for me, strained to resist innumerable contrary pressures, the least bending might have led to collapse. In short, circumscribed and alone as I was, and exactly because I was, I had to reach the summits and never more descend.[11]

However irritating to the Allies, de Gaulle's jealous and stubborn defense of French interests, great and small, substantial and symbolic, was also, as he knew, an important factor in refuting Vichy's charge that he was a British puppet, and eventually it helped him win the support of the French people for his movement.[12]

In the same way, the egocentrism and the "messianism" often laid at de Gaulle's door were expressions of the position he filled. Whatever vision of himself led him to undertake this role, he does no violence to the situation of June, 1940, when he says that, at the worst moment of the history of his country, "it was for me to assume France." It was no more than natural for the role that he thus assumed—"a sort of priesthood" in his own terms—to condition his personal behavior: "The fact that I incarnated, for my companions the destiny of our cause, for the French multitude the symbol of hope, for foreigners the face of a France indomitable in the midst of trials, governed my behavior and imposed on my person an attitude which I could no longer change. It was for me, without respite, a strong internal tutelage and at the same time a most heavy yoke." Thus, when pressed by Churchill to imitate him in displaying flexibility, de Gaulle answered: "You can do it . . . because you are established on a solid state, an assembled nation, a united Empire, with great armies. But I! Where are my means? Yet I am charged, as you know, with the interests and the fate of France. It is too heavy, and I am too poor to be able to bend."[13]

It was thus not merely the rigidities of his character or a deluded notion of French grandeur that led de Gaulle to take positions which gave the impression that he was more often at war with the Allies than with the Germans. On the contrary, this attitude was a calculated response to his situation. He desired, first, to reanimate French pride and nationalism after the blow of 1940. He judged—absorbing the painful lesson of the 1930's—that reliance on others had led France to disaster and that she must henceforth, if necessary, resist and defy her allies, whose interests could not, by definition, always be the same as hers. He saw also that the postwar world would be controlled by the major Allies, and that France, whose future status would be defined in relation to them, must emphasize on every occasion the independent, Great Power role which she expected to play so that they would become accustomed to the idea despite its apparent incongruity with the actual state of France after 1940.

Free France

As early as the middle of May, 1940, when the battle of France was moving to its disastrous conclusion, de Gaulle, according to his own account, had resolved to continue the war wherever and for as long as was necessary, until the enemy was defeated and the honor of France cleared. Promoted to brigadier general in May and named under-secretary of war in the reorganized Reynaud government on June 6, de Gaulle strongly defended the position, in the debates which filled the last days of that government, that France still retained the means to continue the war: "If the situation cannot finally be saved in the metropole, it will have to be saved elsewhere. The Empire is there, offering its support. The fleet is there, which can cover it. The people are there who, in any case, will undergo invasion, but from whom the Republic can raise up resistance, terrible occasion of unity. The world is there, susceptible of furnishing us new arms and, later, a powerful aid."[14] But though Reynaud shared this view, in the end he allowed himself to be overborne and resigned in order to permit Marshal Pétain to seek an armistice.

De Gaulle, who was then in London, at once won Churchill's agreement for the organization of the Free French movement, and on June 18, he raised its banner in his first broadcast. Since Britain continued to maintain relations with the Vichy regime as the legitimate government of France, de Gaulle's organization necessarily was purely military at its inception, without legal continuity or Allied political recognition. Accordingly, his first radio appeals were to the French armed forces in Britain, at sea, and in the colonies, whom he asked to remain in the war as volunteers. As might have been expected, none of the colonial governors whom he requested to assume leadership of the movement consented to do so. More disappointing, none of the well-known French personalities in London or elsewhere accepted his call, so that the team he was able to establish consisted of men who at that time lacked international renown.[15] Even the response of the French military units was hesitant: only a few hundred had enlisted a week after his first appeal, and no more than 7,000 by the end of July.[16] On June 28, however, the British government recognized him as the leader of the Free French and on August 7 signed an agreement with him by which Britain undertook to supply and pay his forces, which by the end of 1940 amounted to about 35,000 men.[17]

Developments within the French empire soon obliged—or allowed—the Free French to assume a political role. The rallying of the New Hebrides, New Caledonia, and French Equatorial Africa to Free France required the creation of a political organization to govern these areas. On October 27, 1940, at Brazzaville, de Gaulle established the *Conseil de Défense de l'Empire,* including, in addition to himself, the governors of most of the territories under Free French control and several other civilian and military personalities. He condemned as illegal the suppression of the Third Republic and denounced Vichy as falsely claiming to be the French government. But neither the original Free French organization nor the new Council of Defense claimed to be a government of France or of the French Empire. Since they could assert neither legal continuity from the Third Republic nor the known, active support of the French people, their claims to speak in the name of France remained largely symbolic.

During 1941, however, the Free French denounced Vichy's "usurpation" with increasing vigor and moved much closer to claiming governmental status.[18] On Septemper 24, 1941, they created the *Comité National Français* under the presidency of de Gaulle, who assumed the power to make treaties and laws. Whereas the Council of Defense had been composed largely of colonial administrators, the new French National Committee, which established functional divisions for civilian as well as military affairs, included French diplomats, civil servants, and politicians. The National Committee of September, 1941, first illustrated a process which was to remain constant with the Gaullist organization down to its return to France in 1944—a continual widening of its base, first among resistants abroad and later among those in France as well.

Throughout this period the Free French organization slowly developed its links with the emerging resistance movement within France. On December 24, 1941, de Gaulle named the resistance leader Jean Moulin as his representative in unoccupied France, with the assignment of unifying the action of the underground groups there. After the conclusion of an agreement between the National Committee and the southern zone resistance organizations in June, 1942, Free France officially changed its name to Fighting France, the better to express its leadership of the resistance abroad and within France. André Philip, a Socialist deputy and resistance leader, joined the National Committee in July as the first direct representative of the interior resistance. At about the same time the siege of Bir-Hakeim, near Tobruk in Libya, represented the first achievement of one of the most important goals of the Free French movement —the engagement of a substantial number of French troops against the German enemy.

Thus, by November, 1942, the Gaullist movement had become a political as well as a military organization, maintaining armed forces, governing extensive colonial territories through a quasi-governmental committee, and closely linked with the internal resistance, which acknowledged de Gaulle as its leader. This recognition by the French resistants gave to de Gaulle an element of strength which had been lacking in his position up to that time and a basis upon which he could properly and realistically claim to represent the French people. His claims to Allied recognition and to governmental authority in the name of France were thereby greatly strengthened, and, in fact, the alliance of the London organization with the internal resistance was to be the key to subsequent developments in French affairs.

The three major Allies, however, remained somewhat reserved in their attitudes toward the Gaullist movement. The greatest degree of cordiality—after June, 1941—was shown by the Soviet Union, who was the most remote from the scene of Free French activities and the least concerned with them. On September 26, 1941, the Soviet ambassador in London, Ivan Maisky, wrote de Gaulle in the name of his government granting him recognition "as the leader of all the Free French" and offering "to accord the Free French aid and assistance in the

common struggle against Hitlerite Germany and its allies." The
Soviet government declared its resolve to assure "the full and
entire restoration of the independence and grandeur of France,"
though no mention was made, as de Gaulle noted, of France's
territorial integrity. In January, 1942, de Gaulle wrote privately
that the Free French felt closest to the Russians who, unlike the
Anglo-Saxons, were waging war without restrictions—by which
he meant, without relations with Vichy.[19]

The relations of the Free French movement with the British
government, to which in the first instance it owed the means of
its existence, were at no time either cordial or smooth. The
British, standing alone against Hitler after the collapse of France,
were not inclined to accept de Gaulle's pretension to equality,
and would probably have preferred a Free French movement
which would have filled a more modest and auxiliary role.
De Gaulle and his associates, on the contrary, inevitably resented
their dependence on the British.[20] In addition, there seems no
doubt that de Gaulle was convinced from the beginning that
the British would, if the opportunity arose, take advantage of
France's weakness to intrude upon her overseas possessions.[21]
The events which followed the occupation of Syria and Lebanon by an Anglo-French force in the summer of 1941 more
than confirmed de Gaulle's fears that the British were pursuing
a policy of settling old colonial scores and attempting to oust
France from her Empire. Friction also arose in regard to Dji-
bouti and the unilateral British invasion of Madagascar in May,
1942. With his realistic view of international relations as the
pursuit of national self-interest, de Gaulle may not have been
overly surprised at these British actions, but he was no less resolved to maintain French interests to the extent of his means.
If, as a British representative claimed, their cause was common,
their positions, according to de Gaulle, were not.[22] In addition,

he no doubt found an occasional public altercation with the British a useful answer to those who held him to be no more than their agent.[23]

As the war progressed the American role grew rapidly, and British policy was increasingly conditioned by that of the United States.[24] De Gaulle took measures to improve Free French relations with the United States, but he was convinced that the Americans took as settled the elimination of France and that they would not hesitate to follow and collaborate with the British in regard to France's possessions and interests.[25] Specific sources of friction arose in regard to St. Pierre and Miquelon, the French Antilles, and American activity in New Caledonia. In June, 1942, de Gaulle, fearing an American or Anglo-American seizure of French West Africa (still held by Vichy), even contemplated a complete rupture with those powers.[26]

The American policy of coolness toward de Gaulle and maintenance of relations with Vichy was the result of an effort to minimize Vichy dependence on Germany and to prepare the way for the North African invasion. Whatever the merits of the policy, de Gaulle was correct in suspecting an active feeling of hostility toward him on the part of Secretary of State Hull and, to a lesser degree, of President Roosevelt. They tended, indeed, to look on de Gaulle as a political adventurer with little support within France. The vigor of their reaction, for example, to the Free French occupation of St. Pierre and Miquelon at the end of 1941 seems to imply, apart from the merits of their position, considerable personal animosity toward de Gaulle.[27]

These major and minor frictions were the curtain-raisers for the full scale and decisive imbroglio in North Africa in which the Free French were most sorely tried and from which they won their conclusive victory. De Gaulle was not informed by the Allies that an expedition was being prepared to seize French North Africa, but he was aware of the fact many months in advance.[28] After all that had gone before—including particularly sharp disputes with the British over the Levant and Madagascar in the late summer and autumn of 1942—he could hardly have been surprised when the Allies concluded that he did not have sufficient support to rally either the officials or the populace to their cause. Casting about for someone who might do so, and after negotiating with General Weygand, they finally selected General Henri Giraud who, after escaping from France, was to be made commander-in-chief of the French forces in North Africa and head of the civilian administration. But when the invasion came in November, 1942, Giraud was in Gibraltar, manifesting, in Anthony Eden's words, "a grasping appetite" for the command of the entire invasion.[29] The Allies therefore felt obliged to make use of the Vichy leader, Admiral Jean Darlan, as a "temporary expedient," in Roosevelt's phrase, to end the fighting. The French forces and the civil administration were left in Darlan's hands but, after his assassination on December 24, 1942, Giraud, at American insistence, was elected head of the Imperial Council which Darlan had established and was named by the council to be civil and military commander-in-chief in North Africa.[30]

The installation of Giraud, despite his non-performance at the time of the Allied landing, appeared to the Gaullists, not without reason, as a deliberate American attempt to bypass the French National Committee and establish a rival French administration which would be dependent on the Allies. The London organization therefore inaugurated a campaign, which lasted for more than a year, to reduce Giraud's power and eventually to replace him with de Gaulle as head of the North African administration. The significance of this long quarrel is larger than mere personal rivalry between the two generals, and it raised, and was ultimately decided by, issues involving both the future constitutional status of France and her foreign policy. Since an important aspect of their divergence concerned their respective attitudes toward the internal resistance movement in France, it is useful at this point to consider the development of that movement and its increasing intertwining with the Free French movement and the complex struggle for power in Algiers.

The Resistance

In the first shock of defeat a confused France turned to Marshal Pétain. Many placed their trust in him who otherwise had no sympathy for the authoritarian regime which his supporters confidently expected him to establish. But from the first hours of the capitulation some refused to accept the defeat of France. The earliest acts of resistance, however, were more symbolic than materially effective; one of the first, for example, was the incident of November 11, 1940, when large numbers of Parisians laid wreaths on the statue of Clemenceau on the Champs-Elysees. Organized resistance began with the appearance of clandestine newspapers around whose staffs clandestine action groups slowly evolved.[31] In the unoccupied zone of France the earliest organizations had already emerged by the end of 1940, but most were formed during 1941. In October, 1942, the three principal southern organizations—*Combat*, *Franc-Tireur* and *Libération-Sud*—without giving up their individual identities formed the intergroup *Mouvements Unis de la Résistance* (M. U. R.) to coordinate resistance activity in the Vichy zone. Resistance in the occupied zone was slower to emerge from the stage of propaganda and journals to that of actual organization, but many groups had sprung up by the end of

1942, notably *Libération-Nord*, the *Organisation Civile et Militaire*, and most important, the *Front National* (F. N.), formed on Communist initiative.

The French Communist Party (P. C. F.) had been severely shaken by the Russo-German pact of August, 1939. Eighteen deputies had resigned from the party in protest, and the General Confederation of Labor (C. G. T.) had expelled all Communists from the offices they held in that organization. The party itself was dissolved by the government on September 26, 1939, and forty-four of its deputies were brought to trial, of whom twenty-seven were imprisoned while the rest went into hiding or, like secretary-general Maurice Thorez, fled to Moscow. The party, gone underground, opposed the war, berated the leaders of the Third Republic both for having initiated and having lost it and, later, denounced de Gaulle as an agent of British capitalism. Communist entrance into the resistance movement was therefore late and was conditioned, in effect, by the relations of the Soviet Union with Germany.

But when they at last joined the national movement, after June, 1941, the Communists did so in a massive and thorough manner. The F. N., which included some Catholics and conservatives but was dominated by its Communist leaders, was organized with a completeness unknown to the other resistance groups. "National Fronts" were organized for women and for occupational groups, and all of these units, as well as several regional fronts, had their own newspapers. With its military arm, the *Franc-Tireurs et Partisans Français* (F. T. P. F.), the F. N. was the largest single resistance group and the most widespread. The Communists hoped to make it the all-inclusive resistance movement, but in this they were not successful, because of the distrust felt by others for the movement's Communist leadership. It is important to note, however, that the Communist Party was the only French party which concentrated all its resistance effort in a single group and which effectively dominated that group, despite the presence of other elements in it. Through the F. T. P. F., which was the most aggressive military organization (including about a third of the maquis, according to de Gaulle), and the many affiliated National Front organizations, the Communists spread their influence into areas and milieux where it had hitherto been slight.[32] In addition, the German tendency to choose principally Communists as hostages and to accuse the entire resistance of being Communist served to increase the prestige and therefore the power of the P. C. F. The party was thus able not only to liquidate the stigma of its equivocal attitude during 1939–1940, but even to lay claim to being the soul of the resistance and the principal defender of France against the invader. The claims subsequently made by the Communists as to the number of their "martyrs" seem to have been greatly exaggerated but the skillful propaganda spread over its resistance record by the party was to be the source of much of its postwar strength.

The Socialists benefited far less as a party from the resistance; indeed, their tactics were the opposite of those of the Communists. Many Socialists participated in the resistance but they did not concentrate their activity in a single group. A *Comité d'Action Socialiste* was formed, but it did not attempt to control or coordinate all resistance activity by Socialists. Partly as a result, the Communists were able, to the disadvantage of the Socialists, not only to secure a widespread influence on the resistance and the control of many local liberation committees but, through the contact of the *Front National* with various labor units, to prepare the eventual Communist ascendancy in the C. G. T.

A third significant element in the resistance was the Catholic left, which, although it held only about fifteen seats in the

Chamber of Deputies of 1939, played a role in the underground
entirely out of proportion to its strength in prewar politics.
Georges Bidault, Henri Teitgen, and François de Menthon
were among the earliest resistants, and the activities of this
small group in the resistance gave its members a confidence and
experience which they had previously lacked, as well as political strength of a magnitude not fully realized until the election
of October, 1945.

The other prewar parties played negligible roles in the resistance, though individual members of each were often conspicuous resistants. The Radical-Socialists and the conservative parties
were both identified with the defeat, and the latter with Vichy
and collaboration as well; none of these groups made a sufficiently clear record in the resistance to enable it to imitate the
Communist achievement of liquidating a discreditable role in
1939–1940. The political atmosphere of the resistance was one
of Jacobinism rather than of liberalism, and the resistants, leading the lives of outlaws and conspirators, were largely without
sympathy for the former parliamentary regime and those who
represented it. Their rebellion was against not only Vichy but
also the discredited system and leaders of the Third Republic,
and they considered themselves a new elite, properly replacing
those swept aside by the defeat.

There was a wide divergence in the political antecedents of
the resistants but there was also some degree of consensus among
them, and between them and de Gaulle, beyond the expulsion
of the Germans.[33] In particular, they all wanted to avoid an
Allied military government in the post-liberation period.
Further, in reaction to the collaboration of the Vichy regime
and to the actual occupation they voiced a resurgent feeling
not only of patriotism but of French nationalism. In both respects the resistance was on common ground with de Gaulle's
determination to defend the independence and the Great Power

status of France vis-à-vis the Allies, if necessary, as well as the Germans.

Nearly all of the resistance organizations emphasized the social, economic, and political renovation of France—whose prewar institutions and leaders were generally held to have been irremediably tainted by defeat. In most of the resistance propaganda, national liberation and national renovation by reform, or, as many said, by revolution, were intertwined. De Gaulle shared or accepted the preoccupation of the resistants with the future reform of French institutions, just as he shared their concern with France's international position. His language on this subject was vague, but its tone was attuned to the wishes and preoccupations of the large mass of the resistants within France.[34]

Considerable thought was also given in resistance circles to the peace settlement, particularly that with Germany. Much of this was less violently anti-German than might have been expected in light of the nationalism of the resistance. Many denied the idea of the guilt of the entire German people and rejected, for example, the radical partition of Germany as traditionally advocated by the French right. There was, however, general agreement on the need for punishment of war criminals, perhaps running to tens of thousands; restitution of stolen goods and the use of German labor and equipment for reconstruction; the disarmament of Germany; control of her essential raw materials and industries for a number of years; de-industrialization of Germany and re-industrialization of France and the other neighbors of Germany; restoration of Alsace-Lorraine; transfer of the Saar to France in partial compensation for the destruction of the French mines; and the transfer of East Prussia and most of Silesia to Poland. In addition, and most significant in the long run, some (but not the Communists) proposed that France increase her economic ties to Great Britain and the Low Countries as the first step toward a European order which might eventually include also a reformed Germany and other countries of Central Europe. This group of ideas, which no doubt marked the beginning in France of the postwar "European" movement, also fit in very well with de Gaulle's thoughts on France's foreign policy.[35]

The resistance in France became large-scale only late in 1942, passing from propaganda and clandestine meetings to sabotage. This was due in large part to the increasingly open subservience of the Vichy regime to the Germans and to the forced draft of French labor for work in Germany, which drove large numbers of men into the maquis. As the scale of resistance activity became larger, the movement toward greater unity of the groups continued, culminating in February, 1944, with the federation of the M. U. R. and several northern groups in the *Mouvement de Libération Nationale* (M. L. N.), whose aim was to unify the non-Communist resistance organizations. But it was de Gaulle who took the initiative to bring all the resistance groups into a single national unit. This effort culminated in May, 1943, when his liaison representative, Jean Moulin, formed and became head of the *Conseil National de la Résistance* (C. N. R.), which included representatives of the principal resistance organizations and the trade unions, and also (in order to increase the prestige of the group outside France) of six political parties, including several which had contributed few members to the resistance.[36] From that date the C. N. R. functioned as the underground government of France, in close contact with Algiers. A year later the French Forces of the Interior (F. F. I.), created by de Gaulle in March, 1944, to unify the resistance for its role during and after the invasion, controlled a secret army estimated by him at over 200,000 men.

The French Committee of National Liberation

During the long negotiations which took place during the first five months of 1943 in an effort to bring together the Giraud administration in North Africa and the French National Committee in London, a number of basic differences between their leaders became clear.[37] Giraud wanted to fight the Germans but had no interest in "politics" nor any grasp of the political side of affairs, which was de Gaulle's preoccupation. In addition, Giraud had no particular political objection to the Vichy regime, and certainly had no understanding of the resistance in France nor any interest in the social and economic reforms advocated in resistance circles. De Gaulle, on the other hand, was the recognized leader of the French resistance and the supporter of its aspirations for a postwar reconstruction of French institutions.[38] In pursuance of his alliance with the resistance he demanded a militant purge of collaborators after the liberation of France and was able to draw considerable advantage from the fact that Giraud, without administrative and political experience, had retained in office in North Africa certain notorious Vichy officials against whom the Gaullists waged an effective campaign that was indirectly aimed at Giraud himself. Giraud's tardy repeal of anti-Semitic and anti-republican Vichy legislation was used to excellent effect by the Gaullist propaganda organization, which was without counterpart in the Giraud camp.

The division of the two generals did not stop short of foreign policy. While Giraud owed his position entirely to the Allies and trusted them to liberate and restore France, de Gaulle had long proclaimed that French forces must play as active and independent a role as possible in the war in order to convince the world that France had never, despite a temporary setback in 1940, relinquished her rights as a Great Power. Even from the beginning of the Free French movement he had considered the group as the trustee for French national interests, and the increasing rapport established with the interior resistance strengthened his claim to speak in the name of France. His reliance on the resistance and his espousal of many of its social and economic aspirations were thus closely linked to his main preoccupation—the maintenance of France's position in the world and that of his organization as the trustee of that position. De Gaulle's insistence on remaining independent of the Allies, as well as his emphasis upon France's status as a Great Power, was one of the factors which won him greatest popularity among resistance groups and representatives in France and Algeria. The Gaullists exploited this popularity shrewdly.[39]

On the day after Darlan's assassination de Gaulle proposed a meeting to Giraud, and negotiations between the two generals were initiated at the Casablanca conference early in 1943, under the patronage of the Allies, and were then continued between London and Algiers. Throughout these talks de Gaulle refused to allow his organization to be swallowed up by Giraud, who in his view did not have the ability, the desire, or the means to maintain any kind of independence vis-à-vis the Allies.[40] As Giraud's position tended to grow weaker in relation to the Gaullists, however, American hostility to them also declined somewhat, and after protracted correspondence and a number of mediatory missions, sufficient agreement was reached between the generals to permit de Gaulle to go to Algiers on May 30. At the conclusion of further difficult discussions, there was organized on June 3, as the successor to both the French National Committee of London and the French administration in Algiers, the *Comité Français de la Libération Nationale* (C. F. L. N.), of which de Gaulle and Giraud became joint presidents. The C. F. L. N.'s assumption of an explicit political role—it declared itself to be "the central French power" which would "exercise French sovereignty on all territories outside the power of the enemy"—obviously answered much more to de Gaulle's intentions than to those of Giraud. De Gaulle at once announced to the French people by radio that "their government was now functioning in Algiers pending its arrival in Paris."[41]

The 300,000 to 400,000 soldiers of the North African army who remained under Giraud's control as commander-in-chief seemed to give him an immense preponderance of force in relation to the Free French units, which remained under de Gaulle's control until the two forces were merged during the summer. But at least seven of the other twelve members of the new quasi-governmental political organ were clearly on the side of de Gaulle and were, as a group, united and more conscious of their purposes. Though de Gaulle was prevented for the time being, by the explicit intervention of the Americans, from establishing the principle of the subordination of the commander-in-chief to the committee, that is, of limiting Giraud's military prerogatives, he lost no time in consolidating his position and setting to work to end as soon as possible the "absurd duality" he had "temporarily" accepted.[42]

During June and July, 1943, the committee annulled various enactments of the Vichy regime. Of particular importance was the repeal on June 25 of the decree which had dissolved the French Communist Party and its organizations in 1939. De Gaulle was certainly not unaware of the reason for the late rallying of the French Communists to the resistance nor of the fact that they, as well as the Soviet government, had denounced him as a tool of British imperialism prior to June, 1941. Nor could he have been unaware that the Communists, who shared his desire to avoid an Allied military government in liberated

France, were acting on the basis of their own calculations, and that the political advantage which their support gave him vis-à-vis Giraud and the Allies at Algiers was balanced by the danger that they might later take advantage of their strength in the resistance and the circumstances that would surround the liberation of France to attempt to establish their own dictatorship.[43] This beginning of an understanding with the Communists therefore testifies clearly to the extreme importance which the Gaullists attached to their entente with the internal resistance, of which the Communists were the largest single element, as a counterweight to the hostility or coolness of the Allies and their "agent," Giraud. A message of July 9 from the C. N. R., published at Algiers, expressed the confidence of the resistance that the committee would end all traces of the Vichy regime and would uphold the principles defined by de Gaulle. That is, the C. N. R. invoked the words and the policies of only one of the joint presidents of the committee; no mention was made of the other.

The American government attempted to increase Giraud's standing by inviting him, strictly in his military capacity, to visit Washington and by showing their clear preference for the "docile visitor," as de Gaulle said, over the absent and publicly unmentioned co-president. But the effort was futile, for as de Gaulle and the C. F. L. N. affirmed their political role, Giraud rapidly faded out. His position was finally hopelessly undercut by the convening in Algiers on November 3, 1943, of a Consultative Assembly—proposed by de Gaulle as early as February—heavily weighted in favor of the resistance and other Gaullist elements. De Gaulle addressed its first session, and the points which he emphasized—the right of the resistance to speak for France, the maintenance of France's status as a Great Power, and the necessity for a postwar reform of French institutions

—were all key themes in the resistance. These themes were echoed in the ensuing debates, in which a reorganization of the C. F. L. N. to include more representatives of the resistance and to subordinate the military to the civilian authority was particularly emphasized.

It apparently became clear now to Giraud and his supporters that his very limited resources—a portion of the French armed forces and a dwindling measure of American support—were inadequate to balance the Gaullist strength in the committee, the Consultative Assembly, and the resistance. Giraud therefore concurred in the expansion of the committee to include more representatives of resistance movements and political parties. He and the Americans also accepted, in principle, the subordination of the military command to the political authority, an aim which de Gaulle had pursued since June. Pursuant to this, a new committee was organized on November 9 of which de Gaulle was sole president, and which included an increased number of resistants and politicians.[44]

For the time being, Giraud was confirmed as commander-in-chief of the French forces. But his position was dependent on the committee, and its estimation of its strength and needs in relation to the Allies in the difficult months preceding D-day could in a sense be measured in terms of its attitude toward him. When, therefore, in April, 1944, after months of negotiations, the committee was further broadened politically by the inclusion of two Communists, it proceeded to assume authority over all land, naval, and air forces and to appoint its president, de Gaulle, to be chief of the armies. It thereby abolished the post of commander-in-chief. Giraud, who declined the honorary post of inspector-general of the army which was offered to him, retired. The Americans, aware by then of Giraud's political incapacity, made no protest.[45] Thus, despite, or perhaps in part because of American opposition to de Gaulle, the long struggle between the two generals and the interests and concepts which lay behind them ended with the complete victory of the Gaullists and the resistance with their common program: a break with the Third Republic, the restoration of French independence and "greatness," and more vaguely, the political, social, and economic renovation of France.

The success of the Gaullists in winning a position of equality and finally of dominance in the North African administration was not fully paralleled in the relations of the Committee of National Liberation with the Great Powers. A number of small states and governments-in-exile recognized the committee before the end of July, 1943, without waiting for the concurrence of the major Allies. Of the three principal Allies, the Soviet Union was verbally the most friendly to the committee, although the actual relations between the two were variable.[46] The Soviet government was ready to extend recognition in June, but held off at American and British request. Finally, in concert with the two Allies, and in more friendly language than theirs, the Soviet government on August 25 informed the C. F. L. N. that it recognized the latter "as representing the State interests of the French Republic, and as the leader of all French patriots fighting Hitlerite tyranny. . . ."[47]

The United States government, as usual, was the least accommodating, for it continued to maintain that no recognition could be granted until the liberation gave the French people the opportunity to demonstrate what they really desired; in the interval, the Allies must not impose de Gaulle or any other regime or leader upon them. The American government seemed to believe, or to hope, that the French would not accept de Gaulle, and that his eagerness for recognition betrayed his awareness of this fact. In addition, the Americans in 1943 did not see an important postwar role for France. They believed that after the defeat of Germany there would be little need or possibility for a revival of French power; in fact, they conjectured, important French bases and outposts such as Bizerte, Dakar, and New Caledonia might be occupied in the postwar period by British and American forces in the name of the United Nations. At Cairo, in 1943, Roosevelt spoke of placing Indochina and even Morocco under trusteeship after the war, and Stalin and Roosevelt both spoke to the same general effect at Teheran.[48] Roosevelt even suggested to Anthony Eden (March, 1943) and to his chiefs-of-staff (November, 1943) that it might be necessary to create a buffer state called "Wallonia" between France and Germany, which "would run from northern France, say, Calais, Lille and Ardenne[s], through to Alsace and Lorraine—in other words, from Switzerland to the seacoast."[49]

The British, on the other hand, resisted American attempts to exclude de Gaulle from North African affairs and demonstrated increasing friendliness toward the committee once it was formed. Already looking to the postwar period, they assumed a relatively early withdrawal of American forces from the continent after the conclusion of hostilities and judged that Great Britain would benefit by having a strong France at her side.[50] Despite their professed regret at seeing de Gaulle oust Giraud, they wished to open no rift between the British government and the group which seemed increasingly likely to govern postwar France. At the same time, although they were ready to recognize the C. F. L. N. in early July, the British tended to follow the American lead in this as in other questions, and it was only at the Quebec conference in August that the two governments decided to extend limited recognition to the Committee of National Liberation.[51] Even then it was not possible for them to reach agreement on a common formula of recognition. The British note, issued on August 26, 1943, was worded as follows:

> His Majesty's Government in the United Kingdom recognize forthwith the French Committee of National Liberation as administering those French oversea territories which acknowledge its authority and as having assumed the functions of the former French National Committee in respect of territories in the Levant. His Majesty's Government in the United Kingdom also recognize the committee as the body qualified to ensure the conduct of the French effort in the war within the framework of inter-allied cooperation.
>
> They take note with sympathy of the desire of the committee to be regarded as the body qualified to ensure the administration and defense of all French interests. It is the intention of His Majesty's Government to give effect to this request as far as possible while reserving the right to consider in consultation with the committee the practical application of this principle in particular cases as they arise.[52]

But the American note, issued the same day, was far more reserved. After welcoming the establishment of the C. F. L. N., it continued:

> In view of the paramount importance of the common war effort, the relationship with the French Committee of National Liberation must continue to be subject to the military requirements of the Allied commanders.
>
> The Government of the United States takes note, with sympathy, of the desire of the Committee to be re-

garded as the body qualified to insure the administration
and defense of French interests. The extent to which it
may be possible to give effect to this desire must however be reserved for consideration in each case as it
arises.

On these understandings the Government of the
United States recognizes the French Committee of National Liberation as administering those French overseas
territories which acknowledge its authority.

This statement does not constitute recognition of a
government of France or of the French Empire by the
Government of the United States.

It does constitute recognition of the French Committee of National Liberation as functioning within specific
limitations during the war. Later on the people of
France, in a free and untrammelled manner, will proceed in due course to select their own government and
their own officials to administer it.[53]

These cool paragraphs express the official American reservations
about the French committee, which persisted down to and after
the invasion of France. They reflect both the legitimate concern of the United States government that no regime be imposed on the French people without their consent, and the
rationalization, in terms of that concern, of the profound distrust which was felt by Roosevelt and Hull for the person and
policies of General de Gaulle.[54]

The committee, despite these Allied reservations, received the
substance or benefits of recognition in such forms as mutual aid,
financial assistance, and admission to the Advisory Council for
Italy (though it had been excluded from any role in the Italian
armistice itself). It was not, however, included in the European

Advisory Commission, which had been established to deal with Germany and other problems. As the invasion of Europe came nearer, the French at Algiers became increasingly preoccupied with the problems of assuring both their prompt assumption of governmental authority in liberated France and France's equal participation in the postwar settlement. De Gaulle, in his opening address to the Consultative Assembly, had asserted the rights of the committee in both areas, and these themes were repeated again and again by him and other French leaders during the winter and spring of 1944. In a speech on March 18 de Gaulle asserted the right of the committee to govern France even before its complete liberation and strongly condemned any attempt to maintain the Vichy administration or the "artificial formation of an authority outside the government"—a warning to the Allies not to repeat in liberated France the policy they had followed in North Africa in 1942, to the local resistance authorities, who might attempt to challenge the central power, and to the Communists, who might try to establish their own power during the liberation.[55]

Apart from this immediate preoccupation, the speech of March 18 is remarkable for the light it casts on de Gaulle's views on the postwar foreign policy of France. After deploring the absence of Europe from the councils of the alliance (which implies, of course, that Great Britain is not part of Europe), he said:

> ... if the old continent, renewed, is to recover a balance corresponding to the conditions of our times, it seems to us that certain groupings will have to be formed, without, however, encroaching on the sovereignty of each element. As regards France we think that some form of Western group realised with us, chiefly on an economic

basis and as extensive as possible, could offer great advantages. Such a group, extended to Africa, and in close relation with the Orient—and notably with the Arab States of the Near East which are legitimately seeking to unite their interests—and of which the Channel, the Rhine, and the Mediterranean would be like arteries, should be able to constitute a vital nucleus in a world organization of production, exchange and security.[56]

These ideas are similar to those of some resistance circles within France which called for French economic cooperation with Great Britain and the Low Countries as the first step toward a European order that might eventually include Germany and other central European states. De Gaulle, however, expanded this to include the African and Mediterranean possessions and associates of the western European nations. Though economic considerations are uppermost in these words, de Gaulle also says that the "western group" would fill a security or political function. Characteristically, he explicitly excludes limitations on the sovereignty of the participants. But this, rather than limiting the application of de Gaulle's idea to economic cooperation, more probably reflects his view that an elaborate super-sovereignty would discourage rather than promote the success of his project and that less spectacular and more subtle means could be found to the same end. What that end is remains somewhat uncertain in this speech. But if, as seems clear, the complaint about the absence of Europe from Allied councils and the reference to the renewed "continent" imply the absence of Great Britain from the "western group," then it is probably a disguised but none the less effective French hegemony over Western Europe which de Gaulle is advocating. More will be heard later—under de Gaulle and after him—of the idea that France might magnify its own voice in world councils and strengthen its Great Power claims by leading and speaking for a grouping of Western European states.[57]

Despite committee claims, the Allies excluded it from participation in planning for either of the operations scheduled to take place in France: Overlord in Normandy and Anvil in the south. It nevertheless made known its military wishes to the Allied commanders in December, 1943: one French division was to participate in Overlord and liberate Paris; the French forces then fighting in Italy and those in North Africa were to participate in Anvil. The committee and the Consultative Assembly worked out elaborate plans during the winter and spring of 1944 to facilitate their assuming control of metropolitan France as rapidly as it was liberated. In an ordinance of June 3, in order to strengthen its position in negotiations with the Allies, the committee assumed the title of Provisional Government of the French Republic. These arrangements, however, depended for their implementation on an understanding with the United States and Great Britain, similar to those which the latter governments had already made with the European governments-in-exile. Algiers proposed such an understanding as early as September 7, 1943, but there was no real negotiation on this subject before D-Day.[58]

De Gaulle had reason to believe that the Allies intended to establish direct military administration of France, and he suspected that, imitating the policy of military expediency they had followed in North Africa, they might well appoint officials of the Third Republic or even of Vichy to administer the liberated areas.[59] Both Churchill and Eisenhower favored a close working relationship with the committee. Roosevelt, however, apparently had little faith either in the military effectiveness of the French resistance or in the ability of the Algiers committee to establish an orderly provisional regime. He therefore concluded that as successive areas of France were liberated they would be governed by Allied officials or by Frenchmen named by them, until such time as free elections could be held throughout the whole of France. The President continued to insist that the attitude of the French people toward de Gaulle was unknown and that no regime must be imposed upon them by the Allies. To de Gaulle, of course, this meant simply that Roosevelt was setting himself up as the arbiter of French affairs.[60] A sharp dispute began in March between the British and American governments on the drafting of Eisenhower's instructions in this respect, and in the end he was left free to deal with such Frenchmen as he might find useful. This hardly satisfied Algiers.

In the absence of an agreement between Algiers and the Allied command, de Gaulle, who was not informed of the date or details of the June 6 landing until the last minute, allowed only twenty of the designated five hundred French liaison officers to accompany the Allied force into France. He also publicly repudiated the "so-called French currency" issued by the Allied command without his approval, having failed to use the issue as a lever to win Allied recognition of his authority. De Gaulle, however, had by this time ensured his entente with the entire resistance by bringing the Communists into the C. F. L. N., and he had also disposed of Giraud, the rival with whom Eisenhower might most probably have tried to deal in liberated France. He was confident that his government was the only authority which the French people would accept and with which the Allies would be able to deal. Having been invested with authority by the French people, he wrote in his memoirs, he did not at this late date have to seek it at the hands of Roosevelt. Indeed, he seemed to feel that the Allied attitude toward him would show even more clearly to the French people the purely French basis of his mandate.[61]

CHAPTER III

LIBERATION AND WAR: JULY–DECEMBER 1944

The Liberation of France

The unexpected speed of the Allied advance across France increased acutely the need for the Supreme Command and the French committee to agree on the administration of the liberated regions. But in the absence of such an agreement ad hoc arrangements, which in effect consolidated the committee's authority, were worked out as successive areas were liberated. A week after D-Day, de Gaulle, visiting the liberated area and receiving a triumphant reception, named François Coulet as regional commissioner of the Republic for the Normandy area. Coulet, who took office without difficulty, worked closely with the Allied authorities; since both his appointment and his actions were accepted by the Supreme Command, the French liaison officers then joined the Allied forces. General Eisenhower made clear that the *Forces Françaises de l'Intérieur* (F. F. I.), commanded by General Koenig, were an integral part of the Allied army and that the Germans would be held accountable to treat the French forces as such.[1] Thus, despite the continued lack of a formal agreement, practical cooperation was established between the Provisional French Government and the Allied command on the military level and, in a less clearly defined manner, on the civil level as well.

But the basic problem of the relation of the French civil administration to the Allied authorities remained to be settled, and after a preliminary Anglo-French discussion of the subject de Gaulle flew to Washington on July 6 to discuss this and other problems with the American government. Presumably assured that events were developing as he wished, he did not press for formal recognition.[2] As a result, de Gaulle was more relaxed and amiable than had been expected, and he made a favorable impression even on some who had been most hostile. The visit was generally accounted a French success. De Gaulle's talks with Roosevelt were cordial and wide-ranging, though he found the President's postwar plans, in which, as he understood them, France played little part, dangerously over-ambitious.[3] But the visit had at least one major result. Since it was obvious by this date that both the French resistance and the general population accepted de Gaulle's leadership, the American government finally agreed in principle to recognize the committee as the *de facto* authority for the civilian administration of France, on condition that Allied military requirements not be interfered with and that the right of the French people to choose their own government be affirmed.[4] After further delays, which again aroused de Gaulle's suspicions that Roosevelt might still be trying even at this late date to find some other French authority, detailed agreements were at last signed establishing the relations between the Gaullist organization and the Allies in France.

The Anglo-French agreement was signed at the political level by Anthony Eden and René Massigli, de Gaulle's commissioner for foreign affairs, on August 25, 1944. The Foreign Office communiqué summarized it in these terms:

This agreement comprises separate memoranda dealing with administrative and jurisdictional questions; currency and mutual aid; the disposal and protection of property, including war material; publicity arrangements; and the distribution of relief supplies for the civil population.

It is intended to be essentially temporary and practical in character. It is designed to facilitate so far as possible the direction and coordination of the assistance which the French authorities and people will be able to render to the Allied Expeditionary Force on the territory of Continental France; the adoption in that territory of all measures deemed necessary by the Supreme Allied Commander for the successful conduct of his operations; and the orderly resumption of full responsibility for the civil administration by the French authorities.

The Soviet Government have been consulted regarding these arrangements and have expressed their agreement.[5]

The Franco-American agreement included similar provisions, but it was signed on the military level by Generals Eisenhower and Koenig. The American communiqué contained the reservations and qualifications habitual to American statements dealing with the Gaullist organization:

General Eisenhower as United States Commanding General has been authorized to deal with the French authorities at Algiers as the *de facto* authority in France as long as they continue to receive the support of the majority of Frenchmen who are fighting for the defeat of Germany and the liberation of France. This authorization is also based on the understanding that as Supreme Allied Commander General Eisenhower must retain whatever authority he considers necessary for unimpeded conduct of military operations and that, as soon as the military situation permits, the French people will be given an opportunity freely to exercise their will in the choice of their government.[6]

These "essentially temporary and practical" arrangements, however, endured nearly until November and it is within their framework that the Algiers authorities, now recognized as the *de facto* authority in France, established their position.

As de Gaulle had long planned, the French themselves were able to make a significant contribution to the liberation of their country. Resistance forces harried the German rear and cleaned up German-held areas behind the main line of the Allied advance; French troops, transferred from Italy, played a leading part in the Allied landing in southern France and the subsequent march northward. Above all, and responding to an early and constant preoccupation of de Gaulle's, Leclerc's Second Armored Division, having marched with the Allies across Normandy, was able to complete the liberation of Paris which had been begun by the resistance. De Gaulle made his triumphant entry into the capital on August 25.[7] By the end of August most of metropolitan France except Alsace and Lorraine had been cleared of German forces. On August 31 the Provisional Government, the ministries, the Consultative Assembly, and the diplomatic corps left Algiers for Paris.

The Provisional Government Establishes Its Authority

The acceptance of de Gaulle's leadership by the interior French resistance had, by the end of August, 1944, enabled the

Provisional Government to establish its *de facto* authority in France vis-à-vis the Allied Supreme Command. By cooperating, the Gaullists, the Communists, and the other resistance elements had achieved their common goal of avoiding an Allied military government. Their success, however, immediately raised the deferred question of the distribution of political power within France between the allied but independent authorities of Algiers and the underground. In general, the internal resistance, with its strong and disciplined Communist component, was considerably to the left of the governmental personnel of Algiers, despite the constant broadening of the latter, and it was far from impossible that the wartime convergence of their aims might quickly prove to be more verbal than real. The immediate appearance of fourteen daily journals after the liberation of Paris showed the great desire of the resistants and others, after four years of silence, to be heard and to press their views on the public and the government. The government, whose strength in relation to the Allies had so largely been based on its entente with the resistance, had now to take into account the wishes of the resistance in the formulation of policy.

If, as has been suggested, de Gaulle intended to canalize the political activity of the resistance organizations into the Consultative Assembly while maintaining the Algiers government virtually without change, he was unable to do so. After protests by the C. N. R. and most of the press, and consultations with resistance and political leaders, who insisted on a larger share in the actual government, de Gaulle agreed to a major reorganization of his cabinet. The new government was announced on September 9:

Charles de Gaulle	President of the Council
Jules Jeanneney	Minister of State
(Radical-Socialist))	

Georges Bidault (Christian Democrat)	Foreign Affairs
François de Menthon (Christian Democrat)	Justice
Adrien Tixier (Socialist)	Interior
André Diethelm	War
Louis Jacquinot (Democratic Alliance)	Navy
Charles Tillon (Communist)	Air
Aimé Lepercq	Finance
Pierre Mendès-France (Radical-Socialist)	National Economy
Robert Lacoste (Socialist)	Production
François Tanguy-Prigent (Socialist)	Agriculture
Paul Giacobbi (Radical-Socialist)	Food Supply
René Pleven	Colonies
René Capitant	Education
René Mayer (Radical-Socialist)	Transport and Public Works
Augustin Laurent (Socialist)	Post and Telegraphs
François Billoux (Communist)	Public Health
Gen. Georges Catroux	North Africa
Henri Frenay	War Prisoners and Pensions
Alexandre Parodi	Labor
Pierre-Henri Teitgen (Christian Democrat)	Information

Of the twenty-one members of this cabinet apart from de Gaulle, twelve had already served in the government at Algiers. The vital posts of justice, which controlled the purge, information, with its authority over the press, and foreign affairs were held by the three Christian Democrats; de Gaulle's long-time associate, André Diethelm, held the army; interior, with the police, was assigned to the Socialist Adrien Tixier, who had been associated with de Gaulle at Algiers for more than a year; the Radical-Socialist Pierre Mendès-France and the conservative resistant Aimé Lepercq controlled the economy. The Communists were obliged to be content with the secondary posts of air and health. From this it appears that de Gaulle, while building an undoubtedly resistant government, was feeling his way toward an entente with the Christian Democrats—a new political factor whose real strength was quite unknown at this time —and, to a lesser extent, with the Socialists. The abolition of the four "symbolic" posts of minister of state which had existed at Algiers, with their implication of party coalition; the significant roles held in this government by so many of de Gaulle's personal London associates; the secondary posts assigned to the Communists, for whom de Gaulle's distrust was not allayed by his desire for their continued support, all indicate that de Gaulle envisaged a government which would be his own. It would not be merely a proportional delegation from parties and organizations, and the decisions to be made on the problems confronting the nation would be national policies rather than party compromises. This attitude reflected de Gaulle's constitutional thinking as well as the needs of the immediate situation. Nevertheless, he did find it necessary to adjust his policies to some extent to hold together the coalition around him.

The give and take between de Gaulle and the parties during 1944 and 1945 on domestic affairs is well documented; in most cases he had his way on major issues, though he sometimes made concessions to the parties. Disagreements over foreign policy are much less well documented, though they surfaced from time to time in debates in the Consultative Assembly. But there is little to suggest that French foreign policy during de Gaulle's tenure of office was anything except his own. The influence even of Foreign Minister Bidault seems to have been negligible. If the president and the foreign minister disagreed on any important issue, little was heard of it until the very end of de Gaulle's term of office.[8] In no case does de Gaulle seem to have changed his foreign policy in any significant respect to accommodate his ministers or their parties.

Liberated France faced a grave economic situation, which also created political problems, but contrary to some expectations, it was neither in anarchy nor economic chaos, and the cabinet's principal task, the establishment of its authority as the sole organ of government, was to that extent simplified. The Algiers government had made detailed provision for the systematic restoration of governmental authority as France was progressively liberated, but the speed of the liberation and the difficulty of maintaining communication between Paris and parts of the provinces resulted in the seizure of *de facto* authority in a number of places by resistance groups and F. F. I. units. The government had correctly foreseen that these local administrations would be reluctant to surrender their authority to the representatives of Paris and had given its regional commissioners wide latitude to adjust to each local situation. However, when local rule persisted in some areas long after liberation and came increasingly under Communist control, the government became more firm in its desire to put an end to a situation which, if it did not actually threaten to lead to a parallel government or a state within the state, at any rate obstructed regular and orderly administration.[9]

On September 14, therefore, de Gaulle undertook a two-month series of tours of France in which he emphasized the need for unity and order and submission to the lawful government. Having thus put forward de Gaulle's personal prestige as the embodiment of its authority, the government on September

23 ordered the incorporation of the *Forces Françaises de l'Intérieur* (about 400,000 men) into the regular army. The F. F. I., including the Communist *Franc-Tireurs et Partisans*, was merged with the regular army without incident, and thus passed under the effective control of the government. On October 28 the government dissolved the resistance gendarmerie known as *Milices Patriotiques* and *Gardes Patriotiques*. Finally, having thus destroyed the independent armed forces of the C. N. R., the government reduced the latter's significance by incorporating it into the organs of the state. The C. N. R. had asked that the Consultative Assembly, which had been almost forgotten since the government's arrival in Paris, be enlarged to take greater account of the resistance. Early in October the cabinet announced that the assembly would hold its first session in metropolitan France on November 7. The size of the assembly was then increased to 248 seats, of which 148 were allotted to the metropolitan resistance, including the entire C. N. R.

While destroying the independent political and military power of the resistance, the government made some attempt to conciliate it and to undercut Communist appeal by nationalizing the Renault automobile works and the coal mines of northern France. It also undertook an ordered purge of Vichyites and collaborators. But the scope of these measures, as well as the government's general policy toward the resistance, did not fail to arouse some bitterness on the part of the more militant and "reformist" resistants. The conduct of the purge, in particular, gave rise to a disillusionment which markedly reduced the enthusiasm and spirit of the resistants, already impaired by the decline of their special position vis-à-vis the government.

The success of the government in imposing its authority and policies on the resistance with so little difficulty was, indeed, a remarkable phenomenon, considering the presence in the summer of 1944 of an underground leadership and program largely oriented to the left, local committees of public safety, and years of bitterness against Vichy and collaborators. The explanation does not lie only in the precautions taken by the government, including some control of the press and radio and the placing of reliable men in key positions, nor in the presence of the Anglo-American forces, though these were, of course, a brake on excessive disorder. An important factor contributing to the government's success was the attitude of the Communist party. It was striking that the Communists, whose negligible representation in the cabinet was the smallest of any important group, were also the best organized and best armed of the resistance organizations and therefore suffered the greatest political loss from the government's measures. Although the Communists occasionally criticized some of these policies, they did not prevent the cabinet from adopting them, and in general they acquiesced with surprisingly little protest in the liquidation of a position from which they might, through the resistance, have challenged the entire Gaullist governmental structure. It can be concluded that, in the face of de Gaulle's great prestige in France, in the presence of an Anglo-American army, and in the midst of a still unfinished war in which the Soviet Union was allied to the Western Powers, the French Communists chose, for the time being, to maintain the "national" role of the war years and to seek power by legal means. They thereby eliminated the danger of being excluded from policy-making altogether, and by respectably and patriotically remaining within the fluid political framework of the Provisional Government they left all doors open to later arrangements with other parties. Thus, Maurice Thorez, granted amnesty from the charge of deserting the army in 1939, returned from Moscow on November 27 and urged support of the government for the war effort and national unity.

In January, 1945, he specifically endorsed the dissolution of the *Milices* and the subordination of the liberation committees to the government's authority.[10]

In addition to the Communist position, a number of other factors within France and within the resistance itself promoted moderation. The resistance comprised only a minority of the French, albeit it claimed to speak in their name, and was widely divided in practice, if not in principle, on nearly every issue except that of expelling the invader and liquidating the Vichy regime. The strength and prestige of the Gaullist government, although dexterously allied to that of the resistance, was never dominated by it. There was no serious focus of opposition to the Gaullist government, since the Communists declined that role and the C. N. R., absorbed into the regime, did not seriously aspire to it. Finally, the objective situation of a continuing war, great material scarcity, and the absorbing tasks of keeping alive preoccupied the vast majority of Frenchmen. In these circumstances the government, by the end of 1944, established itself as the sole legitimate authority in France, having successfully absorbed the resistance into its own structure on a secondary plane of political action. De Gaulle, with his immense prestige and the tacit consent of the Communists, his most formidable potential opponents, dominated his cabinet, and, without elections, both the old and new political parties felt too unsure of their strength to assert themselves against him.

The Foreign Policy of the Provisional Government

Apart from the question of the relations between Algiers and the Supreme Allied Command in connection with the re-establishment of French authority in the liberated territory of metropolitan France, the Provisional Government, in the summer of

1944, faced three separate but related problems in its foreign policy. First, it had to achieve recognition as the government of France, particularly from the major Allies. Second, as de Gaulle had emphasized since 1940, the French government had to win from the Allies re-admission to the circle of Great Powers in whose hands, as the experience of the war indicated, lay the ultimate authority for the making of the peace. When this, which was both an end in itself and a means to a further end, had been achieved, France then had to secure from the Great Powers acceptance for her ideas, which were as yet hardly formulated or revealed, on the European and, particularly, the German peace settlements.

When in June, 1943, the Committee of National Liberation had been organized, it received its first recognition, not from the major Allies, but from the exiled governments of Europe. Perhaps these governments wanted to express their solidarity with a regime similarly situated to their own, to display a certain measure of independence from the Great Powers on whom they were so closely dependent, and also, perhaps, to intimate that they still looked to France as a leader of the smaller states of the continent and their representative among the powers. The same pattern was repeated after the Algiers Committee became the Provisional Government of the French Republic, for it was promptly recognized as such by Belgium, Luxembourg, Czechoslovakia, Poland, Norway, Greece, and Egypt. Despite de Gaulle's efforts to win recognition from the United States and Great Britain during June and July, he was able to secure no more than limited *de facto* recognition and ad hoc arrangements. These, however, permitted the assumption of civil authority in the liberated areas by the representatives of the Algiers government. But it was only on August 25 that these arrangements were embodied in a formal accord between the

French authorities and the Allies, and even then full recognition was not granted to the Provisional Government.

With the unexpectedly speedy liberation of most French territory by September, and the relatively easy and uncontested establishment of the Provisional Government's authority in France during the early autumn, the Allies, and particularly the Americans, had little reason to continue to hope for or to expect the emergence of any substantial group opposed to the Gaullist regime. On October 20, therefore, General Eisenhower and the Paris government agreed on the delimitation of the "military zone" (consisting of nineteen departments and Belfort), which was to remain under the Supreme Commander's overall authority, and the "interior zone," which was placed entirely under that of the Provisional Government. As a sequel to this, on October 23 the United States, Great Britain, and the Soviet Union simultaneously announced their recognition of the Paris regime as the Provisional Government of France.[11] The French government thus formally resumed its place among the nations. But the continued exclusion of France from the European Advisory Commission and the councils of the Big Three was not easily understood by the French and reminded them that only the smaller part of their policy for the re-establishment of France had been achieved.

The act of recognition had been delayed for so long after it had become inevitable that the Provisional Government had properly taken it for granted and had begun looking beyond it to more difficult tasks. Thus, in his first speech in liberated Paris, at the prefecture of police on the evening of August 25, de Gaulle made it clear that he was preoccupied with the restoration of the full international position of France, and, in addition, that he had begun to focus this demand on the specific problem of equal French participation in the settlement of the German problem. The French government on September 14 officially asked the Allies for admission to the European Advisory Commission.[12] These points were reiterated by Foreign Minister Bidault on September 24, in the first discussion of his policy before the foreign press:

> . . . we wish to integrate ourselves into the order to be established by the Allies, but in a manner which will take into account our efforts and our pride. For international peace to exist, it is essential that France shall participate in its organization. . . . Since the Revolution we have been invaded three times, and on each occasion France was the first to feel the shock of the German armies. Once for all we must finish with the problem of Germany; I say that without hate and without fear. . . . France has never ceased to be a humane nation, and just because we are a humane nation we do not want any more German invasions. Neither do you, and for this reason you need French participation in the organization of the peace. The occupation of Germany must be assured not only by the Allied armies but also by our own soldiers; the manner of the occupation cannot be settled without the prior agreement of France. Because France is always the first to bear the brunt of the German onslaught, she must take part in the projects concerning Germany.[13]

Repeated assertions by the officials of the Provisional Government of the international need for France to resume her historic role as a Great Power failed, however, to move the major Allies, and the Dumbarton Oaks conference, which had opened on August 21, ended on October 7 without France's having been consulted. As a result, the main lines of the future United Nations organization were laid down without French participation, and though France was promised a permanent seat on the Security Council "in due course," this theoretical recognition of her equal status only underlined the fact that she was explicitly denied it at present. In a broadcast of October 14 de Gaulle protested the "kind of relegation" inflicted on France by her Allies, and in a press conference on October 25 he again asserted that it would be unthinkable for the fate of Germany or the terms of her occupation to be decided without France. On this occasion, for the first time, he also advanced more or less definite ideas about the future of Germany, including some type of special security arrangement in the Rhineland and the use of the Ruhr as an "arsenal of peace."[14]

French foreign policy was first systematically presented in an interview with Foreign Minister Bidault that appeared in the London *Sunday Times* on November 11.[15] Since Bidault could hardly have made a statement of such detail and magnitude without the agreement of his government, it is clear that by early November, 1944, agreement had been reached on the main lines of French foreign policy. Apart from specific proposals for the German settlement, which are considered in Chapter VII, French policy at this date, as revealed in the Bidault interview, can be summarized as follows: (1) France must be admitted to the councils of the Great Powers where, as Bidault suggested for perhaps the first time, she will be able to serve as a bridge between East and West, reducing their possible friction, because of her "understanding of Russia's conceptions and her spiritual and geographical proximity to the Anglo-Saxon countries." Because France will again be strong, Bidault suggests that the three Great Powers whose company she will inevitably soon join would do well to court her support; (2)

Dumbarton Oaks may "be designed" to form the basis for world peace, but France will seek her security in alliances with Eastern Europe and in some type of regional understanding in Western Europe, including an imperial entente with Great Britain; (3) the partly rhetorical proclamation of French interest in the rights of small nations was probably also meant to imply that France would not close the door to the possibility that, in some circumstances, she might lead them in opposition to the dictatorship, too long prolonged, of the *three* Great Powers. This, in turn, indicated that France was not without diplomatic resources and underscored the importance for the Allies themselves of her being included in their councils.

De Gaulle and Bidault pressed their claims and ideas on Churchill and Eden when, on French invitation, the British leaders visited Paris on November 10–14. The talks were hardly satisfactory from the French point of view. The British backed away from urgent French requests for assistance in equipping the French army. They said that the French should have an occupation zone in Germany, but were not very open about their own or Allied thinking on the subject, and in reaffirming their desire to see France play a role in Syria and Lebanon similar to their own in Iraq, they also pressed the French to make good the pledges of independence which they had made to those countries in 1941.[16]

On a broader level, de Gaulle attempted to persuade Churchill that their two countries, both weakened, both facing the rival American and Soviet colossi, and both imbued with "a certain conception of man despite the progressive mechanization of society," should coordinate their policies for their common good and the good of Europe. Churchill, however, answered in effect that it was better to try to guide the strongest powers than to work against them and that he had hopes of leading both Roosevelt and Stalin in the right path. De Gaulle concluded from these talks that the British, faced with "the voracity of the Russians and the capitalistic ideology of the Americans," would pursue only their own national interest: "The peace which we French wanted to help build according to what seemed to us to be logic and justice the English judged expedient to treat according to the recipes of empiricism and compromise."[17]

Had he expected a different answer from the British? On the eve of D-Day Churchill had said that, whenever he was forced to choose between the open sea and Europe, between Roosevelt and de Gaulle, he would always choose the former alternative. While de Gaulle might think the British misunderstood their national interest in making this choice, he could not have expected that they—or anyone—would prefer "logic and justice" to their national interest as they saw it. His summary of the November meeting with Churchill confirms this: "No trial changes the nature of man; no crisis, that of states." He did not need these conversations to convince him that no one would concern himself with French interests except the French. His policy was always based on no other assumption.[18]

The British leaders did, however, take the occasion to underline the theoretical recognition of Great Power status given to France at Dumbarton Oaks. Thus, speaking on November 12, Churchill said: "It is a moment for France to take her place among the other great powers"; and Eden, reporting to the House of Commons on November 14, spoke also of "France's position as a Great Power."[19]

These words had been partially implemented on November 11 when it was announced in Washington, London, and Moscow that France had been invited to participate in the European Advisory Commission as a full and permanent member and on a basis of complete equality. Ten days later, René Massigli, the

French ambassador to London, was appointed to serve on the commission. Thus, insofar as the Big Three were willing to make use of the Advisory Commission as a policy-making organism for the European settlement, France appeared to have taken a long stride toward her goal of equal rights and status with them. But it was doubtful even at the time that the commission would actually supersede other permanent or temporary decision-making organs of the three major Allies and, as the sequel showed, this French success was of limited importance.

France's inclusion on the commission had been initiated, it was believed in France, by the Soviet Union, and it was announced a few days later that de Gaulle and Bidault had accepted an invitation to visit Moscow and would shortly leave for the Soviet capital.[20] A few days before their departure the Consultative Assembly held a two-day debate on foreign policy —the first since its return to Paris—which forms an important record of opinion on foreign policy in France toward the end of 1944.[21] Bidault's speech to the Assembly was far less explicit and concrete than his interview of November 11. Though he referred to the Rhine as "this French river," he did not elaborate the government's German policy, on the ground that it could be fully developed only when that of the Allies was better known. He did, however, lay particular emphasis on French relations with the Soviet Union and was at pains to dissipate the anxiety of those who feared an exclusive western orientation:

> There is no question of France's participating in some kind of Western cordon, which would cast back into the depths of the continent all those who are not privileged to live beside the ocean. That we shall not do.
> An alliance in the West? Certainly. How could we do otherwise? But also an alliance in the East.

In thus stressing France's good and equal relations with the three major Allies, Bidault reaffirmed his statement of November 11 that France could serve in the councils of the Great Powers as a bridge between East and West.

De Gaulle spoke at greater length, but laid his main emphasis once more on France's equal rights as a Great Power. In regard to the special position to be held in the new world organization by the strongest powers, he stated:

> In our eyes France is, without any possible doubt, one of these powers. She declares herself, from this moment, ready to bear once again the obligations which preponderant duties imply, notably concerning her armed forces and certain of her resources. On the other hand, she clearly judges that she cannot be bound in any way by any measure concerning Europe, and by any major arrangement concerning another part of the world, which she was not able to consider in the same conditions as those who decided them.
>
> We have the conviction, bred in our nature and, we think, shared by a vast part of the world, that by holding to this attitude and accepting the obligations of it we are best serving the general interest.

He was aware, however, that France's position could not be based solely on constant reassertion of her rights, but must have a solid foundation in power:

> Thus, gentlemen, hardly has France come up from the abyss than her rights and duties reappear at the same time as herself. Perhaps, even, she is before one of those occasions of history when a people sees offered to it a

destiny as great as its trials have been severe. Certainly
we cannot sustain our rights nor accomplish our duties
if we renounce the basis of both which is called power.
But all signs, including the debate which has just taken
place here, prove that we have not renounced—much
to the contrary—and this is better for the world.

This attitude adumbrated the preoccupation with military
strength which was to become so important an issue during
de Gaulle's last months in office. But it did little more in November, 1944, than to underline his often repeated determination
to restore France's equal international position—defined as com-
prising her participation in all decisions made in Europe and in
all major decisions made elsewhere.

If the government, on the eve of an important international
negotiation, was reticent about its policy, other speakers ven-
tured somewhat further afield. Most took for granted the creation of a world security organization with control of armaments
and automatic sanctions. But every speaker who dealt with the
German problem refused to place full confidence for French
security in the new world organization—all believed that France
must have more definite and reliable guarantees in military
strength, alliances, and such special measures as the total occupation and disarmament of Germany. The rightist Louis Marin
asked for guarantees of French security on the Rhine similar
to those which, he said, the Soviet Union was already developing on the Oder, and some speakers went so far as to urge the
assimilation into France or deportation of the Germans living
in the Rhineland. It is most significant that, despite the prewar
opposition of much of the left to the classical nationalist policy
toward Germany, many speakers far to the left of Marin now
advocated special security measures and alliances. Even the

Communist spokesman, Florimond Bonte, came very near to the traditional nationalist position by his strong emphasis on the importance of the Soviet alliance. Only the Socialists remained somewhat apart from this general concurrence. Daniel Mayer specifically opposed annexation or dismemberment of purely German territories. At the same time, he was perhaps the only speaker in this debate to suggest, as an alternative to such measures, that increased economic collaboration among the European nations might lead to a federation which in time would be endowed with security functions.

Several speakers, seeking to reformulate the basis for France's claim to a status of the first rank, maintained that she had the right and the duty to lead the small nations of the world in a quest for justice, if not to lead all nations, by the example of her institutions or by the force of her intellectual position. Such assertions reflected the obvious fact that when a nation wishes to maintain a rank for which it no longer possesses the material attributes it will tend to put forward its historical, moral or intellectual importance as a substitute for power. But closely allied to these themes was another idea whose aim was the same but which was expressed specifically in terms of France's relations to the Great Powers whose company she aspired to join. In his interview of November 11, Bidault had argued that the admission of a fourth state to the councils of the major Allies, far from making their work more difficult, would actually facilitate it because "France can play a valuable part in forming a bridge between East and West. France's understanding of Russia's conceptions and her spiritual and geographical proximity to the Anglo-Saxon countries put her into a position in which she could usefully contribute to reducing the possibilities of friction between East and West." Bidault was providing France's demands for inclusion with a basis which they did not have in material strength—the basis of a new role which she alone could fill and in a manner so useful to the other three powers and to the world as to justify their allowing her to play it.

While nearly every speaker in the assembly debate expressed the idea that France must not take sides among the Great Powers but must remain on equally good terms with all of them, no less than five of the orators, representing diverse political positions, went a step further and reiterated Bidault's claim that France had a positive role to play in their councils—the role of a bridge or link between them. Thus, Louis Saillant, president of the C. N. R., called France "the hyphen (*trait d'union*) between the nations," and Maurice Schumann, M. R. P. leader, said that "France is in a way the wedding ring of the great marriage, as she was the forward guard of the coalition. She is its necessary cement. To say it better, she is its soul." Joseph Costa described France as the bridge "between the British Empire and the new Russia." Vincent Auriol, the Socialist leader and president of the Foreign Affairs Commission, called on France to "play her role of conciliator, mediator, to dissipate misunderstandings, reduce frictions. . . ." Finally, Louis Marin, praising the impending trip to Moscow, asked France to link the West and the Soviet Union.

These speakers, like Bidault himself, had to redefine France's claims to Great Power status in the light of her material weakness. They not only vaunted her moral or intellectual superiority, but went on to elaborate for her a possibly unique contribution in the councils of the powers—that of "hyphen" and "wedding ring," of bridge and conciliator between East and West. That they thus assumed friction between the Soviet Union and the Anglo-Saxon powers indicates both their realistic analysis of the international situation—far from universally shared in November, 1944—and also, despite their pleas for Great Power unity, perhaps also their hope for at least that measure of discord which would permit France to assume the role they outlined for her.[22]

The image of a neutral France, linked in the same degree with each of the three Great Powers and conciliating their conflicting interests, offered to each of the three, in the French view, the hope that on a particular issue France would provide that nation with new support against one or both of the others. Insofar as the Western Powers would welcome the presence of a third colleague of similar institutions and civilization in their bargainings with the Soviet Union, and insofar as the latter would welcome the presence of a continental power whose policies on Germany would probably be complementary to her own—to that extent, each of the three powers would see some advantage to itself in admitting France to their councils. Yet, at the same time, the role thus sketched for France, while based upon the firmest realities of power politics, could be clothed in the more benign aspect of conciliator and peacemaker.

Finally, such a policy was in perfect accord with the exigencies of domestic politics; the unity of the resistance could be projected onto the international scene, and the government, formed of elements ranging from the Communists to the right, could maintain its unity on foreign policy through the formula of balance and neutrality. It is true that Bidault's words of November 11—"France's understanding of Russia's conceptions and her spiritual and geographical proximity to the Anglo-Saxon countries"—indicate that to him, at least, France, if forced to choose between East and West, would go more naturally with the West. Yet, as the Assembly debate indicated, an accord with the Soviet Union provided a meeting ground for Communists and nationalists, so that the problem of ultimate alignment was not posed in late 1944. De Gaulle, it is interesting to observe, had not yet enunciated the policy of balance as his own. But the idea fitted well with his preoccupation of restoring France to her Great Power status by giving her a more or less convincing and persuasive claim which she could not make on a material basis alone. Although this policy was clearly evolved and stated before domestic politics had fully crystallized, it was nevertheless a policy which would prove useful when conflicting political interests became more sharply defined and the task of conciliating them within the government became more difficult.

The Franco-Soviet Pact

It has been argued that the Provisional French Government signed an alliance with the Soviet Union in December, 1944 in order to secure the support of the French Communist Party at home. The government needed the support of the Communists, and there can be little doubt, indeed, that the emphasis and phraseology of Bidault's statement to the Consultative Assembly on November 21 had as a major objective an assurance to them that the Catholic president and foreign minister would pursue no anti-Soviet policy abroad. But the Communists had apparently reached their decision to remain within the government and to accept its dismantling of some of their own sources of power early in the autumn, even before Maurice Thorez returned from Moscow. While the signing of such a pact no doubt strengthened the internal position of the government, the primary motivation for it lay in the international arena.

The government was aware that an understanding with the U.S.S.R. would be very popular among Frenchmen of all political views who believed that a Franco-Russian alliance against Germany was a traditional guarantee of French security, the lack of which brought upon France the disaster of 1940. But the most pressing problem before the French government in the autumn of 1944 was not the danger of a new German attack; it was the re-establishment of the international position of France. To de Gaulle and other nationalists preoccupied with this question, the support of the Soviet Union must have appeared almost indispensable. France remained estranged from the United States by years of antagonism and bitterness and from Great Britain by continuing imperial rivalry in the Levant and elsewhere; she herself was occupied by, and dependent on, the Anglo-American army. Under these circumstances, the French government inevitably sought a balance against Western pressure by means of an understanding with the principal ally with whom it had the least contact and therefore the fewest causes of friction. By doing so it would demonstrate its independence of the Western allies and hold before the British, who expected an early American withdrawal from the continent, the prospect of a Franco-Soviet understanding on Germany from which they would be excluded.[23] It was not unreasonable to believe that Great Britain, and the United States in her wake, would then re-evaluate the French position upward and would adopt an attitude—including support of France's claims to Great Power status, acceptance of a satisfactory solution to the question of the Levant, and receptivity to France's ideas on the German settlement—which would preclude France from exclusive cooperation with the Soviet Union.[24]

Such a prospect made an alliance with the U.S.S.R. dazzling indeed from the French point of view. The Russian attitude is more obscure. The Soviet government, as past and subsequent events demonstrate, had a low opinion of French claims and little regard for French interests, but it could not fail to have been aware that a pact with the Provisional Government would greatly enhance the position within France of the French Communist Party. The French government thus basically viewed the pact, not as a bridge to the Communist Party, whose support was already achieved, but as an indispensable international instrument; the Soviet Union, for whom such an alliance was of little significance in itself—and who was unable to win in exchange the one foreign policy concession by France that it had sought—was willing to strengthen the international position of the Gaullist government in order to consolidate the position of the French Communist Party within that government and within France and to demonstrate the gains which the party's cooperation could win for a government which it supported.

De Gaulle and his party visited Moscow from December 2 to December 10.[25] Like the Franco-British talks of November, the meetings were less than satisfactory to the French, though it is difficult to measure de Gaulle's immediate disappointment for lack of knowledge of his expectations. At his first meeting with Stalin his most ambitious hope was blocked: to his proposal that France and the Soviet Union should concert their policy toward defeated Germany and then present it jointly to the other allies, Stalin replied that nothing could be done without the other powers. Thus, when de Gaulle outlined his thinking about the German settlement—proposing detachment of the Rhineland and the Ruhr with, apparently, French control of the former and international control of the latter—and suggested that Stalin agree to support these plans, he met the same response: only the four major allies could handle these problems (though the inclusion of France on an equal footing with the Big Three was some consolation to de Gaulle if he took these words at face value). Despite Soviet refusal to consider these questions, de Gaulle indicated that he would raise no objection to the assigning of German territory up to the Oder-Neisse line to Poland in compensation for Poland's loss of its lands beyond the Curzon line to the Soviet Union—a solution which would prevent a Polish-German rapprochement and would set, he must have hoped, a valuable precedent for Germany's future western frontier.

Though de Gaulle insisted throughout 1945 that no Franco-British alliance could be signed until they had reached agreement on their outstanding political differences, he was less exigent toward the Soviet Union. The importance to him of a treaty as such, whatever the lack of agreement on concrete issues, overrode other concerns. But the French had still to overcome two obstacles to achieve even this in Moscow. In the middle of the conference Churchill telegraphed to Stalin (who had sought his and Roosevelt's opinions on the subject), but not to de Gaulle, and proposed that, instead of there being a Franco-Soviet pact as a complement to the Anglo-Soviet treaty of 1942, there might be a tripartite treaty. Such an agreement would, of course, deprive de Gaulle of both the psychological advantages that he expected from a pact with the Soviet Union and the leverage that he hoped to exert on the British by delay, and he argued strongly, on other grounds, of course, against Churchill's proposal. He finally persuaded Stalin.[26]

Stalin, however, raised a far more serious difficulty, which prevented the treaty from being signed until the last hours of de Gaulle's visit. The Russians led the French to understand, with increasing firmness, that they required French recognition of the "Lublin Committee" set up by the Soviet Union to govern Poland and the de-recognition of the Polish government-in-exile in London as a condition of signature. After many hours of discussion, de Gaulle made it clear that while he favored an independent, democratic Poland, friendly to the Soviet Union as well as to France, he could not accept the Lublin group. At the last minute Stalin agreed to conclude the treaty in any case. It was signed at 4:00 A.M. on the morning of December 10.[27]

The Franco-Soviet pact comprised an introduction, setting forth the purposes of the parties in general terms, and eight articles, the substance of which was as follows:

1. The parties undertake to continue the war against Germany until her final surrender, to lend each other all possible aid in the war (Article 1) and to make no separate armistice or treaty of peace (Article 2).

2. At the end of the war the parties will take by common accord all measures necessary to prevent a new German aggression or any action which might render possible a new attempt at aggression (Article 3).

3. If either party finds itself at war with Germany because of the latter's aggression, or by the play of Article 3, the other will immediately render all possible aid and assistance (Article 4).

4. The parties will form no alliance nor enter into any coalition hostile to each other (Article 5).

5. The parties will lend each other all possible economic assistance after the war, to facilitate their reconstruction and to promote the prosperity of the world (Article 6).[28]

Unlike the Franco-Soviet alliance of 1935, in which action was conditional to the operation of League of Nations procedures, this treaty contained no reference or relation to the future world security organization, but was automatic in its application. To this extent, the treaty of 1944 was meeting the necessities of 1935 or 1939. As suggested above, however, the condition of Germany in late 1944 made it improbable that the real meaning of the treaty lay in the clauses by which the parties pledged mutual support against future German aggression. Nor was it probable that either party feared that the other might make a separate armistice or peace with Germany.

The heart and substance of the treaty from the French point of view lay in the significant wording of Article 3:

> The High Contracting Parties pledge themselves to take by common agreement, at the conclusion of the present conflict with Germany, all measures necessary to eliminate any new threat coming from Germany and to oppose any initiative of a kind to render possible a new attempt at aggression on her part.

From this text two significant implications were drawn by most French commentators: (1) that the Soviet Union would concert with France on the postwar settlement for Germany and therefore, by extension, considered France a state to be reckoned with in the making of that settlement—that is, a major power; (2) that France and the U.S.S.R. would supervise Germany so closely as not only to counter an open aggression against either of them but also to prevent any situation from transpiring in Germany—such, for example, as the establishment of a Fascist or militaristic regime—which might render a new aggression possible.

The feature of the pact which attracted most attention in France was the implication that its signature represented the restoration of France to the rank of a Great Power. This view was given considerable support by the statement of the Soviet ambassador to France, Alexander Bogomolov, in a press conference on December 17:

. . . the Franco-Soviet pact constitutes a first step in the organization of peace in Europe. It is for this reason that it has been received with such favor at Moscow and by all the allied countries. Because all the powers which have been the most active in this war—that is, Great Britain, the United States, Russia and France—understand that they must act in common to reach the goal which they have fixed for themselves.

The role of France in this business is very great. On the continent Germany will remain placed between Russia and France. That is why the Franco-Soviet pact allows us to think that Frenchmen and Russians, with all their allies, will be able to assure to Europe a stable and durable peace.[29]

The new, well-informed daily, *Le Monde*, described the pact as being received in France as ". . . a dazzling sign of her renaissance and her reappearance in the rank of the great powers," and this view was repeated by the president of the Provisional Consultative Assembly, Félix Gouin, in his remarks to that body on December 12, when he described the treaty as ". . . the dazzling sign of French grandeur reconquered."[30]

Opening the discussion of the pact in the assembly on December 21, Bidault emphasized that the treaty was based on both necessity and sentiment, on reason and heart.[31] Germany, he said, had profited more than once from the division of East and West, and this alliance aimed to prevent her doing so again. But opening the door to one of the results which the pact was designed to achieve, he added that while France wanted no Western bloc neither did she desire an exclusively continental alliance, and this treaty represented only the first step in a security system which must include the United States, Great

Britain, and other nations. As for Germany, he said that no security organization or alliance system provided adequate guarantees for France:

> To deprive Germany of the ability to do harm . . . it is appropriate also to take from her the means of doing harm. It is this which our Russian friends and ourselves have decided to accomplish for today, for tomorrow and forever.
>
> We have raised no objection to the tracing of the frontiers which the Soviet government envisages in the East. . . .
>
> As for us, we have clearly, firmly indicated to our interlocutors that we intend definitively to deprive Germany of the territories which have served her, up to now, at the same time as arsenal and springboard for aggression in the West, that is, essentially the Rhineland, including the Rhine-Westphalian basin.
>
> . . . Germany must no longer be able to concentrate troops at Mainz and Cologne; it is on the contrary the forces of the free countries, and above all ours, to whom will belong henceforth the task of assuring the watch on the Rhine; further, the manufactures and factories of the Rhine valley and the Ruhr must henceforth work, not for the Prussian war machine but, first, for the reparation of all the damages it has caused and then to contribute to the prosperity of the peoples.

Bidault thus admitted that the French, while raising no objection to the Soviet plans for the Polish frontiers, did no more than present their own ideas on Germany's western borders. The Russians made no reciprocal commitment on the latter.

De Gaulle's speech was more general than that of the foreign minister, and apart from a discussion of French and Russian experience of the German danger since 1870, he dwelt principally on the "categorical imperative of geography, experience and good sense" which formed the basis for the alliance. But de Gaulle, too, stated that this accord was only the basis for a larger system which must include Great Britain, the United States and other nations. Neither de Gaulle nor Bidault, however, made any mention of France's rights as a Great Power, despite the triumph expressed in the press and the assembly. This was probably due to the fact that while they did not object to increasing the government's prestige by permitting the French people to believe that success had been achieved, they realized the limits of what they had accomplished in Moscow.

The other speakers, on the contrary, were little less than a chorus in proclaiming that the Franco-Soviet pact marked the reassumption by France of her Great Power status. Among many others, the dean of the Communists, Marcel Cachin, spoke of the "sumptuous present" as a result of which "the whole world recognizes that the prestige of France has with one stroke reached the highest summits," and Joseph Paul-Boncour, the veteran diplomat and politician, stated in similar terms that "France has again become a great power with which the greatest continental power treats." Other subjects were referred to during this discussion, including the German settlement, but the belief of all the speakers in the reestablishment of the French position among the Great Powers most clearly stands out from their remarks. There is little doubt, indeed, that both the government and the assembly members, though in varying degrees, considered the pact with the Soviet Union as representing a long step toward the completion of the second phase of France's diplomatic renaissance—her readmission to the councils of the

Great Powers—and as opening the third—the presentation there of her views on Germany and other problems. The pact, in short, appeared or was taken to mean that the Soviet Union accepted France as a full partner and had already developed with her the main lines of a common policy on Germany. It was assumed that the two Western allies would soon be obliged to do the same. But despite Ambassador Bogomolov's statement, the Yalta conference soon demonstrated that many Frenchmen had read too literally a treaty which, to their Soviet partners, probably represented mainly, though not wholly, a move on the board of French internal politics.

CHAPTER IV

WAR AND VICTORY: JANUARY–APRIL 1945

The Revival of Politics in France

Political activity revived rapidly in France in the months after the liberation, but in a somewhat muted and covert manner. Since the Provisional French Government included every important anti-collaborationist group, and since the Consultative Assembly was made up of representatives of the same groups and had no power to control the executive, politics consisted of maneuvering for future position and of disguised conflicts within non-governmental organizations. The most important common factor running through these events was the Communist policy promoting the unification and fusion of the parties, labor organizations, and resistance movements that it hoped to dominate while, at the same time, it refrained from any open challenge to the government of which it was a part.

The Communist line reflected in these developments was laid down at a meeting of the Central Committee on January 21, 1945, in the important speech of Maurice Thorez referred to in the preceding chapter. In this, he explicitly endorsed the dissolution of the *Milices* and other irregular forces and strongly supported the prerogatives of the government against the claims of local liberation committees. At the same time, he called for a French army of one million men and thirty-five to forty equipped divisions. In thus dwelling on the "national mission" of the Communist party, Thorez and other speakers made clear that, at least for the moment, they were determined to seek power within the existing political framework. Unwilling as yet to challenge de Gaulle's power, and falling short of a national majority in itself, the party therefore promoted fronts and groupings with other organizations which, with the P. C. F., might reasonably be expected to provide such a majority but which, at the same time, the Communists could hope to dominate by their superior discipline and solidarity. The potential "left" coalition which the Communists eventually hoped to use as their vehicle for taking power could therefore include the Socialists and even the "bourgeois" Radicals, who could be called "left" only by tradition, but not the more progressive Christian Democratic party, the Popular Republican Movement (M. R. P.), in which the Communists saw a rival too strong, both ideologically and tactically, to be controlled.

As early as December 4, 1944, the Communist and Socialist parties established a permanent entente committee to study current problems in common and to consider the means to achieve the "political unity of the working class." But the Socialists were both attracted and repelled by the idea of union with the massive and monolithic Communist Party and were fearful of losing either their working-class or middle-class adherents. Thus, they cooperated with the Communists on certain specific issues and occasions but avoided explicit consideration of the organic fusion of the two parties. As a result, the *Mouvement de Libération Nationale*, which met in January, 1945, and was largely under Socialist influence, rejected the "unity of the resistance" which was offered to it by the Communist-led *Front National*.

Nor were the Communists successful in their effort to bring about the fusion of the *Confédération Générale du Travail*, which they now effectively controlled, with the Catholic *Confédération Française des Travailleurs Chrétiens*.

Despite this triple setback on the political, resistance, and labor fronts, the Communists did not give up hope of developing close cooperation and eventually fusion with the Socialists. They therefore continued to play their role as a "national party," and, as a corollary to this, they were very restrained in their criticism of the government of which they formed a part. Thus, when the C. N. R. complained late in February that the government had relegated the Consultative Assembly to a secondary role, it received little support from the Communists. Yet, at the same time, the Communists permitted themselves certain well-chosen attacks on the government or, rather, on a number of particular ministers. The minister of justice, François de Menthon, was strongly attacked both in the assembly and in the Communist press for his handling of the purge, and the minister of information, Pierre-Henri Teitgen, came under violent abuse from the Communist organ *L'Humanité* for his management of paper allocation and the press. The issues selected for attack were among those which could be exploited politically, and it was not by chance that both de Menthon and Teitgen were members of the M. R. P. Similarly, during the campaign preceding the municipal elections of late April and early May, the Communists strongly protested the government's decision, against the wish of the assembly, to maintain until July 1 the state subsidies granted to private (largely Catholic) schools by Vichy. The object of this maneuver, which met with some success, was to revive the clerical issue as a bar to cooperation between the Socialists and the M. R. P., thereby attempting to force the former into exclusive cooperation with the Communists.

The most striking example of the Communist attitude toward the government was manifested during the crisis on fiscal and economic policy which divided the cabinet early in 1945. In the months following the liberation of France in August, 1944, the government faced a complex task of importing both raw materials and foodstuffs as well as reviving industrial production, which was far below the prewar level. In addition, since the Vichy regime had recourse to a drastic inflation of the currency to cover occupation costs and the government deficit, the Provisional Government had to deal not only with the basic economic problem of production but with the further difficulties of adjusting prices, wages, monetary circulation, and the public revenues. Two policies were advanced within the cabinet to meet the economic and financial situation. The minister of the national economy, Pierre Mendès-France, supported by the Socialists, advocated reducing monetary circulation by a drastic operation, including exchange of notes, blocking of accounts, massive seizure of illicit profits, and price-fixing. The successive finance ministers, Aimé Lepercq and René Pleven, preferred more conservative methods, including a public loan, with an appeal to the confidence of savers.[1] This view prevailed with de Gaulle and was implemented by the government. Production, however, remained low and inflation substantially unchecked. Therefore, when the government presented its 1945 budget to the assembly, with a planned deficit of over 50 percent, the Socialists strongly attacked the inadequacy of its policies, though without particular success.[2] On April 6, Mendès-France resigned, announcing frankly that his views were in discord with Pleven's and that one of the two therefore had to leave the government. Pleven's policy of encouraging production by permitting price rises was at once implemented by the cabinet and a new spiral of price and wage adjustments began.

The victory of Pleven's policy over that of Mendès-France and the Socialists can be understood only in terms of de Gaulle's position. It seems clear that de Gaulle was interested in financial and economic questions, as in social reform, only to the extent that they influenced the international position of France.[3] Since he desired above all else a unified France to strengthen his position in dealing with the Allies, he was persuaded by Pleven and others that a severe economic and fiscal policy would disrupt national unity, whereas a conservative policy would induce confidence and thus unite and strengthen the nation. The same attitude can be seen in his increasingly moderate view of the purge and his advocacy of "reconciliation" of all but the most conspicuous Vichyites with the rest of the country.[4]

In all these instances, de Gaulle was carrying into the post-liberation era his wartime concept of himself as trustee and guardian of the interests of the whole of France, as opposed to those of any party or faction. The greater his difficulties with foreign powers, the greater his determination to maintain French unity around himself, so that his refusal to meet Roosevelt at Algiers after the Yalta conference and the pursuance of the fiscal and economic policies which ended in the resignation of Mendès-France can both be considered to flow from the same source: the inferior diplomatic status of France which was symbolized by the humiliation of Yalta. It probably did not occur to de Gaulle that these fiscal policies might in the long run weaken the basic economic and therefore political strength of the country; if so, this consideration weighed lightly in his mind against the present need for unity.

One of the most significant aspects of this conflict on economic policy, in terms of domestic and foreign policies, was the attitude of the Communists. It is striking that the strongest support for Mendès-France and the principal opposition to Pleven's policies came almost entirely, not from the Communists, but from the Socialists.[5] The occasional Communist opposition to the government specifically centered around a few chosen issues and ministers—usually M. R. P. members. And it was the Socialists, not the Communists, who were thought—incorrectly—to be likely to resign from the cabinet after Mendès-France's downfall.[6] Though Communist support of the Socialists on this issue might have brought success to the latter and contributed to the alliance of the two parties, which was so important a Communist goal, no such real support was offered. The acceptance by the Communists of so conservative an economic policy can best be explained by their desire to maintain de Gaulle's administration, and this in turn can be interpreted at least in part in terms of foreign policy.

For the Communists, the optimum foreign policy, second to complete alignment with the U.S.S.R., was that being pursued by de Gaulle which, in practice, involved a coolness toward the two western powers. Should de Gaulle be driven from office before the Communists perfected their alliance with the Socialists and were thereby in a position to assume a preponderant share of power, it was possible that an administration under Socialist-M. R. P. leadership would take office, with a foreign policy, even if the Communists remained in the government, which would be more western-oriented than de Gaulle's. The Communists, more flexible than the Socialists in the adaptation of their theoretical position to political realities, therefore found it possible to accept the Gaullist regime, despite Pleven's policies, as preferable to a probable alternative. But since, at the same time, they pursued their efforts to bring the Socialists and others of the "left" into an exclusive alignment with them, their entente with de Gaulle was doubly dependent on the time required for the consummation of this task and on the continued evolution of the government's foreign policy along the same lines.

The Yalta Conference

When the Franco-Soviet pact was signed in December, 1944, the French press, as well as the members of the Consultative Assembly, emphasized that a Franco-British agreement would be the proper supplement to the Moscow treaty. De Gaulle no doubt had the same idea as part of his policy of attempting to maneuver between the U.S.S.R. and Great Britain, and he had indicated as much at Moscow when he insisted on a bilateral alliance with the Soviet Union rather than a tripartite pact such as Churchill had proposed. But despite rumors that Ambassador Massigli had taken a French draft proposal to London at the end of December, or that de Gaulle and Churchill exchanged views on the subject when the latter visited France in the first days of January, no treaty or other agreement was concluded.[7] It is probable that the French government did not particularly press the question, for it remained convinced that the British, isolated before a Franco-Russian understanding, would find an entente with France sufficiently valuable to be willing in due course to agree to a worldwide settlement of all questions outstanding between them, and particularly that of the Levant. De Gaulle said as much to the British in November, 1944, and to the Russians a month later.[8] Thus, in a press conference on January 25, de Gaulle said that one day or another France and

Britain would define the nature of their alliance, by means of a pact.[9] That is, he assumed the existence of an effective, if unwritten, alliance between the two countries and wanted the formal statement of it to go beyond mere mutual defense and embrace more detailed understandings on other subjects—to France's advantage.

But whatever hopes the French had placed in the Soviet government to strengthen their diplomatic bargaining power and to assure their restoration to effective Great Power rank were soon shattered. Even before France was invited to join the European Advisory Commission, the three Great Powers were making plans for another top level conference, and by the middle of January, 1945, it was known that they would meet within a few weeks and that de Gaulle would not be invited to join them.[10]

In the last days of January, Harry Hopkins stopped in Paris and had a cordial meeting with Bidault. Hopkins had hoped to resolve the lingering hostility between the United States and France, but his interview with de Gaulle ended as coolly as it had begun. De Gaulle had formally applied on January 15, without success, to be invited to the forthcoming conference and he believed, with reason, that the United States opposed France's presence.[11] He made clear to Hopkins that the Americans could not hope to improve their relations with France while excluding her from a conference at which the participants would try to settle the fate of Europe. More broadly, de Gaulle accused the United States of holding back the restoration of France's rank as a Great Power—a major consideration of the French, who "feel that their tranquillity and domestic prosperity are at that price." The United States, de Gaulle said, has not always understood that "the very fate of France was linked to this vocation of greatness." Hopkins seems to have been somewhat puzzled that his casual attempt to improve Franco-American relations, which included no concession on the matter of most importance to de Gaulle, produced so little result. But he suggested to Bidault that de Gaulle might meet Roosevelt at some French point in the Mediterranean area after the conference.[12]

In the face of this blow to the hopes that had been raised in France by the Soviet pact, de Gaulle, in a broadcast on February 5, resorted to hyperbole, as in his wartime speeches, to fill in the absence of power, referring to the one hundred million Frenchmen who would be able to secure their interests in war and peace. He warned the Allies that France would not be bound by any decision in whose formulation she had not had an equal role. A similar warning had already been included in notes to the three "other" Great Powers on January 15.[13]

France had been more or less assured that no decision concerning her would be made in her absence, but such assurances meant little, for the Yalta conference was obviously concerned with Germany as well as with other European problems in which France had the deepest interest. The European Advisory Commission had already worked out plans for dividing Germany into three zones of occupation, with greater Berlin as a joint zone. At the Anglo-American meeting at Malta prior to the Crimea conference it had been agreed that France should have an occupation zone in Germany, to be carved from the territory already assigned to the two Western Powers, and should be "integrated" into the German control machinery.[14] At Yalta itself, however, Stalin made very clear, as he had already done at Teheran, that he held a low opinion of France and of French pretensions to equal treatment with the Big Three. At first he would not agree that France should be assigned a zone, even, as Churchill and Roosevelt argued, for reasons of kindness.[15] It was Churchill and Eden who "fought

like tigers for France," arguing the importance of France to
Great Britain in forming the western barrier to a resurgent
Germany and maintaining that the French could not be indefinitely excluded from European councils—though they agreed
that there was no question of admitting them to the exclusive
club of the Big Three.[16] When Stalin yielded on the question of
the French zone—on condition that it be carved from British
and American territory without prejudice to the Russian zone—
the British found it difficult to convince Roosevelt that a necessary corollary of this decision was France's inclusion on the
German Control Council. In the end, Roosevelt was persuaded
of this and Stalin then concurred without discussion.[17]

The status of France was also at issue when the Allies discussed whether the European Advisory Commission should
study the dismemberment of Germany. Eden and Stettinius,
while inclined to leave the matter to the commission, partly because France was a member of it, finally agreed with Molotov
that the question would be referred to a secret committee to be
composed of Eden and Ambassadors Winant and Gusev in London, who would consider the inclusion of France in their work.
Eden also tried, without success, to include France as an original
member of the reparations commission established in Moscow.
The conference agreed, however, to invite France to associate
herself with the Declaration on Liberated Europe.[18] France was
not mentioned when it was decided that the foreign ministers
of the three powers would meet at regular intervals.

Indeed, the entire conference, including the discussions of the
future world security organization, was replete with comments
by all the participants on the importance of the continued unity
—and dominance—of the *three* Great Powers. Apart from the
invitation to France to become a host at the San Francisco conference—after the essential decisions on the new organization

had been made at Dumbarton Oaks and Yalta—the protocol which concluded the conference underlined the fact that the exclusion of France from the Crimea conference was more than a temporary or wartime expedient and that her acceptance as an equal partner by the Big Three was indefinitely deferred. The French press was therefore probably correct in concluding that, while France was granted the rank of a Great Power in formal organizations, such as the new international association, she was not so considered in non-organizational meetings such as those to be held by the foreign ministers.[19] That is, while the five world powers were supposedly to be of equal rank in carrying out international decisions, the Big Three reserved to themselves the authority to make them. France's Great Power rank was therefore more formal than real, and *Le Monde* expressed the general French view very temperately when it stated that "the Yalta decisions perhaps do not give to France the place which, according to the words of the press and of a good number of Allied statesmen, is manifestly hers."[20]

French Diplomacy after Yalta

The Big Three attempted to assuage French sensibilities by communicating the public results of the conference to de Gaulle on February 12, in advance of the release of the communiqué. One note invited France to participate in the occupation of Germany; the second invited her to adhere to the Declaration on Liberated Europe; and a memorandum dealt with the position of France at San Francisco. De Gaulle was, in general, satisfied with the substantial advance in France's position which these documents implied.[21] But he was not at all gratified by the invitation extended to him by Ambassador Caffery to confer with Roosevelt at Algiers. On February 13, de Gaulle declined the invitation, and the next day, while the presidential party was aboard the *Quincy* on Great Bitter Lake, they were so informed by Caffery.[22]

De Gaulle was irritated by Roosevelt's invitation on several counts. He felt that "To go see the President just after a conference at which he had opposed my presence really did not suit me." Then, he feared also that the meeting would imply his acceptance of all the Yalta decisions—and he strongly disapproved not only of those by which, in his view, the Balkans and Poland had been given up to the Soviet Union, but also those which, he suspected, dealt with the Levant and Indochina. In addition, "by what right did the American President invite the French President to visit him in France?"—although, de Gaulle adds, "It is true that, for Franklin Roosevelt, Algiers was perhaps not France." De Gaulle, in any case, did not like to be summoned to Roosevelt's battleship as the potentates of the Near East had been. "I found the thing exaggerated, whatever the present relation of forces. The sovereignty, the dignity of a great nation should be intangible. I was in charge of those of France."[23] In addition, he may have thought that this show of independence would strengthen his position at home.[24]

Efforts were made to conceal this painful incident, but it soon leaked to the press and both the French and American presidencies issued notes on it on February 20. The French statement declared, apart from thin expressions of courtesy and esteem for the American President, that General de Gaulle had been taken "by surprise, at a moment when many matters demanded his presence at Paris and on the morrow of a conference between three Allied chiefs of government, their counselors and their experts, a conference in which France had not taken part and of whose many objects she was still ignorant." Washington merely explained that the President had found it impossible to visit de Gaulle in Paris and was very disappointed when informed that the General could not come to Algiers.[25] Commenting on the incident, *Le Monde* went to lengths to explain that it involved no mere question of susceptibility, "legitimate though it might be," but that the attitude of the French government flowed logically from its prior position: France could not accept a *fait accompli* presented to her in this manner, without time to study or understand the decisions taken. On four points in particular, further information was necessary; zonal boundaries in Germany; the Berlin Control Council; San Francisco; and the charter of liberated Europe. Not having received this information at Yalta, the French government was obliged to resort to diplomatic channels to obtain it and could not commit itself prematurely.[26]

On February 17, Ambassador Bonnet had asked Under-Secretary of State Joseph Grew for further information on the Yalta decisions, and was given it within a few days, particularly on the subject of the liberated countries which, it was stated, the four powers would, in general, handle through the usual diplomatic channels rather than through a special organism. No information, however, was elicited as to what role France might play in the settlement of the Polish question nor on French participation as a regular member of the conferences of foreign ministers. The British government, at the same time, informed Massigli that France would sign the German armistice and would sit on the Berlin Control Council and that her zone would be delimited by the European Advisory Commission.

As a further gesture of courtesy, the British government invited Bidault to visit London for discussion of these issues. All questions, and particularly German problems, were considered during the Eden-Bidault conversations on February 26, and the atmosphere was considered cordial and friendly. But the French foreign minister was unable to gain satisfaction on the key issue of French participation in the periodic meetings of the foreign ministers—which had not been considered desirable at Yalta even in principle or for some future date. No particular reference was made to a Franco-British alliance, and it appears that neither the Levant nor Germany was considered in such a manner as to satisfy the requirements often laid down by the French government as a prelude to any written pact with Great Britain. But one apparent result of these talks was the French decision to accept the invitation to become a host power at the San Francisco conference, and part of the month of March was occupied with negotiations on this subject—which finally ended with France declining to sponsor the conference.

Apart from this, the accelerating Allied advance into Germany from both east and west posed ever more acutely the question of the surrender and occupation regime of that country, and March and April were filled with rumors and plans on this subject. The French position on the future of the Ruhr and Rhineland was stated often and in a fairly detailed manner both prior to and during the Crimea conference.[27] But the decisions of the three powers to grant France an occupation zone and a place on the Control Council for Germany had been made late and, on the part of the Russians, very reluctantly, and while the French welcomed even limited or executory participation in German control, the conference communiqué had passed over any discussion of the final settlement for Germany and did not even specify whether the French occupation zone would be in the Rhineland, as Paris desired. Questions on these subjects were asked in Washington and London, and Bidault repeated them during his brief visit to the latter capital; but neither the British nor American governments made any definite commitment on the occupation zone or the ultimate settlement.

De Gaulle, for his part, made great efforts as the war ended to have French troops occupy as much German territory as possible in order to strengthen France's hand in the bargaining over zonal boundaries.[28] He did this in the belief that he was acting against a determined American intention to restrict France's role in Germany. The commander of the First French Army, General Jean de Lattre de Tassigny, was ordered by de Gaulle, on March 29, to cross the Rhine "even if the Americans disagree and you have to do it on boats."[29] De Lattre did so on March 31, and then pushed on to capture Karlsruhe (April 4), Baden-Baden (April 12–13), and Stuttgart (April 18–21).[30] Unfortunately for the French, de Lattre's superior, General Devers, on April 22 insisted on implementing the plan by which his American forces were to occupy Stuttgart. When de Gaulle ordered de Lattre not to comply, President Truman threatened to cut off supplies to the French units. This painful incident ended with French acquiescence and a further strain on Franco-American relations.[31]

The development of the German situation during the spring corroborated the idea, implicit in the Yalta communiqué, of a hierarchy among the nominal Great Powers. France, whose theoretical position was acknowledged in the sphere of the future world organization, was systematically excluded from the basic decisions on the surrender and occupation of Germany. Such participation as she was promised—a zone and a seat on the Control Council—she received as the result of decisions reached entirely by the three powers, who continued to reserve to themselves exclusive policy-making authority in Germany. The European Advisory Commission, of which France was a member, was bypassed in the planning of much of the German surrender and occupation, and part of its functions were filled by the special London committee of three, established at Yalta, from which France was excluded. It was thus very clear in

March and April that the resumption of Great Power status by France, so triumphantly proclaimed in December, remained more nominal than real, and was particularly lacking in the area of greatest concern to France—the German problem.[32]

While it may not have been wholly clear to the French that their most resolute champions among the Great Powers were the British, with whom their relations were very reserved, they saw clearly that the Russians, with whom they were formally allied, were firm opponents of French claims. The Communist organ *L'Humanité* called Yalta a triumph for France, but ironically it was so only in comparison to the position which the Russians would have assigned to her. General Georges Catroux, assuming his post as ambassador to the U.S.S.R. soon after the Yalta conference, realized within a few weeks that "in high places there was reserve" toward France. When he presented the French request for inclusion in the reparations commission to Molotov, he was told that if France was admitted, then Poland and Yugoslavia should be also. Stalin told Catroux on March 20 that he would accept France, Poland, and Yugoslavia onto the commission—which was, in effect, a rejection of the French claim since the Western allies were not likely to accept Stalin's other candidates. The generalissimo also said that the Soviet Union was keeping its hands free in Germany—sad news indeed for the French, who had hoped that the alliance would at least establish Franco-Soviet cooperation on Germany. After this interview with Stalin, Catroux concluded that: "The Soviet government acted toward her [France] as if the alliance did not exist and as if it challenged her rank as a Great Power. . . . In short, Stalin had little interest in France, which he did not hold to be one of the factors of weight on the chess board."[33]

It was not clear to the French whether the Russians adopted this attitude in order to force them to align their policy with the Soviet Union's (as Stalin had tried to do in December—and

subsequently—in regard to Polish affairs), or to exercise leverage on the British and Americans who wanted to include France
in, for example, the reparations commission, or to restrict allied
policymaking on Germany to as few participants as possible.
But it was obvious to the French that the alliance of December
10 had been worth far less than they had expected and that reliance on it was not a fruitful policy. Circumstances, therefore,
dictated an effort to improve relations with the United States
and Great Britain, and it was precisely this which the Communists wished to avert by presenting Yalta as a French success.
But de Gaulle made no overture to the two Western powers—
perhaps for fear of alienating the U.S.S.R. even more—and in
fact became seriously embroiled with the United States in Germany and Italy, and with the British in the Levant. At the same
time, he was impelled to concentrate ever more strongly on
building France's own strength through military expenditures
which weighed with a crushing burden on the weakened economy of the country. Further, he was convinced that national
unity must be preserved in order for France to confront the
Allies effectively. This, in turn, led to the economic and financial policies which, as was pointed out above, followed a
moderate course for fear of dividing the country by any more
vigorous or reformist policy.

The French government made one attempt, however, in the
months following the Yalta conference, to demonstrate to the
major allies that it was not entirely without diplomatic resources. During the visits to Paris of the Belgian and Dutch
foreign ministers, on February 21–22 and March 18–20, respectively, the French were able to win the general support of these
smaller states for their German policy, particularly in regard to
the Ruhr and Rhineland. France thereby tried to strengthen her
claim to be admitted to the discussions of the Great Powers
on Germany as the representative of Western Europe.[34] In addi-

tion, the French government perhaps meant to suggest by these meetings that it might yet assume the leadership of the smaller states of Europe against the continued dominance of the Big Three. A parallel line of policy was explored to a certain extent by the French in the formulation of their position at the San Francisco conference, but it was abandoned there. Then, after the humiliating exclusion from the Potsdam conference, French thoughts once again turned in the direction of Western Europe.

Despite the rebuffs which France had suffered during February and March, de Gaulle was able to say, in an address made on April 25, that France, little by little, was regaining her rank and weight in the world: "We have always thought and always said that there will be no valid settlements except in the presence and support of France. . . . As for others, whether in Europe, Africa, the Orient, the Pacific, we consider that the fate of none will be really settled unless France is involved in a direct manner in whatever will have been discussed and agreed on the subject."[35] And when, early in May, friction between the three major powers over the establishment of a Polish government reached new heights, *Le Monde* could draw the moral which the policy of the French government implied: "The 'Big Three' can see today that they gained nothing by not admitting our country to the talks at which they have the pretention to settle the fate of the world by themselves. As the friend of each, and having the greatest interest in the agreement of all, France might have been able to play a useful and beneficial role, avoiding clashes and suggesting compromise solutions."[36] Thus, at the moment of German surrender and the gathering at San Francisco of the first postwar conference, the claims maintained by the de Gaulle government throughout the war and the policy laid down by the French government from the end of 1944 remained fully intact, despite all rebuffs.

CHAPTER V

THE FOUNDING OF THE UNITED NATIONS

At the Moscow conference of foreign ministers in October, 1943, the United States, Great Britain, and the Soviet Union undertook to establish a new international organization "at the earliest practicable date." The Chinese ambassador gave his government's concurrence. It was agreed after further negotiation that representatives of these four governments would meet to work out their ideas on the subject (in two separate sessions, since the Russians, who were not at war with Japan, declined to sit with the Chinese). The Anglo-Soviet-American phase of the conference met at Dumbarton Oaks, in Washington, from August 21 to September 28, 1944; the rather perfunctory phase including the Chinese followed. The general structure of the League of Nations was at once agreed upon as the outline for the new organization.

A Security Council, on which the Great Powers would serve as permanent members, was a major feature of the plan. At the Teheran conference, President Roosevelt had spoken of the "four policemen" who would keep the peace, including among them, the participants of the Moscow conference and China.[1] At Dumbarton Oaks, however, the British, consistent with their policy of generally supporting a revival of the power and position of France, proposed that the latter be included among the permanent members of the council. The Americans supported them and together they secured Soviet and Chinese acquiescence. This question, indeed, was a minor problem when compared to the issues on which the conferees were unable to reach agreement: membership in the organization, including the question of multiple Soviet representation; the scope of the Great Power veto in the Security Council; and the status of dependent territories.

The Dumbarton Oaks conference concluded before the Provisional French Government received Allied recognition. The essential features of the future security organization were thus established without consulting France. While the powers recognized France's right to a permanent seat on the Security Council "in due course," her role in drawing up the charter of the organization remained obscure.[2] The French government, however, promptly appointed a committee to study the Dumbarton Oaks proposals, under the presidency of the former foreign minister, Joseph Paul-Boncour. At the committee's first meeting, on December 29, Foreign Minister Bidault publicly accepted the most basic concept of the Dumbarton Oaks plan when he said that primary security responsibility must rest with the states possessing substantial armed forces.[3] This seemed to place France squarely on the side of the Great Powers in the disagreements which were beginning to separate them from certain smaller states that hoped for a more "democratic" international organization.

Even while the committee was pursuing its study, the Allies decided at Yalta, again in the absence of France, that a conference to establish the world organization would be held at San Francisco beginning on April 25, 1945, and that France would be invited to associate herself with the four Dumbarton Oaks powers as a sponsoring nation. At the same time the Big Three settled a principal outstanding problem left over from Dumbarton Oaks by agreeing to "recommend" a formula which established the veto of the five permanent members of the council in all save procedural matters, with the exception that one of them, if party to a dispute, would abstain from voting on measures involving peaceful settlement or recourse to regional arrangements.

The decision of the Big Three to invite France to sponsor the San Francisco conference was important to the French government as support of its claim to Great Power status. But the government, which was unwilling simply to acquiesce in the decisions made at Dumbarton Oaks and Yalta, feared that acceptance of the invitation to sponsor the conference would preclude its presenting amendments to the draft charter.[4] Apparently reassured on this point by Washington and London, the French government announced on February 28 that it would sponsor the conference. The following day it stated that it had accepted the Dumbarton Oaks and Yalta proposals as the basis of discussion at the conference, but would circulate certain amendments to them which it considered necessary. It soon appeared, however, that the formula of invitation agreed on at Yalta seemed to require the sponsoring powers to adhere to the proposals already made.[5] Though the United States and Great Britain seemed willing to soften the formula in order to accommodate France, the Soviet government insisted on the integral application of the Dumbarton Oaks and Yalta agreements. The French government, therefore, announced that it would not be able to sponsor the conference.

Ambassador Bonnet, in Washington, hastened to reassure the Big Three that the French suggestions would involve only "small modifications," and the introduction to the French amendments, published on March 23, confirmed his statement: "[France] admits that during the period which will follow the war, the maintenance of peace will depend above all on the agreement of the Great Powers; she will thus refrain from proposing anything which might, should the occasion arise, compromise such agreement."[6] But while it thus reasserted the policy stated by Bidault on December 29, the French government offered several amendments that involved significant concessions to the smaller powers, as the following analytic summary of these and the other French proposals indicates:

1. The French proposal to insert a phrase in the Dumbarton Oaks text declaring that peace and security must be maintained in conformity with right and justice was little more than a rhetorical flourish reflecting the idea, often proclaimed in the Consultative Assembly and elsewhere, that France had a mission to lead the world toward a just peace. The proposal to require the registration of treaties was carried over from the Covenant of the League of Nations. But the two proposals which insisted on the binding nature of treaties were more substantial and reflected the long struggle of France, the interwar defender of the status quo, to preserve, in the name of the sanctity of treaties, the dominant position given her by the peace settlement of 1919—a consideration which, of course, appeared again at the conclusion of another war from which France emerged as a victor.

2. A commonplace of the day in 1945 was the importance of economic problems in the causes leading to war, and the French proposals to strengthen the position of the Economic and Social Council, including giving it the right to present dangerous problems directly to the Security Council, reflected this consideration.

3. The proposed amendments to Chapter VIII, Section B of the Dumbarton Oaks draft, which aimed to make more concrete and certain the enforcement procedures of the Security Council, again reflected the experiences of the interwar period and sought to remedy the defects of the League Covenant.[7]

4. The French government, in the preamble to its amendments, stated its willingness to go beyond Dumbarton Oaks in the surrender or limitation of sovereignty in order to establish a more efficacious organization, and several of its proposals moved cautiously in this direction. Thus, one aim of the organization would be to watch or see to it (*veiller*) that essential human rights were respected, without distinction of race, language or creed. Further, aspirants to membership in the organization would have to show by their institutions as well as their international behavior that they were peace-loving. Finally, the application of procedures for peaceful settlement of disputes, which were specifically prohibited according to the Dumbarton Oaks text in matters solely within the domestic jurisdiction of the state concerned, would be permitted by France if the "clear violation of essential liberties and human rights constitutes in itself a threat capable of compromising peace."

5. In proposing that half of the non-permanent seats on the Security Council be assigned to states able to participate in the defense of international order to an appreciable extent; that the Military Staff Committee include delegates of members who would be placing substantial forces at the disposal of the organization; and that half the members of the Economic and Social Council should be chosen from among the states economically most important, the French government clearly introduced a new concept of "middle states" into the Dumbarton Oaks plan, which had distinguished only between the "five" and all the others. Apart from a possible increase in the effec-

tiveness of the organs in question by the required inclusion of such states, there is room to speculate on the more subtle motivations that lay behind these proposals.

It was clear by the middle of March, 1945, that the position of France as a Great Power, while more or less formally established in an organizational sense, remained unachieved in fact, and that the hegemony of the Big Three, glaringly asserted at Yalta, was far from ended. Accepting what was offered to them, but desiring also to be included in a more significant manner in the policy-making councils of the Great Powers, the French had not closed the door to the possibility of leading the smaller states in at least some measure of opposition to the continuing dictatorship of the three, from which France, as well as all other states, remained excluded. The French amendments to Dumbarton Oaks make very clear that France contemplated no major assault on the proposed plan and that she had no intention of undermining her own privileged position in the future organization. But at the same time the French government might well have been attempting to make the most of two worlds by defending the prerogatives of the Great Powers in which she had been invited to share while supporting the lesser states in demanding some amelioration of those prerogatives. The government could hope thereby to magnify the French position among the five major powers by speaking, at least on certain issues, on behalf of the states outside that small circle. With France's own strength and position thus increased, the Big Three might then find it desirable finally to include her even in their non-organizational deliberations, either to assuage the other states or to silence them by depriving them of their spokesmen.

From this point of view, the French proposal tending to the creation of a category of "middle states" was one that would win her the support of countries such as Canada and the Netherlands, who had made similar proposals, and, by this fact, enhance her position at the conference. If the plan was accepted, France could look forward to a close collaboration with these states on the Security or Economic and Social Councils, where their collective strength would be not inconsiderable (the analogy to the position of the Little Entente in the Council of the League of Nations is obvious). In addition, as the spokesman and representative of the "middle states" within the councils of the five, France would supplement her own strength with theirs. Further, most of the states in question would be France's traditional allies of Eastern and Western Europe, the British dominions, and a few Latin American countries—all of whom, being stronger by definition than the remaining mass of states, might be expected to be less dependent on the United States, Great Britain, or the Soviet Union and, therefore, more "middle" in position as well as in size and strength. The position of France as the balancer among the Great Powers would thus be re-enforced.

6. In a parallel proposal, the French, while accepting the concept that sanctions could not be invoked by the organization against a Great Power, tried to narrow the area of application of the veto by creating, between "procedure" and "decisions," a middle category of "recommendations" which could be voted by any two-thirds of the members of the council. This, of course, was meant as a concession to the lesser states which might partially satisfy their objections to the veto without seriously impairing the latter.

7. While thus moving to limit the preponderance of the Great Powers within the Security Council, the French also proposed to soften the control of the council itself and of its permanent members over the organization. They suggested that the

General Assembly be empowered to call the attention of the council at any time to situations which it considered capable of endangering the peace.

8. The French considered that even if all their amendments were adopted, the functioning of the future organization under the shadow of the veto presupposed a concord among the Great Powers which might not exist indefinitely. The consequent inability of the organization to guarantee security in all cases, already stressed by several speakers in the December debate in the Consultative Assembly on foreign policy, made even more imperative the problem of reconciling "regional" arrangements —by which the French meant such essentially military or military-political instruments as the Franco-Soviet pact, directed against a single enemy—with the Dumbarton Oaks proposals, which had forbidden the invoking of such treaties without the prior authorization of the Security Council.[8] The problem was much discussed in the French press during February and March, and the French were encouraged by the evolution of the American attitude on the subject which, originally skeptical of regional arrangements, moved with the Chapultepec pact in the direction of the French position.[9] The amendment which France proposed was a very broad derogation of the Dumbarton Oaks plan and permitted parties to a mutual assistance pact to implement it without council authorization.

In the short debate on the San Francisco conference which was held in the Consultative Assembly on March 27, most of the speakers expressed doubts or reservations about the proposed security organization and emphasized the measures necessary to perfect or supplement it, including territorial guarantees such as the exclusive and entire occupancy of the left bank of the Rhine.[10] But such proposals were strongly attacked by the Socialists, who criticized the Dumbarton Oaks proposals less for their lack of reliable security guarantees than for their failure to go far enough toward establishing an international community above the component nations. They objected to considering the Franco-Soviet pact as a mere cynical continuation of the balance of power policies of Francis I or Richelieu but represented it, rather, as the first link in a chain of collective security. Above all, the Socialists maintained that France must provide moral leadership for the world. In an implicit criticism of de Gaulle's "policy of grandeur," one of the Socialist speakers stated to Bidault: "We ask you, Mr. Minister, make the language of eternal France heard at San Francisco, take up again her tradition of serving universal values, seek first the diffusion of international justice, and grandeur will follow."

In striking contrast to the idealistic language of the Socialist orators was the firm, almost rough tone of the Communists. Through the address of their principal speaker, Florimond Bonte, there runs a single theme: the necessary unity of the three Great Powers and the obligation of France to accept any decision they might make. He strongly attacked those who had failed to rejoice at the "generous offer" made to France by the Big Three to be a sponsoring power at San Francisco. Even more explicitly he warned the government against trying to play one power against another or in any way opposing the wishes of the Big Three: "If this negative attitude should persist, only disappointments could accrue to France, because it is impossible to build a policy of grandeur on a league of malcontents, or on the rigid wire of the aerialist, or on a balancing game between the great democratic nations. The foreign policy of France should be a policy based on solidity, that is, on the union of the three great democratic nations. . . . It is thus a policy of close cooperation with these three powers that the

French delegation must have at San Francisco in order to give the world a new security organization." The Communists obviously wanted no French intrigue with the smaller powers at San Francisco to ameliorate the veto or otherwise impair the arrangements which the Soviet Union and its two partners had found satisfactory.

The order of the day which summarized the debate in general terms was unanimously adopted by the Consultative Assembly, but though it proclaimed the unity of view between the latter and the government, it seems clear that in fact there was a wide disparity between the concepts of the Socialists, who leaned far in the idealistic direction of the moral leadership of France and the building of a super-organization; the Communists, who concentrated their attention almost entirely on acclaiming Yalta as a French success—the only group to do so—and on advocating the "unity" of the major powers even at the cost of French subordination to them; and the government, whose proposed amendments indicated that, while it accepted the basic concepts of Dumbarton Oaks, it was willing to go some way in the direction of satisfying the smaller powers and at the same time strengthening the French position by means of their support—in short, of playing the "balancing game" which Bonte specifically deprecated.

In the address which, in effect, concluded the discussion, Bidault carefully confined himself, apart from general and rhetorical statements, to three specific points. First, he reaffirmed France's determination to maintain her colonial empire (a subject which the conference would deal with, at least indirectly, in working out the trusteeship provisions of the charter). He then dealt with the problem of regional arrangements, asserting their importance as a part of the overall security structure:

... peace and, to assure peace, collective security, are continuous creations. Collective security is not axiomatic. It is not decided with a stroke of the pen, particularly when the stroke of a pen does not yet exist.

It is not forbidden to think, to hope, that with time and the growing strengthening of the institutions charged with assuring collective security, special agreements will be absorbed little by little in the general institutions.

But at the present time, on the eve of the San Francisco conference, two observations are called for. The first is that the mechanism charged with establishing collective security does not yet exist. . . . While waiting, our people, ravaged from generation to generation by an enemy who is always the same, needs precise, immediate assurances which enter into effect without conditions.

We must have, in common with those who are menaced by the same peril, arrangements that are rigorously automatic. They exist in the Franco-Soviet pact.

In this, of course, Bidault responded to the wishes both of those who, doubtful of the efficacy of the security organization, wished to buttress it with other arrangements and those who, like the Socialists, hoped that such arrangements could be, as soon as possible, subsumed under the overall structure.

A third point concerned the relations within the new organization between the so-called great and small powers. Bidault did not hesitate to proclaim, once again, that "if it is evident that three great powers met at Yalta, this observation does not exclude another—and I am speaking only for my country— which is that France was, is and certainly will be a great power (strong applause)." If he agreed with the Socialist André Philip that "spiritual grandeur" was important, he did not overlook the "grandeur of power" and added, as an acid commentary on the idealism of the Socialists, that "it is not possible, at the present time, to try to stop armored divisions solely with spiritual grandeur." As for the special position of the Great Powers in the new organization: "It seems to me that that means one thing, and that thing is clear: in the present state of the world the union of the great powers, that is, their unanimity, the fact that they are all in agreement, is an element indispensable to the safeguarding of peace. Let one only of them separate itself out and peace is no longer assured." Though this situation might be ameliorated in time, the government had no hesitation in accepting the proposed system: "If the government, and . . . also the nation, is asked to choose between a formula theoretically perfect at once but inapplicable at the present time, and a proposition of fact for which the evidence is crushing, I think that we must all choose to do the necessary today and tomorrow, and, having done the necessary, to work for the ideal."

Bidault thus remained firmly separated from the ambitious ideas of the Socialists. In this at least he found himself in company with the Communists, and his silence on the government's specific proposals, particularly those concerning the "middle" powers and the softening of the veto, left undiscussed those subjects on which the Communists and the government were clearly less than agreed. But the tone of his remarks showed the realism with which the French government approached the San Francisco conference. This alignment between the government and the Communists was reflected when the cabinet, on March 30, selected Georges Bidault, René Pleven, François Billoux, Joseph Paul-Boncour, and Henri Bonnet as delegates to the conference, with Jean Monnet, Paul-Émile Naggiar, Jules Basde-vant, General Juin and Admiral d'Argenlieu as deputies.[11] The M. R. P. foreign minister, the conservative minister of finance, the Communist minister of health, the elder statesman, and the ambassador to Washington formed a wide and balanced delegation. But the absence of a Socialist from a delegation which included several politicians is remarkable, particularly after it had been rumored that Vincent Auriol, president of the Consultative Assembly's Commission on Foreign Affairs, would be among the delegates.[12] The inclusion of Pleven, whose economic policies were at that moment under strong Socialist attack in the assembly, seemed further to underline the exclusion of the Socialists.

The San Francisco conference opened on April 25, 1945. The first controversy took place in the steering committee on the following day when Soviet Foreign Minister Molotov objected to the proposal that Secretary of State Stettinius, as the foreign minister of the host power, be president of the conference, and suggested instead, the election of four presidents. After much consultation, the four sponsoring powers agreed that each of their chief delegates would preside in rotation over the plenary sessions, but that Stettinius should preside over the steering and executive committees. This was ratified by the plenary on April 27, with the further proviso that Stettinius would preside when the four presidents of the conference met together from time to time, which tended to imply that the basic decisions of the conference would be made in the same way as the decision on the presidency: by the four powers. This was not lost on the French delegation, which realized that its absence from among the sponsoring powers might well, in effect, mean exclusion from the real work of the conference. It may well have been at this time that the French decided—as the sequel showed—to identify themselves to all practical purposes with the major powers.

But the divisions among the major powers themselves did not facilitate the implementation of such a French policy. The fifth plenary session, on April 30, brought the first voting clash of the four powers. A motion presented by the temporary steering committee to seat representatives of the Ukrainian and White Russian Soviet Republics at the conference was adopted, with the concurrence of the Latin American states. But the Latin Americans' desire, supported by the United States and Great Britain, to seat Argentina was strongly opposed by Molotov, who proposed a few days' delay before taking a decision on the matter. His motion to this effect, however, received only seven votes in favor, with twenty-eight opposed, and several abstentions—including France. The motion to seat Argentina was thereupon adopted by thirty-one votes, including France, to four against. This episode, which indicated the great strength of the Latin American bloc at the conference, also revealed the potential weakness of the Soviet Union on any issue which might arise as a direct conflict between her and the Anglo-Saxon-Latin bloc.

In this particular matter, the French delegates preferred, after their initial abstention, to desert the role of "neutral" in order to underline a position which, at least as much as any other, engrossed their attention at the conference—the integrity and importance of regional understandings: "This affair . . . was above all an American affair. France does not wish to intervene in the decisions of a policy which one can consider 'regional.' "[13] This gesture of French support for the Latin American position was therefore thought to be not without value in the effort to win the support of these nations for the French policy on regional agreements. At the same time, the French delegation was obviously trying also to win Soviet support for that policy, and it carefully abstained from participating in the dispute on Poland which ran parallel to the Argentine question. But the position of France in this, as in similar such clashes in the future, was difficult. As *Le Monde* stated: "The position of France is delicate: she has friends of whom she must be considerate, principles and interests which she must conciliate. She can play a useful intermediary role, but it is suitable not to force this role."[14] In general, the French delegates did not force it.

It is perhaps not coincidental that, in his speech to the sixth plenary session of the conference, Bidault made no reference to France as the conciliator of the nations.[15] He made clear, in language reminiscent of de Gaulle's, that France had come to claim her full prerogatives as a Great Power:

> Today France is again on her feet. Each day she recovers more of her military and economic force. She resumes her place not only as a great moral power, which she has never ceased to be, but also as a great power in fact. In the name of the 100 million men of the Metropole and the Empire, a community whose trials have so eloquently shown to the world its unshakeable solidity, I here claim with firmness, at the same time, all the rights and all the responsibilities which are the lot of states of the first rank.

It is true that France was not able to be a sponsoring power at the conference:

> Faced by decisions with which we had not been associated and of which certain were not even known to us, we had to decline the offer which was made to us

concerning the recommendation by us of a system about which we were not fully informed. But that did not mean that at this conference now gathered we did not intend to play fully the role which falls to us, nor that we renounced the rank which is ours and which, I repeat, the misfortune of yesterday has certainly not led us to give up today.

The French delegation, he said, did not consider the Dumbarton Oaks plan to be perfect and, in particular, the role of the smaller powers seemed somewhat minimized in comparison to that of the great—"among whom, I say again, France is counted." The veto, in particular, was far from the ideal of equality to which France was devoted.

But we know what the world is today, and that outside the geometry of theoretical appearances there is the question of the means available to one state or another to place on the line of battle on the day when there is no other recourse.

That is why nothing will be done by the French government which can result in complicating the concerted, common action of the great powers involved.

On this point of the Dumbarton Oaks plan we will not, at present, raise any basic objection.

France, therefore, would make various proposals to ameliorate the plan. But she would be guided by a principle of realism: "To conciliate the demands of the ideal and the possibilities of the real; that is the prime principle to which we want, on our part, to adhere." In conclusion, Bidault emphasized once more that there was no contradiction between the general security arrangements of the new organization, regional accords, and defensible frontiers:

> One might compare them to three walls of the same fortress, and no one in former times asked the abolition of one rampart under the pretext that it was harmful to the effectiveness of the others. On the contrary, if the inhabitants of the donjon were reassured by the existence of three walls of stone between themselves and the eventual enemy, the defenders of each of these walls were for their part encouraged by the presence of two other lines of defense. We think that a question of good sense is involved, and that the international organization of tomorrow will be facilitated and not obstructed if the most threatened countries, to the extent possible, forearm themselves by their own efforts, and if those who feel themselves exposed to the same perils agree among themselves to defend themselves.

Thus, to Bidault, as to his predecessors of the 1920's and 1930's, the circles of French security remained concentric and complementary, with the international organization forming a useful outer wall, as strong as possible, yet not to be assumed unbreachable.

With the conclusion of general speeches at the seventh and eighth plenary sessions, the conference was ready to turn to its basic work: the elaboration of a complete text in commissions and committees. Some of the committees met during the week of April 29–May 5, but little work could be transacted until the proposed amendments of the participating states had been filed, categorized, and distributed by the secretariat. By the deadline of May 4, some 1,000 pages of amendments had been presented, including 22 by the sponsoring powers themselves. Representatives of the powers met constantly during this period to consider the amendments suggested and to adopt a common attitude toward them; the amendments which they themselves presented were obviously designed to cut the ground from under those who demanded extensive changes in the Dumbarton Oaks plan by agreeing in advance to some modification of it— a significant confirmation of the French view, rejected by the four powers in March, that their proposed text should be open to meaningful changes.

For France, May 7 was probably the most important day of the conference. On that day, the Committee on Structure and Procedures of the Security Council voted unanimously to strike from the Dumbarton Oaks text the humiliating restriction which had promised France a permanent seat on the council only "in due course."[16] Even more significant was the fact that on the same day the four sponsoring powers invited France, as a future permanent member of the Security Council and a major colonial power, to join them in considering the trusteeship system to be established by the charter. Thereafter, the five met regularly to consider every important issue as it arose. France thus attained the position which her refusal to sponsor the conference had seemed, during the last days of April, to have put seriously in doubt. It was, therefore, from the position of a major power, equal in conference rank—except for the official attributes of the joint presidency—that France faced the crises of the conference.

The attitude thenceforth of the French delegates on their own amendments and other questions can be understood only in terms of the fact that their status was very different from what it had been when those amendments were put forward in March. This was shown clearly in the fate of the French amendments:

1. On proposals of secondary importance, such as those stating that peace and security must be maintained in conformity with right and justice, and treaties must be registered to be binding, France obtained only partial satisfaction. No specific provision of the charter consecrated the binding character of treaties, though it was claimed that this was implicit in certain passages.

2. The French proposals to strengthen the authority and position of the Economic and Social Council were largely unsuccessful.

3. In the Committee on Enforcement Arrangements, of which Joseph Paul-Boncour was rapporteur, France received substantial satisfaction in her desire to perfect the machinery of coercion.

4. The French proposals that the organization watch or see to it that the essential human rights of members were respected, that prospective members must prove that they are peace-loving by their institutions as well as by their international conduct, and that the organization could interfere in the domestic affairs of the members if the clear violation of human rights constituted in itself a threat to the peace—all these bold proposals to limit national sovereignty made little progress at the conference. The French delegates themselves, in the trusteeship discussions, took a strong stand in support of the application of the principle of non-interference by the organization in the internal affairs of the members.

5. Among the most striking of the French amendments had been those which provided that half of the non-permanent seats on the Security Council be assigned to "middle states." This

proposal aimed both to strengthen the French position at the conference by making her, to some degree, the leader of the restless group of states not entirely satisfied with the Dumbarton Oaks and Yalta proposals and, at the same time, to assure the presence on the future Security Council of a number of states whose power and positions would make them natural allies there of France in her role as conciliator of the major powers. That is, the French government aimed to make use of the lesser states to increase its own stature among the five powers. The four sponsoring powers themselves, however, introduced an amendment which, to some extent, provided for the election of "middle states" to the council.[17] The fact that the French delegates did not seriously press their own or any similar plan, such as had been put forward by some of the smaller states themselves, indicates that they had decided, after the *de facto* acceptance of France among the major powers on May 7, to close the door in effect on the possibility of leading the lesser states against the Big Four.

6. The view that, after May 7, the French delegation had decided to take its stand firmly with the four sponsoring powers is confirmed also by the developing French attitude on the important subject of the veto. Though they had accepted the veto in principle, the French government had proposed to soften it by providing for "recommendations" which could be adopted by a vote of any two-thirds of the council members. But on May 17 the French delegate declared specifically that he would not endanger the success of the conference by opposing the Yalta text. Since the veto issue most agitated the smaller powers, the French decision to stand with the four major powers was a clear indication that France had finally decided to accept the position offered her and to attempt to maintain it without the outside alliance of the smaller states. The French delegates

took part in the preparation of the replies which the other four gave to the questionnaire submitted to them on the veto, and though the French apparently agreed with the United States and Great Britain in their interpretation of the veto as against the more restrictive view of the Soviet Union, they firmly supported the four powers, once they had reached agreement, against the unexpectedly strong opposition led by Australia and New Zealand.

7. The French had proposed that the General Assembly be empowered to call the attention of the council to situations capable of endangering the peace and, after consultation among the five powers, a redrafted text incorporating the French proposal was presented on May 15 and adopted.

8. The French were intensely interested, before and during the conference, in the problem of integrating regional accords into the general security structure, in which, as Bidault frankly stated in his opening speech, they were not willing to place entire confidence. They were able to win satisfaction on this issue.

The subject of colonies and trusteeships had not been included in the Dumbarton Oaks plan nor in the original French amendments to it, but it formed one of the major preoccupations of the French delegates at San Francisco. With the other colonial powers, they were able to achieve what they thought then were adequate guarantees that the organization would not be used as an anti-colonial instrument—though they were placed in the paradoxical position of being obliged to emphasize the non-interference principle which they themselves had earlier proposed to modify in other respects.

With the settlement of the last major point of contention—the scope of the General Assembly's right of discussion—the conference concluded its business and, at the ninth plenary session on June 25, the text of the charter was adopted. At the closing session, on June 26, Paul-Boncour emphasized the superiority of the new organization over the former League of Nations and the importance of harmony among the five major powers.[18]

In a statement to the Agence France-Presse, Paul-Boncour, who had proclaimed in the preceding December that the Franco-Soviet pact had restored France to her former rank, said once more that France, at San Francisco, had resumed her place as a Great Power.[19] This assertion, which was not valid without qualification, was nevertheless true in two important respects:

1) In the charter itself, France took full and immediate possession of the role which had been promised to her "in due course" at Dumbarton Oaks. This, however, constituted no major diplomatic success, since improvement in the internal and international position of the Provisional Government since October had made the striking of the limiting clause inevitable by May.

2) In the actual work and decision-making of the conference itself the four powers found it convenient to offer, and the French delegates found it possible and necessary to accept, the position which had been made available to France in February and which she had declined at that time. The French delegates thereby obviated the danger—very evident in the first week of the conference—of being excluded from effective participation in decision-making, and then utilized their position to win substantial satisfaction in the areas of greatest importance to them: strengthening of the coercive machinery, regional arrangements and trusteeships. Following this shift of their role, the French chose not to strain too far their newly won position and therefore in effect abandoned the proposals—softening of the veto, creation of a category of "middle states," substantial derogation of national sovereignty—which ran counter to the wishes of the

major powers. By doing so, France took her stand on the side of the latter and gave up the possibility of leading the smaller states against the greater even to the extent indicated by her original amendments.

Partly for this reason the conference results and the charter itself were received in France with a certain degree of skepticism and indifference, if not disillusion. French commentators did not conceal the fact that the success of the new organization depended on the concord of the five major powers and, in fact, on that of the Big Two, whose antagonism had dominated the conference.[20] If the policy and achievements of the French delegation at San Francisco are considered in terms of the Consultative Assembly debate of March 27, it is evident that the hopes of those who, like the Socialists, wanted France to lead the world toward idealistic constructions were bitterly disappointed. But the Communists, who had laid their greatest emphasis on the harmony of the three major powers and the more or less modest role of France in promoting it, could have little complaint about the actions of the French delegates at San Francisco. Conservative nationalists, who regretted France's subordinate role, nevertheless could find satisfaction in the actual achievements of the French delegation. De Gaulle, for his part, wrote that France "obtained, at San Francisco, what we most wanted."[21] He could claim no less.

Yet there were many in France who, though aiming less high than the Socialists, believed that despite the French contributions to the conference the substance of real achievement as well as of Great Power status had eluded them. And if, indeed, the motive of the French delegates in allying themselves with the four powers was to secure a voice or support for France in future policy-making meetings of the Great Powers, they were not entirely successful in doing so. For, at San Francisco itself,

France took no part in the consultations of the Big Three on such matters as the Polish question, and as early as May 10 it was reported that another meeting of the Big Three would be held in the near future to deal with the German and other problems.[22] It thus appeared to some that France had won little more at the conference than had already been made available to her in October and February—and yet had paid for this little by separating herself from the smaller states of whom she might have made better use, according to these critics, to obtain the substance rather than merely the form of Great Power status.[23]

But the French government and its delegates, who were not unaware of the inadequacies of their position, no doubt believed that more was to be gained in the long term by winning unquestioned admittance to the councils of the powers than by pursuing the dubious tactic of refusing such participation as they were offered and attempting to force on the three states that held a preponderance of power various charter provisions which the latter were determined not to accept. France, according to this argument, would gain nothing by fighting a battle which could not be won, whereas her presence, even if at first silent, at the table of the decision-making powers would ultimately permit her to play at least some part in the formulating of world policy.

CHAPTER VI

ANGLO-FRENCH RELATIONS AND THE CRISIS IN THE LEVANT

It was generally expected in France that the Franco-Soviet pact of December 10, 1944, would be followed by a similar understanding with Great Britain. But the special factors which made a treaty with the Soviet Union particularly valuable to the French government in its quest for Great Power status were lacking in an alliance with Britain. Apart from the lingering rancors of an ambivalent wartime relationship, which divided France from Britain but not from the Soviet Union, de Gaulle made clear on several occasions in late 1944 and early 1945 that he took for granted a *de facto* alliance with the British and wanted the treaty which would eventually define and formalize this understanding to be signed only after the outstanding issues between the two states had been settled.

The problem of Germany was among the most important of these issues. The French government obviously hoped that the British, when they found themselves faced by the prospect of an early American withdrawal from active participation in European affairs and isolated before a Franco-Soviet entente on Germany, would be obliged to attempt to win France to their own side by supporting her German policies. The British did, indeed, share this view to some extent and at the Yalta conference strongly supported France's inclusion in the control machinery of Germany. They did not, however, accept the French proposals on Germany, nor even seriously attempt to work out common policies with the French government on the occupation and postwar disposition of the Reich. The most serious obstacle to a Franco-British alliance, however, or even to amicable cooperation, was the problem of the Levant, where rivalry between the two powers had persisted since the First World War and had become much sharper since 1941. A month after the war ended in Europe, and while the United Nations conference was meeting in San Francisco, this rivalry brought the British and French to the very edge of armed conflict.

The Grounds of Conflict

Syria and Lebanon had been assigned as Class A mandates to France by the Allied Council of Ambassadors at San Remo in April 1920. But this arrangement was made only after a member of the Hashemite dynasty, which was patronized by the British, had been established on the throne at Damascus and then ejected by French troops. The assignment to Britain of the mandates of Iraq and Transjordan, both of which were given to Hashemite monarchs, and the continued agitation on the part of this dynasty and its supporters among the British agents in the Near East for a "Greater Syria" which would unite the French mandates with the British under a single Hashemite crown, bred a French suspicion of British designs which persisted throughout the interwar decades and easily flared up in acute form after the defeat of France in 1940.

The French administration of the two Levantine states had been troubled from the beginning, for their inhabitants sought to obtain complete independence, while the French persistently resisted such efforts, with force when necessary. Thus, during the uprising of 1925–1926, Damascus was bombed twice, with great loss of life. The French long prevented the adoption of a constitution in Syria or the establishment of a native government. The independence of Iraq in 1932, the Anglo-Egyptian treaty of 1936, and the coming to power in France of the Blum government led to the negotiation in 1936 of a number of treaties between France and the Syrian and Lebanese governments, which provided that the two states were to become independent nations after three years and that France would sponsor their admission to the League of Nations while retaining the right to maintain troops for a time on their soil and to train and equip their armies. Conservative French military and colonial interests prevented ratification of these treaties, however, and Syrian nationalists were further alienated when in June, 1939, France ceded the sanjak of Alexandretta and Antioch to Turkey. The Syrian president resigned his office in protest at this action by France, and the French high commissioner then dissolved the parliament and suspended the constitution.

After the armistice of June, 1940, the Levant states, like most of the rest of the French Empire, remained in the control of authorities responsible to the Vichy government, and Damascus became a center of German intrigue and propaganda which tended to destroy what remained of the prestige of the mandatory power. The Free French had hoped in the spring of 1941 that they might be able to take over Syria and Lebanon with their own forces, but it became clear that the Vichy troops would resist and could not be defeated without important British participation in the effort. The open support given by the Vichy officials in Syria to the Germans during the anti-British Iraq revolt of May, which highlighted the danger to the

British position in the entire area that would result if the Germans should occupy Syria, finally led to a joint military expedition, British and Free French, which entered Syria and Lebanon on June 8.[1]

After a determined resistance, the Vichy forces on July 14 accepted the convention of St. Jean d'Acre with the British who, though they consulted the Free French commander, General Georges Catroux, signed the armistice by themselves. At once the latent conflict between the French and British came to the surface, aggravated now by the fact that the latter had an overwhelming preponderance of military power in the two states and that the former were not only militarily weak and discredited by the defeat of 1940 but were not recognized as a government by London. Some British officials and officers treated the French, at best, without tact, and de Gaulle became convinced that the British, or at least many of those on the spot, aimed to eliminate France from the Levant. More broadly, he feared the dangerous precedent—perhaps to be applied later in North Africa or in France herself—of the British or British and Americans assuming supreme authority in French territory on the pretext of war needs.[2]

The first Anglo-French quarrel arose from the armistice itself, which de Gaulle—who was then in Brazzaville—promptly refused to accept despite the fact that General Catroux had concurred in it. Catroux apparently acted in the belief that the Vichy forces would not sign with the Free French and that the interests of the latter would be taken care of afterward by the British. De Gaulle, it need hardly be said, had no such confidence in the British and no wish to receive from them as a gift what he considered to be France's by right. He at once informed the British that he objected to the exclusion of the Free French from the armistice signing; to the absence of any reference to them in the document itself; to the difficulties the agreement put in the way of his hope of rallying part of the Vichy forces to his own support; and to the fact that the Syrian and Lebanese auxiliary forces in the Levant—the "special troops"— were turned over by the Vichy forces to the British.

As a result of de Gaulle's vigorous action, the Free French were able to obtain an arrangement with the British—the de Gaulle-Lyttleton agreement, signed on July 25—by which the British maintained overall strategic military control in the area but recognized Free French administration in Syria and Lebanon. De Gaulle also took over control of the "special troops" and of the military supplies of the departing Vichy forces, though his efforts to rally these forces to Free France were largely unsuccessful.[3] This agreement established the working relations between the British and the Free French in the Levant, but a more important problem, which remained wrapped in ambiguity in the early days of the occupation, was eventually to lead (in May, 1945) to their most serious clash. This was the question of the political status of Syria and Lebanon.

On entering the Levant states on June 8 General Catroux proclaimed the abolition of the mandates and told the Syrians and Lebanese that they were "free and independent," although he added that "your statute of independence and sovereignty will be guaranteed by a treaty in which, besides, our reciprocal relations will be defined."[4] The British subscribed publicly to this declaration, but it soon became clear that the two sides had very different ideas about what had been promised. In a letter to de Gaulle on July 25 the British resident minister in Cairo, Oliver Lyttleton, stated:

I should like to take this opportunity of assuring you that on the British side we recognize the historic interests of France in the Levant. Great Britain has no interest in Syria or the Lebanon except to win the war. We have no desire to encroach in any way upon the position of France. Both Free France and Great Britain are pledged to the independence of Syria and the Lebanon. *When this essential step has been taken, and without prejudice to it,* we freely admit that France should have the dominant privileged position in the Levant among all European nations. It was in this spirit that we approached the problems under discussion. You will have seen the recent utterances of the Prime Minister in this sense and I am glad to reaffirm them now [italics added].[5]

On July 27 de Gaulle replied:

I have received your letter of July 25. I am happy to take note of the assurances which you have been willing to give me concerning the disinterestedness of Great Britain in Syria and the Lebanon and the fact that Great Britain recognizes in advance the dominant and privileged position of France in the Levant *when these states become* [*se trouveront*] *independent* [italics added].[6]

The matter remained at that point for over two years, but it is clear from these letters that the British—as Churchill said in the House of Commons on September 9, 1941—had in mind a special French position in the two states which would follow and be within the framework of their independence, while the Free French (as Catroux's proclamation suggested) considered that independence (whenever it came) and French privileges formed two parts of a single and simultaneous whole.[7]

The French wanted to maintain a position in Syria and Lebanon analogous to that enjoyed by the British in Iraq and

Egypt, including the right to keep troops there and special relationships in economic and cultural affairs. Instead of attempting at once to establish a solid understanding with the two states, perhaps on the basis of the 1936 treaties, the French seemed to believe that, confronted by a dangerous British preponderance of strength and constant British "nibbling," as de Gaulle said, at the French position, they should await the end of the war before signing the treaties which would, in their view, formally terminate the two mandates and at the same time define France's continuing "special position" in Syria and Lebanon.

The ambiguous nature of Catroux's proclamation of June 8 and of his grant of "independence and sovereignty" to Syria and Lebanon (September 27 and November 26, respectively) became increasingly clear.[8] Governments were set up by the French in both states by the end of 1941 but elections were held only in mid-1943. From these elections, however, there emerged in both states nationalist governments which demanded full sovereignty. The new Lebanese government then took advantage of the absence in Algiers of the French delegate-general, Jean Helleu, who had succeeded Catroux in June, to proclaim the end of the mandate. Helleu, returning to Beirut on November 9, responded by arresting the president and most of the government, suspending parliament, and appointing new ministers favorable to France. Insurrection at once became imminent in both Lebanon and Syria, and with it the prospect of British intervention. De Gaulle considered Helleu's action justifiable but "going beyond what the general situation permitted him to sustain" and sent Catroux to Beirut to re-establish matters. The British, however, interested as always during this period in conciliating Arab nationalism, insisted, with American approval—in what Catroux called a return to Fashoda—on the release of the prisoners within thirty-six hours and the restoration of the ousted Lebanese government. The French were obliged to comply.

The unilateral Lebanese assertion of independence which underlay this crisis was not implemented, however, and the relations between the two Levantine states and France had still to be determined by treaties. During the short tenure as delegate-general of Yves Chataigneau (November, 1943–March, 1944), certain governmental functions were transferred to the two states and some progress was made in the negotiations concerning mixed tribunals, the police, and the army. His successor, General Beynet, was less successful, and as the Provisional French Government gained international recognition (October, 1944) it seemed more determined than ever to secure a "special position" in the two states, both as a part of its general policy of re-establishing and maintaining France's "presence" everywhere in the world and, above all, as the first rampart of defense against any undermining of its position in North Africa. Syria and Lebanon themselves, however, were ever less willing to concede special rights to any power, particularly after the formation of the Arab League in March, 1945. Since the British made clear that they were closely interested in the discussions between the two states and France, the French became increasingly convinced that the British were secretly stiffening the two governments to oppose French wishes in the treaty negotiations.[9] De Gaulle was prompted to remark during his press conference of January 25 that, though France had been the first to recognize the independence of the two states, her intentions were not facilitated by "outside interference."[10]

Negotiations continued between France and the two states, however, and on February 2 the French cabinet approved instructions to General Beynet on the basis, as *Le Monde* put it, that "France is responsible for the maintenance of order in Syria and Lebanon. She is resolved to maintain her prerogatives. . . ."[11] Among these prerogatives of a privileged position in the two states, the disposition of the "special troops"—some 20,000 Syrian and Lebanese nationals who were enrolled in military formations under French command—was already becoming the most critical issue. The desire of the French to retain control of these units, at least until an overall agreement was reached, and of the two governments to wrest it from them presented, in the words of the Lebanese premier on February 6, many difficulties, but both he and the Syrian president apparently believed at this time that a settlement was possible if negotiations proceeded calmly.[12] However, after France's exclusion from the Yalta conference, her irritation at and suspicions of British policy in the Levant became more marked; nor were they reduced when Churchill and Roosevelt, returning from the Crimea, met with Saudi Arabian and Egyptian leaders. In addition, the Syrian and Lebanese negotiators felt—or were believed by the French to have felt—that France's exclusion from the councils of the Great Powers marked the end of her role as a world power, and thereby stiffened their resolve not to grant France any special position in their countries. Speaking in the House of Commons on February 27, Churchill stated that the British attitude to the Levant states was defined by the 1941 agreement which proclaimed their independence but that, at the same time, Britain had no intention of attempting to replace French influence there with her own and, unlike the United States and the Soviet Union, was favorable to a special French position. But de Gaulle believed that the British had long aimed to dominate the Near East and would willingly seize the present occasion to do so, at France's expense.[13]

On March 28, it was announced in Washington that Syria and Lebanon would be invited as independent states to the San Francisco conference, on the initiative of France. This was obviously a conciliatory gesture to speed the negotiations, but there could be little question henceforth that, whatever the technical status of the mandate, France would have to negotiate with the two states on the basis of their independence.[14] This being the fact, France could retain a special position in them only by their free and sovereign consent. If, as was increasingly the case, they were disinclined to give France such a position, she could not offer them their independence in exchange, as Britain had done in Iraq, because she had already accepted if not recognized it without compensation. The physical presence of her troops in the two states was a weak asset in face of the greatly superior British units also stationed there, and when the European war ended before agreements had been reached the French position became increasingly untenable and indefensible.

The Crisis

The nature of the French proposals was not revealed during March and April, with the result that some in the Levant and elsewhere believed that France was pursuing indefinite negotiations to avoid any conclusion. But early in May de Gaulle received General Beynet and provided him with precise instructions concerning the treaties to be signed by France with the two states.[15] On May 18, Beynet met the Syrian and Lebanese foreign ministers at Damascus and presented them with an aide-memoire which recognized the independence of the two states without reservation and outlined the French cultural, economic, and strategic desires. Thus, as Le Monde stated on May 24,

France had already recognized the sovereignty of Syria and Lebanon: "But, before this sovereignty may become fully effective, she intends—as has also been recognized from the beginning by our partners—to assure the safeguard of her centuries old rights and interests in these countries." These rights and interests were to be dealt with by an agreement on cultural questions; a commercial treaty would also cover such economic problems as the flow of oil from Mosul through the Syrian pipeline; and a strategic understanding would provide France with two bases, ports for her fleet, lines of communication to the Far East, and continued control of the "special troops" at least until the war had ended. On this point *Le Monde* declared: "... it goes without saying that France could not, either for her own security or for that of these countries themselves, rely entirely on their forces, manifestly powerless to protect them against all outside danger."[16]

Since, as the cabinet declared on May 29 in the midst of the disorders which had broken out in the two states, "France has made known that she wished to settle these questions before the withdrawal of her troops," it was clear to all parties that France was still trying to make the formal termination of the mandates conditional on the acceptance by Syria and Lebanon of treaties guaranteeing to France a special status similar to that enjoyed by the British in Iraq, including some control of their armed forces.[17] But, unlike the case of Iraq, at the time of its treaty with Great Britain, the Syrian and Lebanese mandates were recognized, even by the French, to have ceased in effect to exist. Therefore, though the French claim for a special position was ostensibly linked to their security needs, it was, in fact, put forward as the price which the two states were to pay for France to relinquish the control which in fact she exercised. It was not unnatural nor unreasonable for France to want to retain a position in the Levant similar to that kept by the British even after the termination of their mandate in Iraq. But, despite official French claims, it cannot seriously be maintained that the French viewed their negotiations with Syria and Lebanon as being with fully sovereign states on whose good pleasure and free consent alone, in fact as well as in law, the French position in the Levant depended.

Beynet claimed later that the first response of the Syrian and Lebanese foreign ministers was favorable to his hopes for a successful negotiation but, in any case, the question of French troop re-enforcements soon arose, as cause or pretext, to end the discussion. At Beynet's request, some five hundred French troops, including a number of Senegalese, were sent to Syria in late April—against British advice.[18] The Agence France-Presse claimed that these troops had been sent to permit France to maintain order in the area and to facilitate the sending of forces to participate in the war in the Far East, and that their presence in no way derogated from the intention of the French government to pursue negotiations with the two states.[19] But popular disorders began as early as May 8, the day after the first of these troops landed at Beirut, in protest against the arrival of the French re-enforcements, and on the 19th there were serious disturbances at Damascus and Aleppo, with loss of life. Whether these events occurred spontaneously or at the instigation of the Syrian government is uncertain. But on the same day the two governments informed the French representative and the diplomatic corps that, because of the content of the French note and of the pressure which was being exerted on them, they had agreed not to pursue negotiations with the delegate-general. The French, of course, maintained that the agitation was artificially promoted and that the arrival of the small number of relief troops—in no way different, they said, from similar movements during the preceding four years—was merely a pretext for the two states to break off negotiations. There was an element of truth in the contentions of both sides, for the French were obviously willing to use a limited coercion to win the special rights which they demanded as the price for terminating the mandates, and the Syrians were no doubt equally willing to utilize popular agitation to frustrate the French policy. The French troops, however, remained in their barracks during the first week of the disturbances and by May 26 Beirut was again calm, though tension persisted in Syria.

On April 30 the British Ambassador, Alfred Duff Cooper, had asked de Gaulle to halt the re-enforcements. De Gaulle refused and accused the British of seeking the elimination of France from the Levant. On May 5, in a message to de Gaulle, Churchill again denied any British ambition for territorial or other advantage in the Levant and recognized the special French position there. At the same time, however, he asked de Gaulle to turn over the "special troops" to the two governments and to cancel the French re-enforcements, which he feared would stimulate disorders that might spread to Iraq. De Gaulle replied the next day, frankly stating the objects France sought to obtain in the negotiations, asserting that agreement could already have been reached if the Syrians and Lebanese had not had reason to think that they could avoid an understanding with France by counting on the British and, finally, asking the latter not to interfere further.[20]

During the first weeks of the disturbances the British, whose forces in the Levant were much larger than the French, remained passive. But on May 28 the Syrian foreign minister informed the British that he could no longer ensure internal security—thereby inviting their intervention against the French.[21] With perhaps suspicious promptness, serious incidents took place in Syria on the following day. French military installations at Damascus were attacked on the night of May 28 by insurgents supported by the artillery of the Syrian army, and a sharp battle raged during the 29th and 30th, in which French artillery and aviation entered the action. Two hundred people were reported hospitalized at Damascus; one hundred were killed and one hundred wounded as a result of a French air raid on Homs. The French claimed later that order had been re-established in most of the area by the evening of May 30.[22]

Both the British and American governments were, by this time, closely following the worsening situation in Syria. Even before the news of these more serious clashes had reached Washington, Ambassador Caffery on May 28 delivered a note to de Gaulle stating that the United States had the impression that France was using force in order to win concessions from Syria and Lebanon and that, in order to obviate suspicions that they do not accept the ideals of the United Nations, the French should revise their policy and treat the two states as free and sovereign nations.[23] Eden discussed the situation in Commons on May 29, stating that, though the British government was in contact with both the United States and France, he preferred to say no more at the moment. To those who demanded the immediate withdrawal of all French forces from the area, Eden pointed out the delicacy of the situation, adding that Britain would do everything possible to promote a settlement. On the next afternoon, after serious battles had begun at Damascus and elsewhere, Eden informed the Commons that Great Britain was engaged in diplomatic contacts on the subject. He said that she would withdraw her forces from the Levant when France had signed and implemented treaties with the two states. He reiterated again that Britain did not seek to supplant France in the Levant.

The British cabinet met twice on May 30 to consider the crisis, and at 8:00 P.M. Churchill and Eden informed Ambassador Massigli that the British would intervene unless the French ordered a ceasefire. Apprised of this, the French government, at 11:00 P.M. on May 30, ordered its forces in the Levant to cease fire and to stand on their positions.[24] It is significant to note, in light of later developments, that the motive put forth by the French in their communiqué of June 1 to account for this action was the hope of creating a better atmosphere for talks with the United States and Great Britain and, eventually, with the Arab states on the entire Near Eastern problem—talks on which the U.S.S.R. would at least be informed.[25]

Massigli was not able to inform Eden that a ceasefire had been ordered until late in the afternoon of May 31. By then the British government had decided to act. On the same afternoon the British embassy in Paris handed to de Gaulle a note from Churchill which stated that, considering the situation in the Levant, the British government with profound regret had ordered its commander-in-chief in the Middle East to intervene to prevent further bloodshed and in the interest of the security of the area, which was a communications zone in the war against Japan. To avoid collision of French and British troops, London therefore requested the French government to order its troops to cease fire and to enter their barracks. When this had been done and order had been restored, the British government would be ready to begin tripartite talks—with France and the United States—in London. The United States, consulted in advance, approved the British action and even the text of the note to de Gaulle.[26] Unfortunately, as if to compound the gravity of the situation by a serious lapse of diplomatic courtesy— or, as de Gaulle thought, by a deliberate, carefully staged attempt to humiliate France and, perhaps, to drive him from power—Eden presented the substance of the British note to the House of Commons nearly an hour before it had been given to de Gaulle in Paris. Beynet, however, was then ordered to stand on his positions and, if he had not already done so in response to the order from Paris on the 30th, he issued appropriate commands on the afternoon of May 31.[27]

The first reaction of official French circles to these events appeared in *Le Monde* on June 1. An editorial expressed great indignation that the small French forces in the Levant could be considered a menace to the two states and noted bitterly that the British intervened only when Beynet had already informed Paris that the situation was under control. The British, it added, knew better than most the nature of disorders in the area and it was difficult to understand how they could strengthen their own position at the expense of France's, whose interests the British government had always professed to respect. "Whether one likes it or not," the editorial stated, "in the Near East as in Europe and everywhere in the world the interest of Great Britain and of France are closely linked. France is too conscious of this solidarity to do anything to endanger it. She strongly desires that our British friends reciprocate in kind."[28] On the same day the French presidency published a communiqué defending France's policy in the Levant and stating that the French troops had been ordered to cease fire and to maintain their positions. In fact, the French troops had already retired to their barracks. On June 2, British forces entered Damascus, encircled the French barracks, and placed sentinels before the French headquarters and other strategic places. Within two days French troops were being evacuated from the Syrian cities to outlying camps, while the British began the occupation of the principal strategic points in Lebanon as well as in Syria. By June 5 a tight British censorship had been imposed and the

Office des céréales panifiables—main organ of French economic control of Syria—had been "temporarily" suspended, which, according to the French press, reflected not a military need but a design to drive France from her economic position in the Levant.

On June 2, the Brtish Foreign Office announced that the United States had agreed to a tripartite conference with Britain and France—prior to the inclusion of the two Syrian states—and that an invitation in this sense had been sent to the French government. The reply of the latter was given by de Gaulle in a press conference on the same afternoon. In a review of French relations with the Syrian states, he did not conceal his view that the French position in the Levant had long been made more difficult by British representatives in the area and that, even if events prior to 1939 were disregarded, new incidents indicated that Britain was trying to take advantage of the temporary weakness of France. He then in effect rejected the British proposal for a tripartite conference, but said that France was ready to negotiate a settlement of the entire Near Eastern problem, not only with Britain and the United States but with all the Great Powers, the Arab states and others.[29] Two days later the French government officially proposed a conference of the five Great Powers to consider the problems of the Near East.

The motives of the French government in thus proposing a five-power conference on the affairs of the Near East appear consistent with its statement of June 1 that it had ordered a ceasefire in the Levant on May 30, at British request but before the British intervention, in order to create an atmosphere in which talks on the entire eastern question might be held with Britain and the United States and, eventually, with the Arab states, and about which the Soviet Union would at least be kept informed. At least from the moment of the British intervention, the French had probably decided to attempt to shift the focus of any international discussion from the Levant alone to the entire Near Eastern situation, in an obvious effort to include Britain's status in Egypt, Transjordan, and elsewhere on the agenda, and thereby to withdraw France from her conspicuous and exposed position as the sole "accused" power. From de Gaulle's statements on June 2, it is clear that the government was already developing its original plan to include a broad international conference, and this was made definite in the specific proposal of June 5.

The chronology suggests that the French had decided, almost from the beginning of the crisis, to attempt to broaden the *scope* of any international discussions of the subject, but that it was somewhat later that they undertook also to enlarge the number of the *participants* in such discussions to include the five major powers. It is very probable that this proposal was motivated in large part by a calculated desire to prevent Britain from drawing down on France alone the full weight of Arab nationalism when she herself faced similar problems in the area, but also simply by spite and a wish to retaliate on Britain in a quarter in which she too was vulnerable.[30] The same desire to make Britain's position more difficult also lies behind the proposal to introduce the Soviet Union into the discussion, for the French realized that the United States would probably be aligned with the British in either three- or five-power conversations, while the Soviet Union, even if it did not support the policies of its ally, France—and it had given little evidence of doing so at San Francisco or elsewhere—at least would not support those of Britain either.

In discussing the French position on June 12, *Le Monde* pointed out that on February 27 Churchill himself had stated that the Levant was of importance to the Soviet Union as well as to the United States: "What appears strange is to want now to keep the Soviet Union out of a problem which, it was said in February, could not be settled without it." And, if Syria and Lebanon were as important in the conduct of the Far Eastern war as the British alleged, then China also was properly interested in them, though, as the journal maliciously added, ". . . her interest in the matter appears very distant—as distant no doubt as the Japanese threat which obliges the British to keep 600,000 men between Iran, the Taurus, and the Nile." *Le Monde* concluded that the French position was dictated neither by spite nor by a desire to introduce powers more friendly to her, but was based on the consideration that, even before the United Nations charter was signed, the five major powers were the sole international authority recognized by the members of the future organization. These powers, from the very fact of their special position, did not need to have any direct interest in a given problem to have the right to take part in its solution.[31] That is, a Great Power was entitled, by definition, to participate in the settlement of any international problem.

Le Monde's reasoning no doubt reflected that of the makers of French policy who, insofar as they were able, in early June, to look beyond the Levant crisis itself, were attempting to establish a principle which, if it involved the inclusion of the Soviet Union and China in the resolution of the present situation, implied also the inclusion of France herself in the settlement of other questions in which she might have no direct interest beyond that which was inherent in the prerogatives of every Great Power. As de Gaulle had stated in his press conference of June 2, this affair offered the first occasion for "international cooperation" to be undertaken, by which he probably meant that the directory or the concert of the Great Powers

—then in process of legal confirmation at San Francisco—should undertake to settle this problem by virtue of its authority to consider *all* problems.

It cannot be overlooked that the French proposal to extend the discussions of the Levant to the five major powers as a group was put forward only after June 1 and, it appears, had not yet been formulated by that date. Since this policy was evolved in the stress of the moment, rather than by advanced planning, it is probable that the elements in it which were based on the specific needs of the Syrian crisis itself were predominant over those which took into consideration longer range policies. The latter, nevertheless, played some part in the French proposal, which at least indicates the general pattern that came to the minds of the French policymakers when confronted by a specific and pressing situation.

Though some circles in Great Britain and the United States received the French proposal favorably, the general reaction in both countries was cool, and the French government had to recognize, by the middle of June, that its plan for a five-power conference would not be accepted either in Washington or in London. During the same period the liquidation of the French position in Syria, which had begun at once after the intervention of the British forces, continued at an increasing pace. On June 12 a French source reported that the evacuation of French military and civilian personnel from Syria would be complete within a few days. A week later the British military authorities assumed control of the *Office des céréales panifiables* in Lebanon as well as in Syria. Underlining the pressure which was thus being exerted on the French to accept the British proposal for a tripartite conference, the British minister resident in the Middle East stated on June 12 that Great Britain, the United States, and the two states of the Levant should impose a settlement on

France if the latter refused to join them in elaborating one. Two days later the Syrian government asked London to call a conference with Syrian and Lebanese representatives at once, with or without France.

The French thus found themselves confronted by the failure of the diplomatic device which they had put forth to facilitate a solution to the crisis and by an increasingly rapid liquidation of the entire French "presence" in the Levant. It was in the face of this mounting pressure to reach a settlement with the two states which was not likely to be very favorable to France in the circumstances that the Consultative Assembly, on June 15, began a two-day debate on the situation.[32] Bidault opened the discussion by recapitulating the history of the French mandates in Syria and Lebanon and emphasizing that the treaties which France wanted to negotiate with them were not to be the price of their independence—which had already been recognized—but were to define, as between sovereign states, their mutual relations with France in terms of the many interests the French had developed in the Levant. He strongly criticized the British for attempting to exploit the weakness of a friendly people and defended the French proposal of a five-power conference, though he stated that France might also appeal to the United Nations. De Gaulle also criticized the British in detail for attempting to direct Arab hostility onto France, but he added that France sought a solution to the problem "which involves no profound alteration in the confident and friendly relations of England and France."

Nearly all of the other speakers in the debate laid some portion of the blame for the situation in the Levant on the British, who were accused by many of continuing the old imperial rivalry and by the Communists of attempting to erect a new *cordon sanitaire* against the Soviet Union. Many speakers, particularly on the left, also criticized the French government's policy as outdated, undemocratic, and even reactionary in its reliance on force. But nearly everyone—and especially the Communists—approved the government's proposal of a five-power conference, and only a few advocated direct Franco-British negotiations, although de Gaulle himself had hinted that he might accept these in lieu of a five-power meeting as preferable to a three-power meeting including the United States.

Despite these divergencies, the Foreign Affairs Commission of the assembly unanimously proposed an order of the day which approved the government's granting of independence to Syria and Lebanon "under guarantee of treaties or accords, freely negotiated" and its invocation of international cooperation for the settlement of the problem. Daniel Mayer, in the name of the Socialists, then proposed the addition of a passage urging that the government "multiply its efforts with a view to the elaboration of a Franco-British pact which, with the Franco-Soviet pact, would be one of the European bases of the collective construction of universal peace." Both this amendment and the entire order of the day were unanimously adopted.

Between the first and second days of the debate, on June 16, the official British refusal of the French proposal of a five-power conference was handed in at the Quai d'Orsay by Ambassador Alfred Duff Cooper. As a Foreign Office spokesman stated in explaining this refusal, a speedy settlement was in the interest of all parties, including France, and the inclusion of additional powers would only delay a solution. The British did offer a minor concession to French prestige by agreeing to hold three-power talks in Paris if this should be suggested. But they rejected the idea of including the Soviet Union in the discussion—

on the subtle ground that the question of the Levant was one which involved the Far Eastern war, in which the U.S.S.R. was not a participant.

The British, however, seemed more and more eager to achieve a settlement of the question before the crisis spread elsewhere in the area. To this end the British government on June 22 issued a declaration which, though it defended British policy in the Levant, was addressed to Syrian rather than to French opinion and constituted an indirect warning to the governments of the two states that they were being given an opportunity to maintain order in their territories and would be judged on their performance. Despite the evident desire of both the French and British governments to find some way out of the impasse into which the dispute had fallen, the situation in Syria, from the French point of view, continued to deteriorate steadily. British officers assumed command of the Syrian "special troops" in the Djebel Druse region, Syrian tribes attacked French military posts near the Turkish frontier, and daily incidents against the French took place at Aleppo. At the same time, the Syrian and Lebanese governments on June 21 reaffirmed their common policy that no special position would be accorded on their territories to any power.

It was thus in the atmosphere of a worsening situation in the Levant that the French government made its last attempt to "internationalize" the question. On June 24, Joseph Paul-Boncour presented an aide-memoire to U.S. Secretary of State Stettinius, the president of the steering committee of the United Nations conference, in which the French government asked that the delegates select a commission to be composed of representatives of three states having no direct interest in the Levant to inquire into the origins of the dispute and to promote a friendly settlement. The French, it added, understood that the United

Nations organization as such was not prepared to deal with the matter, but they desired to take advantage of the presence of the delegations in San Francisco for the selection of the commissioners. This initiative, however, was destined to be dealt with very shortly, for Stettinius informed Paul-Boncour that the conference was not qualified to deal with the French request and it should be referred to normal diplomatic channels. It is uncertain whether the French government had entertained serious hopes for the success of this proposal, made in the last days of the conference, or whether it wished only to demonstrate its continuing belief in the importance of referring such questions to international, in default of Great Power, consideration. In any case, *Le Monde*—and presumably the French government —recognized by June 26 that international consideration of any type seemed definitely excluded and that no real recourse remained for France except direct negotiations either with Great Britain or with Syria and Lebanon.[33]

The Denouement

The prospect for the success of such negotiations was somewhat enhanced by the end of June, when the attention of all the parties to the Syrian dispute was shifting to a larger context in which their mutual relations took other forms. On the eve of the Potsdam conference, at which the Soviet delegates were expected to raise the questions of the Straits and the Middle East, the British government had an interest in liquidating a dispute that would provide a pretext for the intervention of other powers. At the same time, the presentation of Soviet demands to Turkey for a revision of the Straits convention and territorial changes in the East gave rise to rumors that the U.S.S.R. might support Turkish claims to Aleppo in exchange for such concessions. This had the result of diverting the Syrian and Lebanese governments from total preoccupation with their relations with France. In Paris, finally, the importance attached to the decisions in regard to Germany which would be made at Potsdam in the absence of France strengthened the resolve of the government, already indicated in the assembly debate, to abandon an empty policy of recrimination with the British over the Levant. It did not seem too high a price to liquidate at least the French military position there in order to restore normal relations with the one power which might be expected to plead, at least to some degree, France's case in regard to Germany at Potsdam.[34]

Though the French goal in liquidating the crisis in the Levant was in large part the restoration of better relations with Great Britain, the method chosen to escape from the impasse consisted of making a direct approach to Syria and Lebanon rather than to London, presumably in order to strengthen France's hand in later negotiations with the British by slowing down or halting the local deterioration of the French position. The French minister plenipotentiary, Count Stanislas Ostrorog, therefore returned from Paris to Beirut at the end of June with proposals for direct settlements with the two states. Quiet negotiations began at once and, after a series of meetings in early July between Ostrorog and Syrian and Lebanese officials, the French delegation general in Beirut announced on July 8 that because of the end of hostilities in Europe the command of the "special troops" would be transferred to the Syrian and Lebanese governments in a manner to be decided on within forty-five days.[35] Though the withdrawal of the French troops was not affected by this decision, it is clear, in terms of the origin of the Syrian crisis in May precisely around the issue of the command of the "special troops," that the French government was conceding the major point at issue. This decision was well received in Beirut and no less so in London. Though French relations with Syria and Lebanon, as well as with Great Britain, remained strained, it may be said that with the conclusion of this agreement for the transfer of the "special troops" the crisis in the Levant passed its critical point. The actual transfer of the troops took place speedily and without incident.

As the French government had intended and expected, the Franco-Levantine detente soon led to a direct understanding with Great Britain. On July 25, the British and French military commanders in the Levant agreed without reference to Syria and Lebanon that French troops would evacuate eastern Syria at once but would remain on the Syrian and Lebanese coasts and would also retain certain air fields.[36] Two days before, at Potsdam, the Soviet Union had suggested that a conference of the Big Three and France be held to consider the Levant problem, but in face of British reluctance the Russians dropped their proposal. No mention of the matter was made in the protocol or communiqué of the conference.[37]

Despite the wish of Syria and Lebanon that the two western armies would leave their territory, both French and British units remained in the Levant until 1946. Syria and Lebanon, which had welcomed British intervention as an aid in driving out the French, now found that British interests were not identical with their own and that, indeed, theirs were sacrificed when the larger demands of British policy called for a certain rapprochement with France. It is ironic that this dispute, which began with a British rupture with France and a military intervention on behalf of Syria and Lebanon, ended with the restoration of Franco-British cooperation and their consequent joint inculpation by the two Arab states before the United Nations Security Council.

This most bitter Anglo-French clash since Fashoda in 1898, and probably the most painful experience of de Gaulle's tenure of office, passed from the center of the stage by mid-summer of

1945. It is hardly surprising that the forced removal of the Levant question from the agenda of topics which de Gaulle had
insisted be settled preliminary to the signing of an Anglo-French
alliance did not lead to such an agreement. Attempts were made
by the French later in the summer to improve relations with
Britain, but de Gaulle's words of June 4 to Alfred Duff Cooper
should be noted: "We are not, I recognize, in a state to wage
war on you now. But you have outraged France and betrayed
the West. That cannot be forgotten."[38] De Gaulle did not, thereafter, make vengeance on Britain the main business of his career.
But did he forget?

CHAPTER VII

GERMANY AND THE POTSDAM CONFERENCE

Allied Planning for Germany

Little has been said so far about French policy toward Germany, but apart from the general problem of re-establishing French status—without which, in de Gaulle's view, France could hardly even have a foreign policy—there was no question of greater importance for his government than that of Germany's fate. This concern of course became more acute as the war came to its end, but it was only after the German surrender in May, 1945, that it was possible to begin applying a definite policy. As the French soon found, however, their policy had to be worked out within the framework of decisions already made by the Big Three.

During the war the Allies faced three groups of problems concerning Germany, apart from the military victory itself: (1) the modalities of German surrender; (2) the machinery for the occupation of the country; and (3) the entire range of questions related to the settlement to be imposed on Germany in the peace treaties. The Allies devoted little attention to these topics before the summer of 1942, but increasing consideration was given to them as victory came nearer. Since the Provisional

French Government was not recognized *de jure* by the major Allies until October, 1944, and was not admitted to the European Advisory Commission until the following month, France was totally excluded from Allied planning on Germany up to that date. But the agreements which the Allies had reached during this period on the surrender, occupation, and future status of Germany, and the decisions they continued to make even after France was at last seemingly admitted to Allied councils at the end of 1944, were obviously of critical importance in defining the possibilities of action which remained open to the French when they were finally able to make their voice heard.

The most basic formal decision on the actual capitulation of Germany was made as early as the Casablanca conference of January, 1943, when the unconditional surrender of the Axis powers was laid down as the goal of Allied military policy. Roosevelt proposed this formula in order to avoid the possibility that the Germans might again, as after 1918, contend that they had been betrayed on the terms of their surrender; to obviate Russian suspicions that the Americans and British might negotiate a separate peace with Germany; and, probably, to assure public opinion that there would be no Allied understanding, such as the very unpopular arrangement which had been made with Admiral Darlan in North Africa, with some clique which might seize power within the Axis states and attempt to conclude an armistice. Churchill concurred in this policy at Casablanca, as did the Soviet government later, and, despite attempts to modify it, unconditional surrender remained the official Allied war aim. In this matter French ideas hardly differed from those of the principal Allies, so that the non-participation of France in this decision did not seriously affect her actual interests.

The first important contact between members of the Big Three on the subject of the Allied occupation of Germany appears to have been made during Foreign Secretary Eden's visit to Washington in March, 1943, when the American government proposed to him that the areas to be occupied by the three Allied armies in Germany should be delimited in advance. No substantive decisions were made at that time, however, nor at the foreign ministers' meeting at Moscow the following October, but the European Advisory Commission was created to study questions related to surrender terms and their execution. This body was to formulate recommendations on problems referred to it by the three governments, but it had no executive authority.

The commission held its first formal meeting on January 14, 1944, to consider its two principal tasks—the preparation of the instrument of surrender and the making of plans for the occupation of Germany.[1] Work on the surrender was completed by July 25, but the zones of occupation were not finally settled for more than a year. (The proposals for joint occupation of all Germany that were offered from time to time made no headway.) It was generally agreed that the Soviet army would occupy the eastern portion of Germany and that the remainder of the country would be divided into northwestern and southwestern zones. But Anglo-American disagreement soon arose over the assignment of these two zones. The British wanted the northwestern zone—including, significantly, the Ruhr—partly in the expectation that there would be an early American withdrawal from Europe and that the American zone would then devolve on the French. Roosevelt, however, was strongly opposed to American occupation of the southwestern zone because he was convinced, for some reason, that the occupant of this zone would have to deal with Danubian and Balkan problems and, in addition, because he feared that the supply lines to this zone across France might be disrupted by internal disorder in that country. The three actual zones were delimited by July,

1944, but it was only at the second Anglo-American conference at Quebec in September that they were finally allocated in principle. By this date the danger of civil disorder in France had practically disappeared and southeastern Europe was so effectively under Soviet control as to reduce Roosevelt's fear that the United States might be called on to assume primary responsibility there. Therefore, when Churchill proposed to grant Bremen and Bremerhaven to the Americans as ports of entry to Germany, Roosevelt accepted the southwestern zone.

Even after this agreement the Americans and British continued to haggle over the terms of American control of Bremen and Bremerhaven, so that the protocol on zones approved by the E. A. C. on September 14 left the two western zones unassigned. Because the Americans and British wanted to complete work on this protocol (and also on the one on control machinery) before France took her place on the commission, they allowed the Quebec agreement on zones to be written into an amended protocol which, together with the protocol on control machinery, was approved by the E. A. C. on November 14.[2] The British government approved both on December 5, but the American military were still unhappy because the details of access to the southwestern zone were not fully worked out. Faced, however, by the speed of the Soviet advance into Germany in early 1945, and by the prospect that the Russians might occupy an area greater than that specified in the as yet unratified zonal accord, the American government approved the control protocol on January 24, 1945, and on February 2, at the Malta meeting with the British, approved the protocol on zones as well. On February 6 Soviet approval of both was given at Yalta, and the occupation agreements were finally signed by the three powers. They provided for three zones of occupation, joint occupation of Berlin, and an Allied Control Council, which would be composed of the three commanders-in-chief.

The role in the occupation which the major Allies anticipated would be assigned to France remained uncertain. The British at first looked forward to France's relieving the American forces when they withdrew from Germany, but when Churchill visited Moscow in October, 1944, he suggested that France be included on the proposed Control Council. Neither the Soviet government nor the Americans seemed inclined to include France in their plans for the German occupation and she was excluded from the Yalta conference, at which the question was considered. The British, however, were increasingly preoccupied with the problem of confronting Russian strength in Europe after the Americans, as they had often announced, withdrew from the continent. Therefore, at the Malta conference which immediately preceded that in the Crimea, they and the Americans agreed that France should be given an occupation zone in Germany, to be carved from the territory already assigned to them. At Yalta itself Stalin resisted assigning an occupation zone to France even on this basis and, when he had yielded, opposed her inclusion on the Control Council. Despite Roosevelt's initial opposition, however, the British finally won their point. The details of French participation were left for negotiation in the European Advisory Commission. Thus, although France was slighted in other dispositions which were made for the settlement of the German problem, she won the most important point: admission to the occupation of and to the control machinery for Germany.

Allied planning for the occupation was thus well advanced by the time of the German surrender. Their ideas on her ultimate fate were far less developed. Both the British and the Russians, at least, were already looking sufficiently far ahead to realize that the disposition of Germany would be of the greatest importance for the power distribution of the postwar world. Apart from the problems of the surrender and the occupation of Germany, some attention was thus given by the Allies during the war to the peace settlement.

The first serious inter-Allied consideration of territorial problems probably took place during the visit of Eden to Washington in March, 1943. On that occasion the British and Americans considered the partition of Germany into several states and the cession of East Prussia to Poland. By the time of the Moscow conference of the three foreign ministers in October, 1943, the Americans appear to have had second thoughts on the subject of partition, and the other governments were also still undecided. It was agreed there, however, that Germany should be reduced to her 1938 frontiers and that East Prussia should be taken from her. The rest of the problem was referred to the European Advisory Commission. Later, at Teheran, Roosevelt produced a plan for the partition of Germany that received some discussion. More concretely, Churchill and Stalin agreed in effect on the Curzon line and the Oder River as the eastern and western frontiers of Poland. Roosevelt indicated clearly to Stalin that he had no objection to such an arrangement but for domestic political reasons could not agree to it before the 1944 elections.[3] In this way, the decision for the dismemberment of Germany in the east, with all the implications of this for the rest of the German settlement, was made a year and a half before the end of the war. Though overall partition plans had been considered, this partial decision was made as a by-product of the Polish settlement and in isolation from other aspects of the German problem.

There was, indeed, little detailed planning on the overall German settlement at this time. The United States, in particular, was reluctant to raise difficult postwar problems when the war was still far from won and had objected, for example, to the European Advisory Commission's being charged with the preparation of plans for postwar Germany. Within the United States government itself there was no coordinated planning for the postwar period, although several departments produced their own proposals for the German settlement. No firm American policy had been worked out prior to the Anglo-American conference at Quebec in September, 1944. On that occasion Roosevelt accepted Henry Morgenthau's plan for the destruction of German industry and the transformation of that state into a pastoral and agricultural country. Churchill, who may have been thinking of the importance of the Secretary of the Treasury in Britain's quest for postwar economic assistance, also endorsed the Morgenthau proposal, but Roosevelt was soon persuaded by Secretary of War Stimson and others to renounce the plan. A principal result of this episode was that the President, having once over-committed himself, discouraged further planning for the postwar settlement. As a result, no definite Allied plans for Germany were worked out before the end of the war.

The Yalta conference, however, in addition to its decisions on the occupation of Germany, established a secret three-power committee in London to consider plans not only for the disarmament and demilitarization of Germany but also for its dismemberment, on which the Big Three now for the first time apparently agreed in principle. Further, it was agreed that reparations would be laid on Germany, to be paid in labor, annual deliveries of goods from German production, and capital goods. The United States and the Soviet Union agreed that twenty billion dollars should be the basis for the discussion of reparations, of which half should go to the latter; the British, however, declined to be bound by any total or allotment.

This summary of wartime Allied decisions about Germany indicates that at the moment of surrender the only definitive agreements related to the German eastern frontier, which had

been more or less fixed on the Oder, and, less definitely, to reparations, on which two of the Big Three had tentatively established a total sum and partial allocation. Other questions had
been referred either to the European Advisory Commission, of
which France was a member, or to the special committee in
London, from which she was excluded. But no Allied agreements had been made on the western frontiers of Germany, nor
on more than the principle of her dismemberment or partition
(if, indeed, even on the principle), nor on the level of her industrial production. The French theses on these subjects were
thus not excluded before the German surrender, nor were
further Allied agreements made in the months which immediately succeeded it.[4]

As early as July, 1944, during his trip to the United States,
de Gaulle had indicated that France would in some manner seek
to estabish her own authority in the Rhineland, and in October
he reiterated the need for a special security regime in that area.[5]
He also held that the Rhine basin formed an economic unit,
including the Ruhr, which should be used for the benefit of all
Europe. Apart from these suggestions that French policy on
Germany was already rather well defined within a few months
of the liberation, the detailed interview by Foreign Minister
Bidault in the London *Sunday Times* of November 11 constituted France's first formal statement on the subject. Bidault asserted he had been loyal to Briand's policy toward Germany "as
long as there existed a civilized Germany." He then stated:

> One thing, however, is certain: there must be a Ger-
> many. Not an enslaved Germany, but one which will
> be unable to wage another war. This is in everybody's
> and particularly in France's interest, because she is her
> direct neighbor. Peace with Germany should not be one

of vengeance; it must be just and humane. Germany will have to be controlled for years to come, but I am not for trying to make her harmless by dismembering her artificially. Germany in her death struggle against unconditional surrender may fall bit by bit, like the walls of a house, and thus find herself naturally and organically dismembered—but to force it would be ill-advised. On the other hand, the early establishment of a central authority in Germany may impede the natural desire to dissociate themselves from Prussian influence that may exist to-day in other parts of Germany.

We do not want to incorporate any German territory. We do not want any German minority within our borders. Our greatest interest lies in the control of the Rhineland, because it represents our frontiers. International control has been suggested. We would not object to that, but there are different kinds of international control, and if such are set up, France, as a direct neighbor, perhaps ought to be given a privileged position in this control. British and Americans will one day want to go home. We will remain. We, therefore, must have a full share in the control of Germany. I do not believe it would do good to convert her into an agricultural country, but her industries, and especially her laboratories, must remain indefinitely under Allied supervision. Germany has given us on our own soil a very good example of how to control industries efficiently without making the control too obvious to the public. This method deserves to be studied carefully.[6]

In rejecting radical plans for the partition or pastoralization of Germany, Bidault was being consistent with the thinking of the

French resistance. At the same time, his remarks indicated that the French government had already evolved clear-cut ideas about the nature of the settlement it desired for Germany. Their plans included the two elements of a prolonged military occupation of the Rhineland, a classic maxim of French security policy, and an international control of Ruhr industry, which responded to more modern concepts.

During his talks in Moscow in early December, de Gaulle outlined French thinking on Germany in some detail. He called for (1) the detachment of the left bank of the Rhine from German sovereignty and its establishment as an autonomous area which would be a part, "from the economic point of view, of the Western zone"; and (2) a similar detachment of the Ruhr and the establishment there of an international control.[7] The Russians made no commitment on these points. In his subsequent report to the Consultative Assembly, Bidault said the French had accepted the Polish frontiers proposed by the Soviet Union, including the Oder line, and had stated their intention of depriving Germany of the Rhineland and Ruhr, her springboards for aggression. German industry, he added, must work first for the restoration of the damage caused by the war and afterward for the prosperity of all nations. Bidault denied—accurately—that definite plans had been worked out, alleging that other interested parties had not been represented at Moscow. The French soon learned, however, that far from accepting their plan for Germany the Soviet leaders had not even agreed to support France's inclusion in the deliberations of the Great Powers.[8]

Lacking a diplomatic forum in which to develop its ideas, the French government was obliged to state its German policy in the form of public speeches and declarations. Thus, in a press conference on January 25, 1945, after it had become known

that the Big Three would soon meet once again, de Gaulle reiterated France's desire to occupy the Rhineland and, apparently, at least a part of the Ruhr also.[9] In the days before and
during the Yalta conference, the Paris press gave considerable
attention to Germany. The semi-official paper, *Le Monde*, repeated that France desired ". . . the occupation of the Rhineland and Ruhr, and the establishment of an international control
over the economy of the Rhenish-Westphalian basin, the sole
means to reduce the military power of Germany and to insure
the effectiveness of whatever collective security organization
there may be." Commenting on a plan attributed to Churchill
for a four-power consortium to administer the Rhineland and
the Ruhr, the paper stated: "This plan was not up to now
known in Paris. It envisaged a distinct regime for the left bank
of the Rhine, which might have been a territory of French occupation. This zone is not to be confounded with the industrial region of Westphalia, situated on the right bank of the
river, which, as much by its geographic situation as by its economy and population, presents a different character. An allied
control of the Ruhr basin is an absolute necessity."[10]

In a broadcast on February 5, de Gaulle stated once again
the now habitual theme of French policy: "I can make clear
once more that the definitive presence of French forces from
one end to the other of the Rhine; the separation of the territories of the left bank of the river and of the Ruhr basin from
what will be the German state or states; the independence of
the Polish, Czechoslovak, Austrian, and Balkan nations, joined
in friendship with each of the peoples who will have to bear the
principal weight for the maintenance of peace in Europe, are
the conditions which France judges essential."[11] These ideas
were also pressed on Harry Hopkins by Bidault and de Gaulle
during Hopkins' visit to Paris before the opening of the Crimea

conference.[12] French attitudes toward the postwar treatment of Germany were rounded out by a number of non-territorial prosposals that were reported in the press in mid-February, two weeks after the conclusion of the conference. These included destruction of German armament factories; prohibition of the manufacture of airplane engines and control of the importation of other types of machinery; reduction of the production of other war potential to a minimum and control of it; control over laboratories and research; and confiscation of German-owned industries abroad.[13]

In April, de Gaulle reiterated to the American assistant secretary of war, John J. McCloy, that he did not favor a scorched earth policy in Germany, but that control of her economy was essential, and international control of the Ruhr valley was particularly important. He once again stated that the left bank of the Rhine, as far north as Cologne, should be under French political control. Bidault said much the same to Acting Secretary of State Grew on May 19.[14] French thinking about postwar Germany had thus been rather fully worked out and persistently pressed on the major Allies when, with the end of hostilities, the time came to pass from planning to implementation.

The Establishment of Allied Control in Germany

The Allied occupation machinery was not established without considerable difficulty and delay. At the time of the German surrender at Reims on May 7, 1945, the armies under the command of General Eisenhower occupied considerably more territory than had been allocated to the western zones of occupation. Churchill wanted the American and British forces to hold their positions in order to exert pressure on the Soviet Union, whose policy in Eastern Europe increasingly disturbed him. In addition, the British were concerned with the problem of feeding the industrial area which constituted the British zone, and they wanted to bargain with the Soviet government for food from its zone in return for the withdrawal of Allied forces to the agreed boundaries. The Americans, however, rejected Churchill's ideas and wanted to implement the German control machinery as quickly as possible.

Allied relations were at a low point during May because of the sharp divergence of Soviet and Anglo-American policies on Trieste, the Balkans, and particularly on Poland. Although Generals Eisenhower and Montgomery were named by their governments to the German Control Council on May 22, no Soviet member was appointed. However, the mission of Harry Hopkins to Moscow at the end of the month concluded with, among other results, an apparent understanding on the Polish problem which was sufficiently satisfactory to the Russian government to facilitate the settlement of other outstanding difficulties. Marshal Zhukov was therefore appointed to the Control Council at the end of May. As for French participation, the document providing the basis for Allied control that had been drawn up by the European Advisory Commission and approved at Yalta was amended on May 1 to provide for the inclusion of France in the occupation.[15] The French cabinet approved this on May 10 and created a commandership-in-chief for Germany to which General Jean de Lattre de Tassigny was named. The Soviet Union ratified the arrangements on the following day. With the authority of the Control Council thus settled by the end of May, the commanders-in-chief met in Berlin on June 5 and issued the documents by which the four powers assumed supreme authority in Germany.[16]

In the first of these declarations they formally assumed control of Germany, as well as the right to settle her frontiers and government at a later date. The second declaration formalized the division of Germany into four zones, in each of which the occupant would name a commander-in-chief, while Berlin would be governed jointly by a four-power Kommandatura. The third provided that each commander-in-chief was supreme in his zone and that the four of them, each assisted by a political counselor, would form the Control Council which would, by unanimity, make decisions for all zones. Under the Control Council there was to be a permanent coordinating committee and a control staff organized into specified functional divisions.

The establishment of this machinery was dependent, however, on the final adjustment of the zonal boundaries, and most of June was taken up by Allied negotiations on this subject. The French wanted to occupy the left bank of the Rhine and a zone on the right bank as far north as Cologne—with the clear intent of detaching this area from Germany. They also wanted to include Hesse and Baden in their zone of occupation.[17] After bilateral discussions with the Americans and British they finally agreed on June 22 to take a good deal less: the left bank of the Rhine south of Bonn (including part of the Prussian *Rheinprovinz*, a small part of *Rheinhessen*, the Palatinate and the Saar), a small segment of Hesse-Nassau on the right bank, about two-thirds of Baden, and about half of Wurttemburg.[18] The French thus gave up Stuttgart and Karlsruhe and did not get Cologne. Because the United States wanted to hold the Karlsruhe-Stuttgart-Ulm-Munich autobahn, the French had to accept the division of the historic states of Baden and Wurttemburg, which not only diminished their zone but undercut their hopes for the emergence of separatism or federalism in this part of Germany on the basis of the established states. By the evacuation of Karlsruhe, which the French army had captured in April, the French zone was split into two disconnected sectors. At the same time, the United States and Great Britain decided to evacuate the territory which they occupied within the zone originally assigned to the Soviet Union. The appropriate troop movements were made during the first days of July. On July 4 French troops entered Berlin and two days later they moved into the Saar and the portion of the Rhineland assigned to them. The French zonal headquarters was established at Baden-Baden, and on July 31 General Pierre Koenig succeeded General de Lattre de Tassigny. Under him General Louis-Marie Koeltz was named to serve on the coordinating committee in Berlin, General Goislard de Monsabert to command the French occupation forces, and Emile Laffon to act as civilian administrator-general.[19]

During May and June each of the Allies began to develop separate occupation policies in its own zone. The most important attempt to form a coordinated policy was in the area of reparations. It had been agreed at Yalta that representatives of the Big Three would meet in Moscow to consider this problem. The United States and Great Britain, however, which were advocating the collection and distribution of reparations on an all-German rather than on a zonal basis, were convinced that France, as an occupying power and a member of the Control Council, should be included in the work of the Reparations Commission. They therefore pressed for her admission.[20] But the Soviet Union, which had opposed the admission of France to the Control Council until the very end of the Yalta conference, was no more willing to accept her as a fourth member— and claimant—on the Moscow commission.[21] The Russians parried the Allies request for the inclusion of France by demanding the admission also of Poland, whose government the Western Allies did not recognize. As a consequence, Britain and the United States had to accept the exclusion of France, and they finally agreed that the three-power commission should meet in

Moscow on June 21. The French government was of course aware of the reason for its exclusion, for the Soviet leaders had long since explained their point of view to General Catroux, the French ambassador in Moscow.[22] In an obvious effort to break down Soviet opposition, France, responding to hints which the Russian leaders had given since December, 1944, and anticipating the United States and Great Britain, recognized the Polish government of Warsaw at the end of June; in addition, she expressed a willingness to see Poland included on the Reparations Commission.[23] Since the Allies, as the Russians surely foresaw, could not accept this condition, the problem of France's role in the reparations question, as well as the bases of the settlement itself, was left to the Potsdam conference.

Another Conference Without France

The evident need to resolve the continuing tension between the Big Three over Poland, Trieste, and other European issues; to complete strategy for the Far Eastern war; and to lay down in greater detail the policies to be followed in Germany—all contributed in mid-May to the widespread belief in France that the leaders of the principal Allies would soon hold another personal meeting. Indeed, on May 6, Churchill proposed a three-power meeting to President Truman. The conference was prepared by the preliminary missions of Joseph Davies to London and, particularly, of Harry Hopkins to Moscow, and it was during Hopkins' visit that July 15 was fixed for the opening of the meeting. Within a few days it became publicly known in France that the conference would take place near Berlin in July.

The French government, which had strongly resented its exclusion from Yalta, of course wanted and tried to be invited to the Berlin conference.[24] France's claims to be included were by then far stronger than they had been in February. If it could be argued that the French role in the Pacific war was minimal, it was more difficult to maintain that, though a permanent member of the Great Power directory which was at that moment being embodied in the structure of the United Nations Security Council, she had no direct interest in the settlement of the Polish, Trieste, and other European problems. Above all, it is not easy to understand how the three Great Powers, having given France a zone of occupation in Germany, a seat on the Control Council, and a veto on its activities, could have thought it possible to lay down the main lines of a German settlement, to be applied by that council, in France's absence.

The explanation for Soviet opposition to French participation appears to lie in the same quarter as their objection to France's inclusion on the Reparations Commission; they stubbornly refused to grant France any substantive role in Allied decision-making, and particularly in the government of Germany, which was quickly emerging as the principal problem and index of Allied relations. The Soviet demand for the admission of Poland as a counterpart to that of France—a demand which the United States and Great Britain obviously could not accept, since, among other evident reasons, the composition of the Polish government was itself an important subject of contention among the powers—indicates that the Russians may have anticipated that France would prove hostile to their policies and would add her voice to that of Britain in opposing them. It is probably not far from the truth to conclude that the Soviet desire to exclude France from a significant role in German affairs was based on the same postulate as the British wish to include her: the belief that, despite British arguments to the contrary, the United States would soon withdraw from effective participation in European affairs. In this case the British hoped to have France by their side in the anticipated struggle with the Soviet Union. The U.S.S.R. obviously wished to see Britain isolated in Europe by establishing as a fixed rule that European and German policy would be made only by the Big Three or, after the anticipated lessening of American participation, by Britain and Russia alone —a contest whose outcome neither the former nor the latter could have doubted. The role of France in Europe and in Germany thus became an important factor in both British and Soviet policy, and at Yalta and Potsdam the British recruited American assistance on behalf of French participation, as if to make maximum use of American influence before it disappeared from the European scene—a prospect increasingly alarming to Churchill.[25]

Unfortunately for the French government, its standing with both Britain and the United States, as well as with the Soviet Union, was very low during May, and they, too, did not favor inviting France to the conference.[26] While the American government recognized the French preoccupation with questions of national prestige and was to a certain extent inclined to assist France in recovering her Great Power status, various French actions during that month were strongly opposed by Washington. The French refusal to surrender Stuttgart to the American army according to plan until Truman threatened to cut off support to the French units, and the even more serious episode of the French occupation of certain border cantons in northern Italy against the wishes of the Allied military government there, which ended finally in the same manner as the Stuttgart affair, gravely compromised de Gaulle's position in the eyes of the Truman administration.[27] In the Italian incident, Truman's policy was fully approved by Churchill, who went so far as to cable Washington on June 6—at the height of the crisis in the Levant—that, after five years of experience, he was convinced that de Gaulle "is the worst enemy of France in her troubles" and "one of the greatest dangers to European peace."[28] The American government, it should be noted, fully backed the policy of intervention adopted by the British in the Levant.

Bidault therefore received a less than cordial reception when on his return trip to Paris from San Francisco he was received by Truman on May 18. The President stated in general terms that the United States wished to see France resume her place as a Great Power but, when Bidault pressed for a specific commitment on the use of French armed forces in the Far Eastern war, Truman was frank to say that he was not pleased by recent French behavior in Germany and Italy and that any French participation in the war against Japan could only be on the basis of the supreme authority of the American command in the Pacific.[29] Bidault also hinted at France's great interest in the work of the forthcoming Great Power conference. But though Acting Secretary of State Grew urged Truman to approve de Gaulle's participation, the President told Bidault only that "in the event of such a meeting the participation of France might be given consideration by the three heads of government."[30] Bidault could have had few illusions about what this meant, for, in his remarks to the press before leaving Washington, he said that the French considered themselves a Great Power and assumed that at the coming international meetings that point would be definitely settled.[31] Although Bidault had perhaps understood—or hoped—that the American government would press France's claims during the conference, he clearly knew there was little prospect that they would be established prior to it.

When, on July 6, Ambassador Bonnet urged Truman at least to assure him that no decision would be taken at the conference on matters affecting France, notably Germany, the President only "expressed the opinion that no matters of interest to France would be finally decided at the coming conference until the French Government had been consulted."[32] The parties were hardly of one mind, however, as to what matters were of interest to France, the nature of the consultation promised, or the meaning of "finally decided." At Potsdam, as at Yalta, major decisions were to be taken by the Big Three which, if they had been implemented, would have severely limited French freedom of action on matters of major concern to France. It is obvious, therefore, though somewhat ironic, why a study of French foreign policy must give so prominent a place to the proceedings of a conference in which France did not participate.

The Potsdam Conference

Each of the three participants brought to the Potsdam meeting fairly definite ideas about the German and European settlements. The Soviet leaders were preoccupied, as they had been at Yalta, with the question of extracting maximum reparations from Germany, and they had already begun to implement their views even before the conference began. In addition, they wanted their control of Eastern Europe to be accepted by the Allies and confirmed by recognition of the new Communist-dominated governments of Poland, Rumania, Hungary, Bulgaria, Yugoslavia, and Albania, which would serve to discourage the domestic opponents of these regimes. Finally, the Russians wanted to round out their zone of influence by extending Poland's frontiers on the west and by pursuing a forward policy toward Turkey and Iran.

The British, whose government changed from Conservative to Labour halfway through the conference, and whose economic situation was becoming increasingly difficult, were in a much weaker power position at the Potsdam meeting than at previous Allied conferences. They recognized the extent of Soviet ambitions and the menace which this constituted to the distribution of power on the continent, but with the Red Army in occupation of most of the disputed areas there was little to be done beyond protest. Much of the conference, therefore, took the form of sharp verbal battles between the British and Russians regarding the "democratic" nature of the regimes in Poland, the Balkans, and Italy. But the British were preoccupied above all with the problem of feeding the population of the highly industrialized zone which they occupied in Germany. On the one hand, they hoped to obtain American aid for the support of their occupation forces, as well as food supplies from the Soviet zone; on the other, they had become convinced that some measure of German economic revival was necessary if the European economy itself was to be rebuilt, and if the occupation was not to represent an intolerable drain on Britain's much reduced resources. They therefore tended to oppose the extreme Soviet demands for reparations and to favor an overall economic policy for Germany which would permit exchanges between the industrial western zones and the more agricultural east.

The American representatives do not appear to have been entirely conscious of all the implications of this incipient struggle between the British and Russians. Their principal concern was to lay down the principles of the German occupation, provide for the negotiation of peace treaties with the former satellites, and, in general, promote a sufficient degree of stability and order in Europe to facilitate their own early departure from it—not, certainly, in the sense of completely cutting themselves off from world affairs, but rather of at least reducing their principal responsibility for European problems. In Germany the United States favored the re-establishment of local self-government and the encouragement of political activity in all zones, the formation of a central administration—not a government—under the Control Council, and the treatment of Germany as an economic unit. The Americans were ready, further, to participate in Allied missions to supervise elections in Eastern Europe in the hope that the resulting governments could be recognized and could sign peace treaties. But they felt no particular responsibility in Europe apart from Germany. The Americans to some extent still appeared, at least to themselves, somewhat in the role of mediators, and Russo-American differences remained muted behind the glaring Anglo-Russian divergences.

The Potsdam conference lasted officially from July 17 to August 2, with a suspension during the absence of the British leaders in London. At the first plenary session Truman proposed that a council of foreign ministers be established, made up of the ministers of the five permanent members of the Security Council, to prepare the drafts of peace treaties for the defeated enemies. Behind this proposal lay (1) the American desire to have France as well as the Big Three participate in the essential work on the European peace treaties; and (2) the hope that the use of the Big Five of the Security Council for this purpose would fend off Soviet objections to including France.[33] According to the American proposal, the five ministers would serve in the same relation to the drafting of the peace treaties as the Dumbarton Oaks conference had served in relation to the United Nations Charter. The Italian and Balkan treaties were to be the first items on the agenda of the new council.

Both Stalin and Churchill clearly indicated that they were not enthused at the idea of including China in the council; Stalin also was skeptical about the role of France. The matter was referred to the foreign ministers, and it was agreed at the second plenary session that the council, for the drafting of each treaty, would be composed only of those states which had signed the armistice with the enemy in question. On the following day, July 19, Secretary of State Byrnes pointed out to Eden and Molotov that the formula that had been agreed on was too narrow and would exclude France from work on the Italian treaty. Molotov asked whether France, under the formula Byrnes proposed, would take part in the drafting of the Rumanian treaty, to which Byrnes replied that "if France were not at war with any country she would be present during any discussion but would not necessarily participate in the decisions." Apparently satisfied, Molotov agreed to change the formula as Byrnes suggested. The next day the foreign ministers altered their earlier text to state that France would be considered, in the work of the council, to have signed the Italian armistice. The heads of government then approved the new text. By this agreement China would participate actively only in the drafting of the Japanese treaty, if the council ever came to consider it, and France only in the Italian and German treaties. The Big Three would deal with the former satellites. In addition, their continued primacy was confirmed by the decision to keep in existence the three-power Council of Foreign Ministers established at Yalta, which of course undercut the success France had scored in the establishment of the five-power body.[34]

The problems of Germany, Poland's western frontier, and the Balkans were far more difficult. It was fairly simple to agree on common political instructions to the four commanders-in-chief, utilizing the work of the European Advisory Commission. These, however, were largely negative, calling for disarmament, demilitarization, and the destruction of Naziism. But after agreement on these points on July 19, the conference made little progress until its final days. The succeeding plenary sessions were marked by constant Anglo-Soviet wrangling on the Balkans, Poland, German shipping, the Italian colonies, the Straits, and other subjects. Disputed problems were referred to the foreign ministers, who were no more able to resolve them than their chiefs. Even more complex was the controversy over reparations policy in Germany. The Americans, as well as the British, feared starvation and disorder in their occupation zones and wished to be sure that reparations would not reduce the German standard of living excessively or require Anglo-American subsidization of reparations. The Russians, however, insisted on the ten billion dollars in reparations which they claimed had been accepted by the Americans at Yalta as the basis of discussion.

Acrimonious dispute on the major topics of reparations and Soviet policy in the Balkans, as well as on various subsidiary questions, continued until the departure of the British delegates to London to receive and act upon the results of the parliamentary elections. During their absence, Byrnes tried to find satisfactory compromises on all outstanding questions. The deadlock was broken only on July 31, when Byrnes, after preliminary talks with the British and the Russians, presented to the eleventh plenary meeting of the conference three proposals dealing with reparations, the Polish border, and the former German satellites, all to be treated as an interdependent whole.[35]

By the first proposal, the Soviet Union would satisfy its own reparations claims (and, significantly, Poland's also) by removing capital assets not needed for the peacetime German economy from the Soviet zone. The other three zones would provide reparations for all other claimants. In addition, the Soviet Union would receive 7.5 percent of the "surplus" capital from the western zones gratis and 12.5 percent in exchange for food, coal and other raw materials from the Soviet zone. "Surplus" was to be defined by the Control Council, subject to the veto of each commander in his zone on implementation. The Russians found this proposal far short of the ten billion dollars in reparations which they had sought—indeed, it contained no sum at all—but, since the Ruhr was physically under the control of the Western powers and since the Americans indicated that they would leave the conference without any agreement rather than yield on the reparations issue, the Soviet delegates had little choice but to accept in principle. At first, however, they made several other claims, including demands for 30 percent of German foreign assets, 30 percent of the gold captured in the western zones, and 500 million dollars worth of shares in western zone enterprises. Truman then said that if the Russians would renounce these new claims, he would agree that the proportion of capital goods from the western zones which the U.S.S.R. was to receive would be increased. The British, more reluctantly, concurred. On this basis, it was finally agreed that 10 percent of surplus German capital from the west would be transferred gratis, and 15 percent in return for other goods. Further, the Russians were authorized to seize German assets in all the ex-satellite countries of Eastern Europe. They renounced all claim to German assets elsewhere. The difficult questions of defining "surplus" (in terms of what German standard of living?) and "reparations" (only capital goods or current production also?) were left unanswered.

Since reparations were to be drawn on a zonal basis, and the Soviet Union had a material interest in those in all the western zones, the Russians were reluctantly obliged to admit France, as an occupying power, to the Reparations Commission, although Stalin once again attempted, without success, to have Poland included also. The Big Three agreed further—and most significantly—that Germany "shall be treated as a single economic unit," that central administrative machinery should deal

with economic questions, and that "certain essential central German administrative departments" would be set up, although "for
the time being no central German Government shall be established." Later in the session the Russians brought up their proposal to establish a four-power authority over the Ruhr, a plan
which was similar to that long advocated by France. In May,
Harry Hopkins had told Stalin that Truman favored international control of the Ruhr as well as of the Saar and the west
bank of the Rhine. But at the Berlin conference neither the
Americans nor the British showed any interest in the Soviet
proposal. The Russians did not persist and the matter was referred to the new Council of Foreign Ministers.[36]

Once German affairs had been disposed of, Byrnes's second
proposal was taken up. The Western powers accepted the *fait
accompli* of Polish administration of the German territories east
of the Oder-Neisse line, which the Russians had already granted
to Poland—purportedly until the fixing of Germany's frontiers
at the peace conference. The third part of the package included
a commitment by the three powers to give priority to a peace
treaty with Italy and to its early admission to the United Nations, and a rather meaningless verbal formula by which the
powers undertook to study, separately, establishment of diplomatic relations with Rumania, Hungary, Bulgaria, and Finland.

These proposals saved the conference from breakdown and
represented a certain measure of common understanding on
German administration and a rather firm provisional policy on
the problem of reparations. Other contentious matters, however,
were either referred to the Council of Foreign Ministers or
glossed over by compromise formulae with little substance.

Most important, the bargain which resulted in the settlement
of the reparations question also practically closed the door on
four-power control of the Ruhr. It was clear that neither the

British, who occupied the area, nor the Americans were willing to permit Soviet participation in the economic direction of the western zones. One of the key points of French policy was thus in effect rejected in the absence of France. The same was true of the dismemberment of Germany and of the detachment of the Rhineland. Though the Potsdam agreements were supposedly only temporary, pending a final peace treaty, the provisional zonal arrangements, as the French had feared, were already beginning to crystallize into permanent *de facto* settlements.

The French Response

In general, French reaction to the conference tended, with a certain satisfaction, to emphasize the subjects on which the communiqué was vague or silent. In its first editorial comment on the subject, on August 3, *Le Monde* noted: "One will perhaps judge that the Potsdam decisions contain few positive elements, at least to our knowledge. The conference postpones many problems, especially that of population transfers. It passes over others in silence. The only ones which it takes up, concerning Germany, are more posed than settled. Some broad lines are drawn, according to which there may be action, more or less. Is it because they could not do more or because they were not in agreement? The future will tell us."[37]

The creation of the Council of Foreign Ministers was of course welcomed in France, since it would permit her to participate in the German and Italian settlements, but the possibility of French exclusion from the work on the Finnish and Balkan treaties, and the continued existence of the three-power foreign ministers' group established at Yalta, which many feared would retain real decision-making power, were adversely commented on. Above all, in light of these last facts, there was no illusion as to France's being admitted even yet to a full place among the Great Powers. Speaking on August 11, de Gaulle conceded that France's position was not entirely satisfactory, but each nation, he said, was measured by its power alone, and France must hope for both a mellowing of this brutal rule and an increase in her own power.[38]

Shortly before the end of the Potsdam conference, the American, British, and Soviet ambassadors informed the French government of the decisions made there, inviting it to associate itself with certain of these decisions and to accept membership on the Council of Foreign Ministers and the Reparations Commission.[39] The French government replied to these proposals in six notes handed on August 7 to the ambassadors of the Big Three in Paris. The substance of these notes was as follows:

1. France agreed to participate in the Council of Foreign Ministers. But despite the Potsdam decision, which seemed to exclude her from the work on the Balkan and Finnish treaties, she asserted: "France is evidently interested in every important question concerning Europe, or any region whatever of Europe. This applies, in particular, to the settlements concerning Rumania, Bulgaria, Hungary and Finland." In addition, France, who was not a signatory of the Italian armistice, saw no reason why she should now consider herself as such.

2. The French government regretted that decisions on a subject as important to it as Germany should have been taken by three of its Allies in its absence. It could not accept the reconstitution which seemed to be envisaged of a central German government. It approved the stated aims of the occupation but remained reserved on the formation of all-German political parties and the creation of central administrative departments for the whole of Germany, whose frontiers remained undefined.

3. The French government agreed to participate in the work of the Reparations Commission, where it would be represented by Robert Coulondre and Jacques Rueff. It reserved the right to present its views on the economic control of Germany and the bases for a reparations settlement.

4. No objection was raised to Polish administration of Germany east of the Oder-Neisse line, nor to Soviet administration of part of East Prussia. But the question of German frontiers constituted a whole which should be examined by all the interested powers. France also had no objection to the transfer of German populations from Poland, Czechoslovakia, and Hungary.[40]

France, by thus accepting membership in the Council of Foreign Ministers while declining to associate herself artificially with the Italian armistice, implicitly reasserted her right to participate in the Italian and other peace settlements not because the Big Three invited her to do so but on the basis of her status as a belligerent and, particularly, as a great power properly concerned in all European problems. Even more significant was the attitude expressed in these notes on the German question, for the French government promptly and at one stroke destroyed the facile expectations of the Allies, who presumably had believed that France would accept the policies laid down at Potsdam in her absence. In only one respect—that of the Polish frontiers—did France agree on an important substantive matter with the conferees; this, of course, was not only in harmony with her own policy of weakening Germany but also provided a precedent for parallel operations on Germany's western border. But though the French government approved the ostensible aims of the occupation of Germany, it opposed the creation of a central administration; and though it was obviously pleased to become a member of the Reparations Commission, it reserved the right to present its own views on the questions before that body, including the economic organization of Germany.[41]

The French thus gave clear warning, and not for the first time, that they would not necessarily accept decisions made in their absence from Allied councils. Once France was armed by the three major powers with a veto in the implementation of the policies on which they, but not she, had agreed, it should have surprised no one that she would use it to press her own views, hitherto disregarded, on the Allies.

De Gaulle's Policy to the United States

CHAPTER VIII

FRENCH DIPLOMACY AFTER POTSDAM

The French welcomed the gains they made at Potsdam, but they had no illusions that they had achieved the unquestioned right to participate as an equal in Allied councils or that their German policy stood much chance of acceptance. The hope of support from the Soviet Union, so high in December, 1944, had dwindled by the summer of the next year. In the period immediately following the Potsdam conference, therefore, de Gaulle made some effort to improve French relations with the United States and even with Great Britain. In addition, he tried to strengthen France's position in relation to all three of the major powers by developing, in the new form of the "Western bloc," the policy of "magnification" of France's voice which had been thought of and then discarded during the San Francisco conference. Little was accomplished in Washington and London, but much would be heard in time to come of the unity of Western Europe. In the meantime the first Great Power conference to which France was invited, the London meeting of the new Council of Foreign Ministers, ended with a cruel setback to French hopes.

De Gaulle's Visit to the United States

The reserved attitude of the American administration toward de Gaulle and his government, exacerbated by the Stuttgart and the Franco-Italian frontier episodes and by American hostility to French policy in the Levant, did not change notably during the Potsdam conference. President Truman indicated the minor role he assigned to France by rejecting a Soviet proposal to invite Yugoslav representatives to the conference when Yugoslav affairs were being considered on the ground that it would be necessary to do as much for France. When the Russians raised the question of the Levant, Truman expressed his belief that France should not enjoy any special position in Syria and Lebanon because of her recent conduct there.[1] At the same time, however, the Americans and British realized the necessity of securing French agreement for the implementation of the policies which had been laid down for Germany. De Gaulle, for his part, had no reason to reject an opportunity to press his views on the new American president. It was thus agreed that he would come to Washington on August 22, 1945.

During the talks, which lasted four days, Germany was the main subject of discussion.[2] De Gaulle urged the importance of "autonomy" for the left bank of the Rhine, though without explicitly demanding annexation to France, and of international control of the Ruhr, whose coal and industry, he said, should be used for the reconstruction of Western Europe. He agreed with Truman that Germany should not be allowed to sink through misery into Communism, but he argued that there must be guarantees for French security. More broadly, he said that only a decentralized, federal Germany offered any hope that the Russians might eventually allow their zone to rejoin a German state. Bidault, for his part, pressed on Byrnes the danger to France of the shifting of Germany's center of gravity toward the West (requiring, he said, territorial changes on that side also), the risk of communization of all Germany, and the French objections to the establishment of central administrations in Germany.[3] The French also stressed France's preoccupation with the return of Indochina to their control after the Japanese surrender, and de Gaulle spoke of a new, liberal regime to be established there. In addition to these questions, a most urgent French interest at the conference was economic, for on the day of de Gaulle's arrival in Washington lend-lease had been terminated.

The atmosphere of the talks was cordial but the results were vague. The French views on the German settlement elicited no commitments and little encouragement from the Americans. Even the French described the discussions as no more than preparations for the consideration of the German problem, which they assumed would be on the agenda of the September meeting of the Council of Foreign Ministers. The Americans at least did not object to the economic attachment of the Saar to France. They also listened with sympathy to France's concern over Indochina, and during de Gaulle's visit it was announced that French officers would accompany the British and Chinese troops who were to receive the Japanese surrender there. Perhaps the most significant result of the visit was the grant of American credits to France.

De Gaulle's visit to Washington was thus useful to France in establishing a basis for the personal rapport and cordiality in Franco-American relations which had long been lacking, in permitting the French to explain their German and other policies, and particularly in providing the occasion for serious economic discussions. But the "American observer" quoted by *Le Monde* as saying that the United States "would with a favorable eye see

France take its place as the principal European power" seems to have reflected the attitude of the American government less accurately than the Associated Press, which on August 25 stated that if the United States was determined to prevent France from dying of hunger during the winter, the balance sheet of de Gaulle's visit was dominated by the fact that the Americans did not show themselves in much of a hurry to treat France as a major power.[4] The elusive search for Great Power status, denied to the French at Potsdam as at Yalta, was still far from success, and the American government made no commitment to support additional French claims in this respect.

Franco-British Relations

The restoration of the pre-war status of the international zone of Tangier, a problem which received relatively little public attention during the summer of 1945, contributed to some improvement in Franco-British relations after the Syrian crisis. Tangier was a part of the Moroccan Empire, of which France was the principal protecting power.[5] On June 14, 1940, 1,200 Spanish soldiers had entered the zone on the pretext of maintaining its neutrality, but probably to prepare for its seizure by Spain since the Mendoub, who represented the Sultan of Morocco, was expelled and replaced by a representative of the Caliph of Tetouan in Spanish Morocco. Both the French and British protested this action throughout the war, but it was only in June, 1945, on French initiative, that they began to take steps for the termination of the Spanish occupation. For France, of course, the matter was of particular importance because of her treaty obligations to maintain the prerogatives of the Sultan of Morocco and her desire to demonstrate beyond any shadow of doubt that, notwithstanding the defeat and surrender of 1940, the protectorate treaty remained unimpaired. As *Le Monde* said on June 13: "One thing at least seems evident to us, and that is that we must start from these two premises: on the one hand, the zone of Tangier has never ceased to be an integral part of the Sherifian Empire, and, on the other hand, this empire as a whole is bound to France by a protectorate treaty which also is still in effect."[6]

An exchange of views was begun in the middle of June between the British, French, and American governments in regard to the ending of the Spanish regime. France from the first insisted that any conference called to deal with the question recognize Moroccan sovereignty over Tangier. These exchanges led to the decision that representatives of the three governments would meet to consider means by which to annul the Spanish action of 1940. The Americans and British wanted an interim regime to be established; the French, who feared a reduction of their prewar role, wanted to revert to the statute of 1923. All agreed that a general conference of the signatories of the Act of Algeciras—with the exception of Italy, and of Spain, whose rights were deemed to have been forfeited by her action in 1940—would be called later to establish a new permanent statute. The first tripartite meeting was scheduled for July 2 in Paris.

But the Soviet Union, when informed of the plan, indicated that it wished to take part in this stage of the discussions. The meeting of the technical experts was therefore postponed until the governments had considered the question. The Americans favored the Soviet request, the British did not, and the French, who hesitated to admit new factors into a situation that had been entirely satisfactory to them, attributed the difficulty to the other two, who had wanted a new interim regime rather than, as France had desired, the restoration of the 1923 statute to which

the U.S.S.R. was not a party. During further exchanges between the three governments in early July, the British indicated
that, with the Big Three meeting so near, the Tangier talks
should be postponed until August. In the meantime the question
of Russian participation—but nothing else dealing with the
problem—could be discussed at Berlin. Their view prevailed,
though the French feared (and the American ambassador in
London apparently agreed) that the British might try to use
Tangier to bargain with the Russians for some advantage to
themselves (as, for example, on the Straits question). The Soviet
Union did, in fact, raise the subject at Potsdam, and the Big
Three agreed that their representatives and those of France
should meet in the near future in Paris. The conference protocol—but not the communiqué—included this arrangement,
with the understanding of the participants that the zone of Tangier should remain international.[7]

French, British, American, and Russian representatives accordingly met in Paris on August 10. On August 23 a communiqué from the conference of experts announced that they had
agreed on (1) the re-establishment at Tangier of a provisional
regime based on the status of 1923; and (2) the convocation,
within six months, of a conference of all the signatories of the
Act of Algeciras (including, presumably, Spain) to consider
modifications of the statute.[8] On August 31 the conference
adopted a group of resolutions to the effect that Spain must
evacuate Tangier; the sovereign rights of the Sultan of Morocco
would be re-established; the international administration would
be restored and would include the United States and the Soviet
Union; and this regime would continue until the conclusion of
a new convention at a conference composed of all signatories
of the Act of Algeciras. Great Britain and France, as signatories
of the 1923 convention, made a joint demarche to the Spanish

foreign minister on September 4, requiring Spanish evacuation of the territory. When this had been completed, it was stated, the Control Committee would be restored; the Legislative Assembly would be elected; the Sultan would name the administrative officers; and a police force, recruited locally and trained by officers of the powers, would replace the Spanish-officered gendarmerie. After diplomatic exchanges with Spain, the troops of the latter were withdrawn from the zone and the international regime was formally restored at Tangier on October 10.[9]

The problem of Tangier was thus settled not only with the restoration of France's own important position in the government of the international zone, and with that of the legal position of its nominal sovereign, the Sultan of Morocco, but also with the international recognition of the legitimacy and continuation of the French protectorate of Morocco and of France's right to conclude foreign agreements on behalf of the Sherifian Sultan. The increased importance attached by the French to their North African territories and protectorates after the practical liquidation of their position in the Levant need not be emphasized. Despite certain difficulties along the way, the British attitude in the matter had some effect in reducing the French animosity aroused by the crisis in the Levant. Probably it was designed to do so by Britain's new Labour government.

Despite the emergence of an irritating if temporary new source of friction in the circumstances by which British and Chinese rather than French forces received the Japanese surrender in Indochina, the restoration during July and August of a certain entente between Great Britain and France in regard to the Levant and Tangier reflected the importance attached by both to the removal of barriers which stood in the way of understanding on subjects of greater intrinsic importance. But neither the speeches of de Gaulle and Bidault in the Consultative

Assembly debate in mid-June on the Levant nor any subsequent statement by the French government indicated the form which the idea of a Franco-British entente assumed at that time in the minds of French policymakers. Though de Gaulle visited Washington after the Potsdam conference he made no attempt to establish a parallel contact with Great Britain. Some in Britain interpreted this as indicating his preoccupation with courting the Soviet Union and the United States at the expense of Britain.[10] In fact, French policy had been somewhat reserved toward Britain for many months in the belief that the British would be forced to support French claims and policies in order to avoid isolation; it is therefore not surprising that de Gaulle continued to follow the same line after the violent disruption of Franco-British relations during the Syrian crisis. Nevertheless, shortly before the first session of the Council of Foreign Ministers, the French government made one attempt to strengthen its ties with the British by sending Léon Blum, the Socialist leader, on an "unofficial" visit to London.

It is uncertain whether this represented an initiative on the part of the French Socialist Party in which the government concurred, or whether Blum was chosen by the government as best qualified to deal with the new British Labour government. In any case, Blum's arrival in London on September 5 was described by Le Monde as having "a particular importance . . . at the moment when the ground seems to have been minutely prepared for broad Franco-British conversations with a view to the conclusion of an alliance between the two countries."[11]

The Blum mission, however, had no such significance. He presented to the British leaders France's views on Germany in particular, and on other problems which the Council of Foreign Ministers would consider, but no agreements were reached. Nor was there any direct French initiative toward a full alliance, and de Gaulle, in an interview to the London *Times* on September 10, reiterated at length the views on that subject which he had expressed many times before.[12] According to de Gaulle, the alliance between France and Britain against the German menace in the recent war as in the previous one had been automatic and inevitable and would be so again if the same danger recurred. It was useless to commit such a self-evident relationship to paper as an "alliance." A true Franco-British alliance must involve, instead, the laying down in advance of a common basis of policy. "This has been lacking to date," he said, "and this lack would have made the signature of a treaty a meaningless and unwholesome gesture because it would have been belied by every diplomatic vicissitude."

That de Gaulle considered a treaty with Great Britain which was not based on specific policy agreements to be meaningless and unwholesome after having signed precisely such a treaty with the Soviet Union suggests that he continued to feel that a French alliance was as important to Britain as a Soviet alliance had been to France, and that France could therefore obtain better terms for her signature in London than she had in Moscow. It may suggest also that de Gaulle believed real policy cooperation was possible and obtainable between the two nations, which were, he said, Western European, imperial, and democratic, whereas such cooperation was hardly possible with the Soviet Union. He made very clear once again that agreement on Syria and, above all, on Germany was a prerequisite to improved relations between France and Britain, and spoke very severely of the British attitude on the German problem: "That Britain should have consented to a settlement of the German problem without France is not only galling for France, General de Gaulle said, but an absurdity with regard to Europe. For Britain to declare that she desired a treaty with France and at the same time to leave France out of these discussions was a contradiction in terms."

After outlining France's case in regard to the Rhineland and the Ruhr, de Gaulle returned to the problem of Franco-British relations. "The British people, he said, have never been as near to the heart of the French people as they have been since the battle of Britain. But unless a settlement is found which puts an end to the difficulties which have tended frequently to arise between Britain and France on questions which Frenchmen knew to be vital to France, Britain will not be able to win or to hold this national feeling, and any treaties or alliances will be castles built on the sand." It was clear, therefore, that if the Syrian problem had lost much of its acuteness by early September, the question of Germany had become increasingly critical both in itself and as a prerequisite, as far as the French government was concerned, to any real understanding with Great Britain. Such an understanding remained as elusive as ever.

A New Policy: "The Western Bloc"

In the late summer of 1945 the French government found that, although it was slowly recovering its formal position as a Great Power, it continued to be baffled in its efforts to achieve the full substance of that status. The alliance with the Soviet Union had not brought Russian support for French claims or major policy goals, the United States showed no readiness to accept either, and the type of basic understanding with Great Britain which de Gaulle would accept was unobtainable.

In these circumstances, de Gaulle began to elaborate a policy to which he had earlier alluded: the building around France of some kind of relationship among the nations of Western Europe which would strengthen French claims to participate as an equal in world councils and, particularly, in negotiations on the European settlement. The French had earlier taken tentative steps to "magnify" their weakened voice by attempting to some extent, in the amendments they proposed to the Dumbarton Oaks draft of the United Nations Charter, to speak for and lead the smaller powers against the hegemony of the Big Three. This attempt was given up almost at once, but in the late summer and fall of 1945 a parallel effort was undertaken on a more realistic basis. This effort produced little result during de Gaulle's remaining months in office, but it had a most significant impact on future French foreign policy.

In March, 1944, de Gaulle had said that "Europe" was not really present in Allied councils and that if it was to hold its place in the postwar world the countries of Western Europe would have to establish, without infringement on their sovereignty, some kind of grouping which would also have overseas extensions in the Mediterranean and in Africa. Little was heard of this idea later in the year, though Bidault alluded to it in his November 11 interview. Indeed, during the foreign policy debate in the Consultative Assembly at the end of November, Bidault was at pains to reassure his listeners—notably the Communists—that France did not contemplate any exclusive Western ties, but wanted alliances in both the West and the East. In Moscow a few days later, de Gaulle turned aside Stalin's pointed inquiries about the "Western bloc" by saying that France of course desired close ties with her neighbors but that these would not constitute a bloc, and that the only bloc she wanted was an Anglo-Franco-Soviet bloc against German aggression.[13]

De Gaulle would hardly blush if it were pointed out that this disclaimer—which served the purposes of his visit to Moscow— is contradicted by other passages in his memoirs which specifically assert that his purpose was indeed to build just such a Western European bloc. Speaking of the end of the war in Europe, "the hour of settlement," he wrote:

> This moment of truth exposed to the light the state of weakness in which France was still plunged in relation to the aims it pursued and the interested calculations of others. The latter, naturally, will make use of the situation to try to constrain us in regard to disputed matters, or else to relegate us to a secondary place in the concert that will build the peace. But I want to try to prevent them from doing it. Moreover, judging that the collapse of Germany, the disintegration of Europe [and] the Russo-American antagonism offer to France, saved by a miracle, exceptional chances of action, it seems to me that the new period will perhaps permit me to undertake the execution of the vast plan which I have formed for my country.
>
> To assure it security in Western Europe, by preventing a new Reich from again menacing it. To collaborate with the West and the East, if necessary contracting on one side or the other the necessary alliances, without ever accepting any kind of dependence. To ward off the risks, still unfocused, of dislocation, to have the French Union progressively transform itself into a free association. To lead the states that touch the Rhine, the Alps, the Pyrenees to group themselves from the political, economic, strategic points of view. To make this organization one of the three planetary powers and, if it is one day necessary, the arbiter between the Soviet and Anglo-Saxon camps. Since 1940 what I have been able to accomplish and say has nourished these possibili-

ties. Now that France is standing I am going to try to attain them.[14]

Was this in fact the foreign policy of the French government in 1945? The contemporary record is less explicit but, read in light of the Algiers speech of March, 1944, and the goals and methods of French policy, this 1958 formulation is probably a reasonably just summary of de Gaulle's thinking—if not of his concerted actions—in 1945.

In the interview published by the London *Times* on September 10, on the eve of the first session of the Council of Foreign Ministers, de Gaulle spoke at length of his conditions for an Anglo-French alliance, but also of the geographical, economic, political, and cultural factors which made Western Europe a "natural complex," including Holland, Belgium, Italy, western Germany, and, normally, Iberia, as well as Great Britain and France. These countries, he said, have the means to form an "economic aggregate," and though it would not be self-sufficient "it would have the same sort of completeness that is possessed by the other economic masses of the world in face of which it would not be in a position of inferiority." Later in this interview de Gaulle spoke of the common interest of these Western European countries in the disposition to be made of Germany: "if the Ruhr and the river Rhine are internationalized they become the focus of European cooperation."[15]

The idea of some kind of Western European grouping was not exclusively de Gaulle's in the summer of 1945, though thinking varied as to the form it might take. A remarkable article appeared in the semi-official *Le Monde* of July 31, above the signature of its chief editor, Hubert Beuve-Méry. It partially reflected and was possibly inspired by the views of the M. R. P. entourage of Foreign Minister Bidault, with whom the paper's relations were closest, as well as of the Socialists, to whom close relations with Britain became even more important after the victory of the Labour Party in late July. According to Beuve-Méry, Great Britain had long been in the process of losing her extra-European character, and the Labour victory probably would only increase this trend. Like France in 1919, he wrote, "She is glorious, victorious and . . . diminished." Mastery of the sea and air had been lost, financial supremacy was gone, and the Dominions tended to become more and more independent of the mother country. "In sum, the old British lion retains all its majesty, but in a world in which colossi are coming up it has lost much of its power." Britain must now decide whether to attempt to retain the old patterns or to yield to geography and history and forge new ones. What form would the latter take?

The nations of Western Europe are among the most developed still. They group 200 to 250 million souls. The African continent, long neglected, presents a vast field for their activity. They have analogous conceptions of man and society. The indispensable conditions appear to be present for us to be able to hope for the necessarily slow and difficult construction of a third world organization, comparable in importance to the United States of America and the Soviet Union, within which England in the nature of things would play the leading role.

Such a policy, Beuve-Méry stated, would involve the sacrifice of anachronistic attitudes, such as were recently manifested in the Levant. A more serious objection to the formation of a Western European bloc was the possible reaction of the United States and the Soviet Union. The United States, according to

Beuve-Méry, could only welcome a large economic bloc if it were not closed to American commerce, but the U.S.S.R. seemed fearful of any grouping of which it was not a member.

> The Western union or association is possible and desirable only if it displays toward America and Russia an equal understanding and an equal independence. If England, for example, leaned too strongly on America, it is to be feared that France might balance this by turning too strongly toward Moscow, and vice versa. If England was to become a sort of American bridgehead in Europe, France, though it might be temporarily included in an immense Atlantic community under American direction, would nearly inevitably tend, sooner or later, to become the Western extremity of Eurasia. London and Paris would then be playing a game of dupes, because they would pay the price very often of the agreement or the disagreement of their too powerful protectors, and the peace of the world, need it be said, would not gain thereby.[16]

Similar views were expressed in the same paper on September 7 in an unsigned editorial which urged a Western European entente, not to rival the great power blocs but to serve as a liaison between them in order to prevent a clash of which Britain and France would be the first victims.[17]

It is evident from these very suggestive articles that what were later to be known as "the idea of Europe" and "neutralism" or "third forcism" had come into existence in France at least as early as the summer of 1945 and were closely linked with each other from their inception. They constituted both a repetition and a new definition of the idea of France as the "wedding ring" or "hyphen" of the alliance which had been set forth at the end of 1944. But these ideas were also characterized, as early as 1945, by the diversity or ambiguity of detail which has since marked them. If the editor of Le Monde assumed that France and the United Kingdom should together lead the Western European grouping, it is far less likely that de Gaulle, whose object was similar, had the same concept of the means. In particular, it is doubtful, despite the language of the September 10 interview, that he thought that the British should or could be part of the group. It is more likely than not that de Gaulle, after his talks with Churchill in November, 1944, did not believe that Great Britain could become part of the kind of European bloc he wanted to establish. The long quarrel in France between the advocates of Europe-with-Britain and of Europe-without-Britain, which was so notable a problem in French foreign policy in 1950, and 1954, and 1963, was thus underway in the summer of 1945.

De Gaulle invoked the idea of a Western European grouping repeatedly during a speaking tour of the French zone of Germany in early October. To the Germans, whom he said he addressed as Europeans and "Westerners," he held out the idea of cooperation with France to build "our" Europe and "our" West. Thus, speaking in German at Saarbrucken on October 3, he said that France would assist the people there and that they must work together with her: "If it is thus, it will be much better for the West and for Europe, of which you, like us, are the children." At Mainz he said: "Here, such as we are, we spring from the same race. And here we are today among Europeans and Westerners. So many reasons for us, henceforth, to hold close together." And at Strasbourg, on October 5, he spoke of the Rhine as "the link of Western Europe" which should be free from end to end for trade, ideas and civilization.[18] In these speeches, de Gaulle was trying to place France's separatist policies in Germany in a more presentable framework.[19] But it seems clear that he was not only competing for German support but was also trying to bring Germany, or at least a part of it, into the service of his wider European policy. At the same time de Gaulle may have judged that the German problem would be solved best from France's point of view by offering the Germans, as well as other Western Europeans, the prospect of recovering an important place in world affairs at France's side.

A few days after his German tour de Gaulle visited Belgium. French and Belgian ideas on Germany were discussed. De Gaulle called for cooperation between the two states and, he writes, met a sympathetic response from his Belgian interlocutors.[20] Though he did not detail his thought publicly, *Le Monde* amplified it:

> Those who heard his speeches have noticed that the union of the West recurred in them, like a discreet leitmotiv, simply indicated by the orator. We should guard against seeing in this, as certain people with more or less good faith are tempted to do, a political formula. It is a question for the moment of a tendency which the General has defined many times, recalling the basis of civilization, the common political institutions, the economic interests that unite the Western peoples. Whether one likes it or not, these links exist, they distinguish these peoples from others, and it is appropriate first to take account of them and to fortify them.[21]

In a press conference on October 12, de Gaulle developed the idea of a Western grouping even further. To a journalist who asked whether such an entente would prejudice French relations with Eastern Europe, he answered:

> I do not see why those in the first category would deny their character of Westerners, and I see no inconvenience if the others proclaim their character of Eastern Europeans. All are Europeans. But the rivers which interest them are not the same, the economies are not identical, the frontiers are not always common to all, the same oceans do not wash every shore at the same time. There are natural elements, and there are also acquired ones which should not be misunderstood. Otherwise, how can the world be organized? And we must organize the world.
>
> A Western organization does no wrong to a European organization, quite the contrary; and a European organization can do no wrong to a world organization, quite the contrary.[22]

In this frank presentation of his idea of a Western European grouping, de Gaulle tried to cover himself, as he and his foreign minister had had occasion to do more than once before, from the accusation that he wished to build an exclusive bloc which would be hostile to the Soviet Union or to all of the other Allies. De Gaulle was only the first of the postwar French statesmen who had to try to reconcile attempts on this line to magnify France's role in world affairs with existing French ties to the major powers. But his emphasis on Western Europe in his September 10 interview and in later statements occasioned much discussion in the French press, and many spoke of it as representing a proposal for a "bloc" against the Soviet and American blocs. It is probable that the Russians—whose interest in the subject had been expressed at Algiers in the spring of 1944 and at Moscow in December—had de Gaulle's words in mind when, at the London conference, they insisted once again on excluding France from her newly won position in Allied councils.[23] In any case, though de Gaulle was not able to carry this policy any distance toward implementation, he at once met strong Communist hostility to it. There thus arose the controversy concerning "the Western bloc" which ran through the November political crisis and played its part in finally dissolving the political foundations of de Gaulle's rule.

The London Meeting of the Council of Foreign Ministers

The communiqué of the Potsdam conference provided that the new five-power Council of Foreign Ministers was to meet no later than September 1 to prepare draft peace treaties for Italy, Finland, Rumania, Hungary, and Bulgaria. For France, this meeting was of the first importance, less for the substance of what it was to consider than because it was the first Great Power conference to which she had been admitted since 1940. However, the conflict between the Anglo-Saxon powers and the Soviet Union over the Balkans and other questions grew more rather than less acute after the Potsdam conference, and it was to dominate the London meeting. Although the French maintained a discreet silence during most of the foreign ministers' sessions, it was their mere presence which furnished the pretext on which the conference finally broke down. Therefore, as a by-product of the disagreements of the Big Three, France's formal status as a Great Power was once more called into question.

The French government had hoped to be able to discuss the German question in the course of the conference and tabled a memorandum on this subject on September 14.[24] It recognized, however, even before the meeting opened, that this topic would not receive much consideration. In addition, France wanted several minor rectifications of her Italian frontier, and recovery of that part of the Fezzan area in southern Libya which Pierre Laval had ceded to Italy in 1935.[25] Her only other interest in the Italian colonies was to prevent their achieving independence, since an independent Libya, for example, would constitute a dangerous model for Algeria and the adjacent French protectorates, Tunisia and Morocco. This concern, however, was presented in the form of a gesture of magnanimity toward Italy, which, the French stated, should be given a United Nations trusteeship in Libya.[26] While the French expressed detailed interest in the Italian and German settlements, they appeared to have no firm position on Balkan problems. In his lengthy interview of September 10, General de Gaulle made no reference to these problems—presumably because he was still courting Soviet support.[27]

The French delegation arrived in London on September 9. It was led by Foreign Minister Bidault, Maurice Couve de Murville, the new political director of the Quai d'Orsay, and Hervé Alphand. Because of a delay in the arrival of the American delegation, the conference, to be held at Lancaster House, did not open until September 11. It was agreed at the first session, which was devoted to procedure, that all five of the participating ministers could take part in the preliminary discussion of each treaty, but that only those states which had signed each armistice (together with France on the Italian treaty) would be able to vote on each clause. This was a reasonable if not quite literal application of the Potsdam decision that created the council and was adopted without controversy.[28] The five deputies were to meet each morning to prepare the work for their superiors; the ministers themselves would meet in the afternoon at sessions over which each of them would preside in turn. Though Molotov apparently wanted to discuss the Balkan treaties first, it was decided to begin with the Italian treaty, presumably because the government of that country was recognized by all the participants of the conference.

After a preliminary exchange of views on the Italian problem, a British draft was taken as the basis of discussion. The Italian colonies were the first subject considered in detail. The interest of the British in Cyrenaica and Italian Somaliland, of France in the Fezzan, of Greece in the Dodecanese, and of Ethiopia in Eritrea was already known, and at Potsdam the Soviet delegates had indicated that the U.S.S.R. was also thinking in terms of assuming a trusteeship in one of the Italian colonies. But the four other participants, and particularly the British, appear to have been taken aback when on September 14 the Russians expressed a serious interest both in the Dodecanese and in Libya, including the port of Tripoli. Secretary Byrnes's formal proposal provided that each colony be placed under international control, with a governor responsible to the United Nations and an advisory council whose members would be named by each of the four principal European Allies, Italy, and the local population. The Chinese delegate agreed to this plan at once. After some discussion, British Foreign Secretary Bevin also accepted it for Libya, although not for Eritrea and Somaliland where, he stated, the interests of Ethiopia must be taken into consideration. Bidault, however, was not favorable to Byrnes's plan, nor, of course, was Molotov, who—obviously to improve his bargaining position later—refused to agree to the cession of the Dodecanese to Greece, as desired by the other four powers, until all aspects of the Italian colonial question had been agreed upon.

After two days of discussion, the entire problem was referred to the deputies, who were to report their conclusions two weeks prior to the second session of the council. Thus, the first topic taken up by the conference, and presumably the most simple to resolve, had opened up a new area of disagreement among the participants and was, in effect, removed from the agenda lest it disrupt whatever progress might be possible on other problems. It is not surprising that *Le Monde* found the first week of the conference rather discouraging: "The balance sheet of the work of last week has caused a certain disappointment in diplomatic circles in London: two days to agree on procedure and three days to decide to postpone the problem of the Italian colonial empire for later examination."[29] It was already being said in London, on the basis of the first week's achievement, that this first session of the Council of Foreign Ministers would discuss all questions and settle none.

On September 17 the conference turned to the problem of the Italo-Yugoslav frontier. It was generally expected in the West that the city of Trieste would become a free port, but Yugoslavia asked that the frontier be, in effect, the Austro-Italian border of 1915, which would give her possession of Trieste as well as most of the province of Venezia-Giuilia. In this she was supported by the Soviet Union. After two days of discussion the ministers agreed in principle that the basic frontier should be the ethnic line and that Trieste itself should be placed under an international regime which would guarantee that the port itself and the transit facilities to it would be available on equal terms to Yugoslavia, Italy, and the states of central Europe. But the drawing of the frontier and the elaboration of the international statute were deferred pending further study.

During the first ten days of the conference, other parts of the Italian settlement were also considered. The Soviet Union, Yugoslavia, Greece, and Ethiopia all demanded substantial sums from Italy in reparations. But the United States, which was spending much money in Italy through the United Nations Relief and Rehabilitation Agency, was naturally reluctant to assume, in effect, the burden of Italian reparations. On this issue, therefore, the Ministers were no more able to reach any real agreement than on the problems of the Italian colonies or of Trieste. French sources claimed that the rectification of the Alpine frontier was agreed to in all but detail by the other ministers, but beyond this the French delegation seems to have played no significant role in the discussion of these questions.

The French, however, were not blind to the fact that they were witnessing, if not participating in, a struggle for influence in the Mediterranean between the Soviet Union, which was expanding where it could, and the British, who were attempting to limit this expansion. In this struggle the interests and wishes of other states were no more than secondary. As Le Monde noted: "The negotiation on Italy appears more and more like a bargaining between two or three great powers. The countries directly interested (Greece, Albania, Yugoslavia, Austria) play no more than an accessory role. It is a question of knowing in what measure, by what concessions the U.S.S.R. will take a place in the Mediterranean which its partners want to be as small as possible." France, said Le Monde, was not a participant in this contest, nor was she to be considered, of course, a pawn in it.[30]

What, in fact, was France's role in this situation? Though rivalry between the Anglo-Saxon powers and the Soviet Union had been foreseen and in a sense welcomed by French leaders as early as the end of 1944, its sharp emergence in the first days of the peacemaking seems to have taken the French delegation somewhat by surprise. The occasion might have seemed appropriate to them to attempt to play that mediatory role which had been proclaimed long since as France's—though, indeed, the weakness of France was such as to give any proposals of her delegates very little weight in the calculations of the Big Three. But there is no evidence that the French attempted, as they were to do increasingly during 1946, to present compromise solutions to the conference. Apart from their own interests in the Italian settlement—the Alpine frontier, the Fezzan, the status of Libya—the French seem to have been nearly as silent during the Italian discussions as their Chinese colleagues.

On September 20 the council turned to the Balkan peace treaties. The substance of the formal issues was less complex, but the refusal of the Western Allies to recognize the Communist-dominated governments of the Balkan states raised a major obstacle to the speedy conclusion of peace. After a short discussion it became clear that it would be impossible to confine the conference to the technical details of the treaties and that the political issue of the Balkan governments could not be avoided. On September 21, therefore, the American and British delegates raised the question of the request made by King Michael of Rumania for Allied assistance in establishing a more representative government than the Groza regime, which the Russians supported. After a sharp discussion of this subject, Molotov accused the Western powers of mounting an offensive against him. The same issue was raised when, after a deadlock was reached on Rumania, the Bulgarian treaty was taken up. The Russians supported Bulgaria's claims to a territorial adjustment at the expense of Greece and took the occasion to counter the Western charges of lack of democracy in Hungary, Rumania, and Bulgaria by strongly attacking the Greek government.

Beneath this skirmishing lay the basic issue: the determination of the Soviet Union to maintain the control of the Balkans which it had established by military force, and the reluctance of the United States and Great Britain to recognize Soviet control. After several days of fruitless discussion around this single point, which appeared beneath all surface issues, Molotov suddenly raised the procedural issue which finally put an end to the conference. On September 22 he informed Bevin and Byrnes that a mistaken interpretation of the Potsdam agreement had been made at the beginning of the conference and that the Soviet Union could not continue to discuss the Balkan treaties with France and China, which had not signed the armistices with the states in question.[31] It had been agreed at the first session of the council that all five members of the council would be permitted to take part in the preliminary discussion of each treaty, though only those that had signed each armistice would be able to vote on the treaty for the given state. The sudden Russian attempt to exclude France and China was clearly in large part a device either to terminate a conference which was not proceeding well for them or to apply pressure on the United States and Great Britain to force them to yield on more substantive points—particularly the Balkans—in order to keep France and China in the conference.

The Chinese were willing to be excluded from discussions of subjects which were only remotely of interest to them. But Bidault received the Russian demand with extreme ill temper and, with the support of his government, reasserted France's right to participate in the discussion of all European questions. He argued that the decisions made by the five ministers on September 11, and not the Potsdam agreement, formed the basis of the conference procedures and that these could be altered only by unanimous agreement, in which France would not participate.[32] Bidault was dissuaded from walking out of the conference with a strong attack on the Soviet attitude only when Byrnes explained that efforts were being made at Moscow to secure a reversal of Molotov's position.[33] Two sessions of the conference were therefore held on September 24, at which secondary subjects were discussed by the full council, including the Austrian food supply, European waterways, and the repatriation of Soviet nationals. But even these topics raised divergences among the powers. By the end of these sessions, the *Daily Herald*, organ of the British Labour Party, asserted that the Russians were not really seeking agreement at all, but only advantages for their Eastern bloc. The United Press went so far as to speak dramatically of World War III already hovering over the conference room.[34]

In an attempt to avert a breakdown of the conference, Byrnes, on September 22, had asked Truman to intervene directly with Stalin in order to obtain a change in Molotov's position. Truman accordingly cabled Stalin to the effect that, although France and China perhaps did not have a clear right to participate in the discussion of the Balkan and Finnish treaties, they had been invited to do so on the first day of the conference and their exclusion two weeks later would not be well received in the world. But Stalin replied two days later and firmly supported Molotov's attitude.[35] With this failure, which was reflected in the continuing deadlock in London, it was generally expected that the conference would end shortly. But the ministers decided to work to the end of their agenda, while apparently agreeing tacitly to avoid any substantial formal consideration of basic problems. A day was thus passed in a discussion of the repatriation of Soviet nationals, the work of the Reparations

Commission, and the French memorandum on the restitution of goods stolen by the former enemies. Suddenly, however, the Russians reopened the Balkan question by proposing that (1) the Western powers renounce all active intervention in Balkan affairs; (2) Rumania, Bulgaria, and Hungary, whose governments the U.S.S.R. considered democratic, be recognized by the United States and Great Britain; (3) Balkan frontiers be settled by the parties themselves, without the participation of the five major powers; and (4) an Allied commission be named to assist the Supreme Commander in Japan to elaborate a common policy for that country and the Pacific. These proposals, which meant the exclusion of the West from the Balkans and the intrusion of the Soviet Union into the Japanese occupation, obviously contained nothing to commend them to the United States or Britain and received no serious consideration.

The council, however, continued to take up one after another all the points of its agenda, without approaching agreement on any, and the French were finally able to participate in a discussion of the German question on September 26 and 28. Bidault was able, for the first time, to present officially to the other Allies the French thesis on the German settlement—the permanent occupation of the Rhineland and the establishment of an international regime in the Ruhr—and to repeat to his colleagues that France would not concur in the establishment of a central administration in Germany until she had received satisfaction on these proposals. But the matter was put off for further study, and the French delegates were under no illusion that any of the Big Three was very much inclined to accept these policies.[36]

These general and inconclusive conversations on Germany were of secondary importance when compared to the efforts being made privately between the British, American, and Soviet delegations to arrive at some formula to break the procedural impasse on the question of the Balkan treaties. The willingness imputed to the American government to recognize the existing Hungarian government if it undertook to hold free elections and the announcement from Moscow that elections would be held in Hungary on November 6 were thought to indicate that some compromise on the Balkans might be possible. In addition, Byrnes, on September 28, presented a procedural plan aimed at satisfying the Russian objections: several sub-commissions of the council would be created, each of which would deal with a particular treaty; France would participate in the sub-commissions on the main Italian treaty, the Italo-Yugoslav treaty, and those concerned with the Italian colonies and with Austria; neither France nor China would be members of the sub-commissions dealing with the Balkan treaties; and the council itself would presumably continue to be constituted in the manner agreed to at the beginning of the London session.[37]

This plan, however, was not accepted by the Russians, and the council, at its meetings on September 29, turned to consideration of the conference communiqué and the protocols which would form the basis for the continuing work of the deputies. Discussion of these topics continued for two days, but it soon became apparent that the questions they raised were as difficult of solution as the substantive issues which had already been taken up and laid aside. Molotov's refusal to admit France and China to any role at all in the Balkan peacemaking, or even to agree to any mention of the part which they had actually played in the discussions, revealed his desire to return to the three-power system of Yalta. Members of the delegations of the Big Three, as well as the council itself, met constantly in search of some formula for the communiqué and protocols, but without success. Despite all proposed compromises and concessions to the Soviet position, it appeared to many that the Russians, who constantly brought forth new demands, were deliberately trying to put an end to the conference and with it to the five-power machinery which they had agreed to on September 11. The council met twice on October 2, principally because none of the participants wished to be the first to admit failure by moving adjournment. But at the end of the second meeting, which lasted five hours, the Chinese delegate took the initiative to declare the session ended. The terse communiqué stated only that the council had decided to terminate its present session.

In a communiqué published after the breakup of the conference, the American delegation defended the right of France and China to participate in the making of the peace, but indicated also that the United States was willing to accept a preliminary treaty drawn up by a few powers provided that this was then submitted to a conference of all interested states. Molotov, for his part, emphasized the need to abide by the Potsdam decisions and denied that any agreement had been made on September 11 by which France and China were to participate in the drafting of the Balkan treaties.[38] In his own press conference, Bidault attempted to point out that the meeting had not been entirely unfruitful and that considerable agreement had been reached on specific points in the Italian, Austrian, and Balkan treaties. But he clearly indicated his strong objection to the course of the Soviet delegation and the determination of France not to be excluded in any manner from the work of the peacemaking:

> . . . certain people have wanted to return to the outdated
> conception of a directory of three powers. It was
> normal in wartime that the three powers which had

assumed the main burdens and had the principal responsibilities should periodically hold three-power conferences and adopt important decisions there. This
procedure no longer has any justification. France definitely intends to be present in the deliberations whence
these decisions are now to come. She does not ask that
anyone be excluded but she insists on being present.[39]

Bidault naturally did not open a public discussion of why the
Soviet Union had so abruptly decided to treat its ally, France,
in this manner. Probably, the French did not know whether it
was de Gaulle's recent allusions to a "Western bloc" that had
led the Soviet government to take this step or whether it was
simply another manifestation of the basic Russian willingness to
sacrifice French friendship and interests if Soviet purposes could
better be served by doing so.[40] He added, however, in words
similar to those of the French note of August 7, that France
had not been a participant in the Potsdam conference, and although she had accepted the invitation made to her there to
take part in the drafting of the Italian treaty, she considered
herself entitled to participate, not because of this invitation,
but because she had been a belligerent against Italy. For the
same reason, and because of her long interest in Rumanian affairs, she was equally entitled to participate in the preparation
of the treaty with Rumania, the conclusion of which without
France was, he said, inconceivable.

Despite these claims, and the hope that the presence of France
at the London conference marked the resumption of her Great
Power status, her delegates played no more than a secondary
role even when substantive matters were being considered.
They made little attempt, for example, to mediate the disputes
of the three principal powers or to propound compromise

proposals. The United States and Great Britain, despite their support of French and Chinese participation in the discussion of the Balkan treaties, did not hesitate to attempt to meet the Russian objections to this by suggesting proposals which would have excluded those two states from much of the effective work of the conference. The French thus found themselves excluded from many private three-power meetings during the London conference itself, and the latter ended in circumstances which indicated that the three powers might well come to some agreement which would surmount the ostensible cause of the breakdown of the conference by once again excluding France from the substantive proceedings of much of the peacemaking. The French left London with clear notice that the Big Three, for all their divisions, might yet be able to agree to maintain their wartime directorate of affairs—at France's expense.

FRENCH DIPLOMACY AFTER WORLD WAR II

proposals. The United States and Great Britain, despite their

CHAPTER IX

CHALLENGE AND REPRIEVE AT HOME: THE POLITICAL CRISIS OF NOVEMBER, 1945

It is clear from the first paragraph of de Gaulle's memoirs that
he believes a vigorous foreign policy is essential to the maintenance of French national unity. It is equally clear that he
believes a strong government in France is essential to the country's success and, indeed, to its survival as an independent nation. While the greater part of de Gaulle's attention after the
liberation of France was no doubt given to foreign affairs, he
did not neglect those steps which were required, first, to establish his own power in the country, and second, to prepare the
permanent basis for the kind of regime which he believed
France needed. His first purpose had been accomplished by
the end of 1944. The second purpose, which he failed to accomplish, gave rise to a series of skirmishes and battles, sometimes muted and sometimes out in the open, between the
General, who was almost without any organized political support, and most of the political parties. It is often said that this
was a battle between de Gaulle and the Communists, apparently the two main power centers of French political life after
the liberation. On the surface there is some plausibility to this

idea, but it should not be overlooked that the ultimate winner—
the holder of political power in France between 1947 and 1958
—was the group of non-Communist parties. That they should
have bested both de Gaulle and the Communists despite their
own weaknesses and divisions is something of a minor-key
political epic. The very improbability of such an outcome, in
the eyes of de Gaulle and many others in 1945, was a factor
in the political history of that year.

The effort of the Communists to drive the Socialist Party into
fusion or at least an exclusive alliance with them continued
through the spring and summer of 1945. In June the Communists went so far as to publish in *Humanité* a draft charter of
unity for the two parties. The Socialists, however, were increasingly unwilling to abdicate their identity in this manner,
and their refusal was reflected in the formation, during June,
of a new non-Communist resistance organization, the *Union
Démocratique et Socialiste de la Résistance* (U. D. S. R.), which
quickly allied itself with the Socialist Party. At the same time,
the Communist desire to maintain the existing government until
their alliance with the Socialists could be established was put
to a severe test when it became clear that de Gaulle had definite
ideas of his own on the form which the imminent electoral
consultation should take. On June 3 he indicated that a referendum should be held in order that the country might decide
whether it wanted to restore the Third Republic or establish
a new constitutional regime. By promptly condemning the very
principle of a referendum and demanding the election of a
sovereign constituent assembly to which the government would
be responsible, the Communists attempted to assume leadership
of the large body of French opinion for whom plebiscites and
a strong executive power, which de Gaulle favored, recalled
the anti-republican Bonapartism of Napoleon III and other

"men on horseback." So strong was this sentiment, indeed, that the Socialists and even the M. R. P. more or less shared the Communist view on the question of the referendum.[1]

After de Gaulle had informed his ministers that he would accept the resignations of those who disagreed with him, and after the parties had decided that no crisis would be opened on this issue, the cabinet on July 9 unanimously accepted a law which provided that an assembly would be elected in October; the voters would decide on the first question of a referendum, to be held at the same time, whether the assembly was to be a Chamber of Deputies or would have constituent power, that is, whether or not the Constitution of 1875 would remain in force; and on the second question of the referendum they would decide whether the assembly, if constituent, would be unfettered and wholly sovereign or would be (1) limited in duration, (2) able to elect but not overthrow the president of the government, and (3) obliged to submit the new constitution itself to ratification in a later referendum.[2] De Gaulle's success in imposing this project on the parties, already on record as opposing its main features, is a striking proof of his ascendancy —based on his personal prestige and his threat of resignation— and the reluctance of all the parties, and particularly of the Communists, to maintain their position at the risk of disrupting the government.

The parties were not wrong in believing that de Gaulle wanted this temporary arrangement, involving a separation of powers and an independent executive which were unknown to the practice of the Third Republic, to serve as the basis for the constitution of the future Fourth Republic; that is, he wanted popular approval of his plan to serve as a guide and mandate to the authors of the new constitution.[3] From his observations of pre-war political conditions de Gaulle was convinced that chronic government instability was incompatible with the needs of the French state; and from the disaster of 1940—during which, as he later noted, ". . . the President of the Republic abstained from raising his voice, even in the Council of Ministers, to express the superior interest of the country"—he carried the permanent image of a regime so infirm as to be totally divorced from the interests and honor of France.[4] Concerned as de Gaulle was with France's place in the world, his constitutional conceptions were rooted in his belief that the supreme interests of the state must be entrusted to an executive who would guard them firmly above the passions of parties and politics, as he himself had done during the war.

But in addition to this long-term and basic concept, de Gaulle had other preoccupations in the summer of 1945. He wished that within the proposed provisional framework, "the country may as soon as possible give itself solid new institutions, without being thrown arbitrarily during the transition into the risk of adventure."[5] And at Brest on July 21, in pleading for an equilibrium between the executive and the assembly, he added that, "I should judge it deplorable that it [the assembly] might be sovereign without any brake or limitation."[6] In this fear of an assembly unchecked by any other authority and of the "adventures" to which it might lead, de Gaulle was surely thinking not only of the dangers incident to such a regime in times of international crisis but also of the dangers embodied in the French prototype of such a system, the all-powerful revolutionary Convention of 1792, dominated and driven to ever greater excess by a small and determined group. There is no doubt that de Gaulle saw in the Communists such a group— and indeed their own tactics and policy on the constitutional issue indicated that they saw themselves in such a role. De Gaulle thus moved to counter the Communist purpose without, however, breaking with them at a time when such a rupture would have entailed most grave internal and international repercussions. The Communists could not have failed to understand the purpose of his attitude, but for the reasons noted above they were willing for the time being to oppose de Gaulle's policy only within the existing governmental framework.

Although they had agreed to this project in the cabinet, the Communists and others felt free to oppose it when it was submitted for the opinion of the Consultative Assembly, and, as a result of the assembly's adverse judgment, it was modified to permit the overthrow of the cabinet by the future Constituent Assembly. The double referendum finally adopted, therefore, called upon the voters to decide if the assembly they were electing on the same day was to have constituent powers and, if so, if it was to be bound by the attached draft of law. If, as was expected, the voters answered the first question in the affirmative, the Constitution of 1875 would be formally dead and the newly elected assembly would thereby be charged to draft a new constitution. If, in addition, they also approved the second proposition, the Constituent Assembly would be limited in duration to seven months, with the right to elect the president—who would organize his own cabinet and submit it to the assembly's approval—and to overthrow him by vote of an absolute majority taken forty-eight hours after the filing of such a motion. In this form the Socialists and the M. R. P., as well as de Gaulle, supported an affirmative answer to the second question as well as to the first. The Communists continued to demand an unlimited, fully sovereign assembly and therefore a negative response to the second question.

The October election campaign added little new to the political situation as it had developed during the summer. Since de Gaulle had played a predominant role in defining the form and issues of the election, the Communist opposition to an affirmative answer to the second question of the referendum made the latter in effect a personal plebiscite. Nevertheless, de Gaulle refrained from endorsing or supporting the candidates of any party or parties and intervened only once in the campaign, to urge approval of both questions. His wishes were more than gratified by the results of the election of October 21. Ninety-six percent of those voting approved giving the assembly which they elected the same day constituent powers, thereby formally putting an end to the Third Republic. This was not unexpected, since all political groups except the Radical-Socialists had favored such a response. But 66 percent also voted in favor of the second question, providing for the "corseting" of the assembly, a result that the Communists had strongly opposed and which therefore represented a major political victory for de Gaulle and, to some extent, for the Socialists and the M. R. P. The Communists, however, emerged as the largest single party, with 151 seats in the new assembly. The M. R. P., to general surprise, won 150 seats, indicating for the first time that it was a major political element. The Socialists, who had expected to be first, actually won only 139 seats, while their resistance ally, the U. D. S. R., won 31. The Radical-Socialists received only 29 seats, the right-wing parties between them won 64, and Algerian Moslems held 7.[7]

It was generally assumed that de Gaulle would be chosen to head the first elected government of the Fourth Republic and his victory on the referendum question strongly supported this supposition.[8] But since, despite his electoral victory, he made no initiative on behalf of his own candidacy or for the formation of a government, the parties took upon themselves to work out a program on which some as yet uncertain number of them would be able to cooperate within the next government. The

Communists and Socialists together commanded an absolute majority of the new assembly, and since the Communists had long made clear that they would be willing to govern alone with the Socialists, it was evident that the nature of the majority and of the government would depend on the Socialists. Taking the initiative in favor of a Communist-Socialist government "in the image of the nation and . . . of the Assembly," the Communists at once instigated a meeting of the *Délégation des Gauches*. The latter was a coordinating device of the pre-war left, created during and reminiscent of the Dreyfus era and including, in addition to the Communist and Socialist parties, such "classically" left and anti-clerical groups as the *Confédération Générale du Travail*, now under Communist control, the Radical-Socialist party, socially rather conservative but opposed to de Gaulle, and the League of the Rights of Man. Such a meeting as the Communists proposed had no purpose other than to entwine the Socialists in a combination which would have a historical and sentimental appeal to their anti-clerical rank and file, and thereby isolate them from the M. R. P.—and perhaps, ultimately, from de Gaulle too.

The Socialists, although they wanted to share governmental responsibility with the M. R. P. as well as with the Communists, agreed to participate. Foreign policy, however, soon proved to be a principal subject of discord between the Socialists, who favored some type of regional understanding in Western Europe and particularly with socialist Britain, and the Communists, whose central committee declared the party's policy to be "the pursuit of a foreign policy tending to assure peace through collective security, loyal cooperation with the three great Allies, and the application of the clauses of the Franco-Soviet alliance; *refusal to participate in a Western bloc*, which would be a return to the spirit of Munich that must be made totally to disappear. . . ."[9] [Italics added.] After several meetings, the members of the *Délégation* approved a long document embodying their common program, which dealt in detail with the liquidation of the Vichy regime; the increase of democratic liberties of thought, press, and education; and the nationalization of large banks, insurance and public utility companies, and other industries. On foreign policy, apart from assertions of support for the United Nations and collective security, and detailed proposals for the democratization of Germany, they agreed on a broad statement, largely acceptable to any group, which condemned both participation in any bloc and the formation of a new bloc against—or between—others, while at the same time citing the approbation of the United Nations Charter for regional ententes: a careful verbal compromise between the Socialist and Communist attitudes on this subject.[10]

The Communists opposed presenting this program to the M. R. P. but finally agreed that the Socialists could do so on their own behalf. The M. R. P., however, despite its cavalier treatment by the Communists and Socialists, was not passively accepting the Communist attempt to exclude it from power. Georges Bidault asserted that neither the clerical question nor social and economic problems divided the M. R. P. from the two parties to its left. As for foreign policy, he declared, speaking as M. R. P. leader rather than as foreign minister, that the dispute over the so-called "Western bloc" was tilting at windmills. There is, he said, no talk of an American bloc when the United States discusses the Western hemisphere, nor are the Russian pacts with Poland and Rumania referred to as an Eastern bloc, and France has as much right as these states to make agreements with her neighbors, particularly since the United Nations Charter itself sanctioned such understandings.[11] But despite the fact that there was little difference between the programs of the M. R. P. and of the two left parties, the Communists, who were obviously concerned less with the details of specific issues than with their attempt to eliminate the M. R. P. from office, continued to refuse to enter into direct contact with them. The Socialists finally succeeded in bringing about a three-party meeting, but far from producing a common program, which could be presented to de Gaulle as a *fait accompli* before his election, it ended in deadlock.

By this time the assembly had validated the credentials of a sufficient number of deputies to permit it to elect its permanent officers and, on November 7, Félix Gouin, the Socialist leader who had been president of the Consultative Assembly, was chosen to preside over its successor. The next order of business was the election of the president of the government, but when the assembly attempted to fix its agenda a serious debate arose as to the date for this election. For the Socialists, Daniel Mayer stated openly that since the major parties had not yet agreed on a program, the election should be delayed until they had done so. The M. R. P., though hesitant, finally voted to defer the election until November 13. But the Communists, who had already repudiated all responsibility for the failure to arrive at a program, abstained on this vote, allowing the two parties which had supported the second question of the referendum to violate its letter and spirit and to bear the onus of delay. The Communists, however, obviously had no objection to a postponement which tended by its nature to reduce the importance of the presidency and thus lessened the chance that de Gaulle would finally accept it on the terms presented to him by the party leaders.

The Communists continued to raise obstacles to a three-party program. But in the face of Socialist reluctance to embark on the adventure of a two-party government, which would probably have meant the elimination of de Gaulle as well as of the

M. R. P., they decided to delay forcing the issue of the composition of the government and consented, in their own words, to "a manifestation of national unity around a candidacy which arises naturally from the results of the referendum."[12] On November 13, therefore, the assembly unanimously elected General de Gaulle as president of the Provisional Government. Because the Communists chose to wait, de Gaulle, who had remained on the periphery of the political scene during the weeks since the election, was able once more to return to its center as he began official consultations on the formation of his government.[13] After two days of discussions with party leaders, however, de Gaulle's office revealed that, though no obstacle of principle or program stood in the way of the formation of a government, "certain difficulties have appeared concerning the assignment of ministerial departments."[14] The publication of several letters exchanged between de Gaulle and Maurice Thorez soon explained the nature of the difficulty: the Communists had asked that one of what they claimed to be the "key" ministries —war, foreign affairs, and interior—be given to them as a condition for their participation in the government, and de Gaulle had refused their request.

Thorez had then written to him in these terms:

> This morning, during the interview which you gave me, you made known to me that you did not find it possible to give a Communist one of the three stated ministries and invoked arguments which challenged the national character of our party and of its policy.
>
> We might have been able, once again, to accept a new sacrifice for the cause of national unity by giving up one of the posts legitimately claimed by our party.
>
> But we cannot accept the reasons you have cited, which we judge to be wounding to our honor as

Frenchmen. That would insult the memory of 75,000 Communists who died for France and liberty.

In these conditions the political bureau has charged me to inform you that it holds to its proposals as regards the form of Communist participation in the government.

To this de Gaulle had answered:

I cannot admit in any way that the conversation . . . which we had this morning on the subject of the foreign policy of France and of the attitude of the Communist Party in this respect might in any manner insult the memory of any Frenchman who died for France. On the other hand, it is necessary that the country have a government as soon as possible. Having received the unanimous mandate of the Assembly to form it, I asked of you a large representation, naturally reserving to myself the attribution of the ministerial departments.

Thorez finally replied to de Gaulle's letter as follows:

Conscious of its responsibilities before the people of France, the Communist Party can only hold to its proposals as regards the form of its participation in the government, that is, a division—equitable in number and importance—of the various ministerial departments and the assignment to a representative of our party of one of these three great ministries: interior, foreign affairs, war.[15]

The motivations both of the Communists and of de Gaulle were complex. It is not surprising that the Communists would attempt to secure posts which were as important as possible in return for their support. Their claim that foreign affairs, war, and interior were the "key" or major ministries in comparison to all others had no historical foundation, but the Communists hoped at least to obtain control of the army in a tripartite government, even if they considered it most unlikely that they would be permitted to control the police or to represent France on the international scene. On the other hand, if de Gaulle refused to entrust them even with the armed forces, to which he attached so much importance, the Communists would be able to claim that a three-party government under him was impossible. At worst, they would force their will on de Gaulle or his successor, weaken the presidency, and emerge from the crisis with a ministry which would be very valuable to them. At best, if de Gaulle were driven from office, they calculated that the M. R. P. might well follow him into opposition, forcing the Socialists finally to accept a governmental alliance with the Communists.

On his side, de Gaulle, to judge by the terms of his letter, was making use of the occasion to demonstrate his independence of the parties. Having been obliged to stand to one side as they vainly sought to establish a common program to force upon him, it is not surprising that as an advocate of a strong and independent executive power he would attempt to construct his own cabinet. With minimal interest in domestic affairs, and no substantial objection to the policies which were presented to him by the parties, he had no occasion here for an act of independence. Even on foreign policy there was little in the program of the *Délégation des Gauches* to which he could take serious exception. But after having more or less dominated his past cabinets, de Gaulle obviously did not want to accept the personnel forced upon him by the parties. He was also well

aware of the record and aims of the French Communists and
of their relations to the U.S.S.R., and even by November, 1945,
the example of the Eastern European states, where the Communists had taken possession of the police and other key ministries, was evident.

In addition to these preoccupations, de Gaulle himself advanced another reason for excluding the Communists from the
ministries they sought. In a broadcast to the nation on November 17 he said:

> . . . naturally I intended to distribute the ministerial
> departments myself . . . on the one hand, according to
> the talents of each one, on the other, according to the
> policy which men who come from parties necessarily
> represent within and without. If the head of the gov-
> ernment did not act thus, what would his function be?
>
> Now, I found myself faced by the demand of the
> heads of one of the three principal parties, which pre-
> sented a categorical condition for the participation of
> its members in office. This party asked that I give one
> of its members one of the following three ministries:
> foreign affairs, war, interior. I could not accept this
> condition.
>
> Much as I was disposed to associate largely with the
> economic and social work of the government the men
> of the party in question, and to assign them ministries
> appropriately, I did not think it possible to give them
> any of the three levers which command foreign policy,
> that is: diplomacy, which expresses it; the army, which
> supports it; the police, which cover it.
>
> In acting otherwise, in today's international circum-
> stances, I should have risked jeopardizing, if only in

appearance—and in our tense world appearances count for much—the French policy of equilibrium between two very great political powers, which I think absolutely necessary for the interest of the country and even for that of peace. It happened also that this question which was put to me coincided, by chance, but nevertheless coincided, with a difficult moment between these two very great powers, particularly grave for the future of peace. . . .

In my negative attitude toward what was asked of me, there was not, you see, insult for anyone, but simply a superior interest of the State. I ask all French men and women to weigh that. As for me, I should hold myself unworthy to be head of the government of France if I failed to recognize, for the convenience of a combination, this principle of supreme national interest.

In the face of this situation, de Gaulle said, he had chosen to resign. If the assembly elected another president he would retire without bitterness; if it re-elected him he would continue to work for the best interests and the honor of France.[16]

The domestic reasons for refusing the Communists the ministries they sought and the constitutional thinking which underlay the classic exposition in de Gaulle's broadcast speech of his concept of the presidential role were probably decisive for him in themselves, but the references to foreign policy in his address were not entirely a rationalization. Though he had not hitherto so firmly endorsed the idea of French neutrality between the two blocs, this policy had been expounded by his foreign minister for a year and was perfectly consistent with his own outlook on foreign policy. Further, the Russian attitude at the Council of Foreign Ministers had not been such as to improve de Gaulle's relations with either the Soviet Union or the French Communist Party, and he may have thought it prudent to secure continued Anglo-American support for French participation in the council's work by a bold demonstration of his independence of Communist and Soviet influence—without, however, falling into dependence on the Western powers or burning bridges to either the U.S.S.R. or the French Communist Party.

The day after de Gaulle submitted his resignation to Assembly President Gouin, fifteen members of the three principal parties met and all reaffirmed their previous positions: the Socialists said they would support no candidate for president not supported by all three major parties; the Communists refused the Socialist proposal to send a new delegation to de Gaulle; and the M. R. P. declined to accept any president other than de Gaulle. No agreement had been reached when the assembly met on November 19. The U. D. S. R., however, moved that the assembly request de Gaulle to attempt again to form a tripartite government. The Socialists indicated that they would support this motion if an amendment were added to the effect that the assembly desired the three parties in the new government to divide the portfolios equitably among them. After considerable discussion the Socialist amendment was adopted by 358 to 38, with the Communists abstaining, and the entire motion was then approved by 400 to 163, with the Communists voting in the negative.[17]

The concurrence of the M. R. P. as well as of the Socialists in the amendment favoring the equitable distribution of portfolios implied that both these parties were willing to have de Gaulle accede to the Communist demands in the matter of ministries. But the firmness with which the M. R. P. had refused to serve under anyone but de Gaulle, which in itself pleased the Communists, and the determination of the Socialists not to enter any two-party combination, which gratified them much less, apparently convinced the Communists that nothing was to be gained by drawing the crisis out further. Their attempt to drive de Gaulle out of office and the M. R. P. into the opposition had failed in the face of Socialist determination, and they therefore permitted a surprisingly speedy resolution of the crisis.

De Gaulle at once resumed his consultations and the new cabinet was announced on November 21:

General de Gaulle	President, Minister of National Defense and of War, Chief of the Armies
Vincent Auriol (Socialist)	Minister of State
Francisque Gay (M. R. P.)	Minister of State
Maurice Thorez (Communist)	Minister of State
Louis Jacquinot (Democratic Alliance)	Minister of State
P.-H. Teitgen (M. R. P.)	Justice
Georges Bidault (M. R. P.)	Foreign Affairs
Adrien Tixier (Socialist)	Interior
Jean Michelet (M. R. P.)	Armies
Charles Tillon (Communist)	Armaments
François Billoux (Communist)	National Economy
René Pleven (U. D. S. R.)	Finance
Marcel Paul (Communist)	Production
François Tanguy-Prigent (Socialist)	Agriculture and Food Supply
Jacques Soustelle (U. D. S. R.)	Colonies
Paul Giaccobi (Radical-Socialist)	Education
Ambroise Croizat (Communist)	Labor and Social Security
Jules Moch (Socialist)	Transport and Public Works

Eugène Thomas (Socialist)	Posts and Telegraph
André Malraux (non-party)	Information
Raoul Dautry (non-party)	Reconstruction and Urbanism
Robert Prigent (M. R. P.)	Population[18]

The most striking feature of the ministry, in light of the crisis which had preceded its formation, was the distribution of responsibility for national defense. De Gaulle himself assumed this post, as well as the portfolio for war, while actual administration was divided between control of the armed forces themselves, which was given to the M. R. P., and control of armaments production, which the Communists received. The meager return which the Communists got from their campaign for one of the "key" ministries can be understood only in terms of de Gaulle's continued refusal to give them control of the army and their acceptance of this defeat because of the failure of their attempt to persuade the Socialists to enter a two-party government with them. De Gaulle's success in forming a government in which the Communists were held to the role he desired, despite the wishes of a majority of the assembly, represented a large triumph for his conception of an independent executive, as well as for his own resolution.

De Gaulle gave the Communists an appreciable role in economic affairs, including the ministries of national economy and production. But interior, and the police, remained in the hands of the Socialist Tixier, and foreign affairs was kept by Bidault. De Gaulle's success in forming his cabinet did not stop with the exclusion of the Communists from posts which it would have been dangerous to entrust to them. He was able, in addition, to confide most of the important ministries to politicians whom he had found reliable during the preceding year and to keep in office a significant number of his wartime associates, who had little party support. It was surely obvious to the Communists, among others, that in de Gaulle's hands the executive authority was an independent force which was not to be bound by and dependent on party alliances and transactions.

At the same time, the success of de Gaulle's personal policy in regard to the construction of the cabinet was made possible only by the fidelity of the M. R. P. to him and of the Socialists to tripartism. The attitudes of these two parties in November were, however, no guarantee, as de Gaulle may have believed, of their continued cooperation with each other and with him either in the writing of the new constitution or in the governing of France. Nor were the Communists reconciled, despite their defeat in this episode, to the permanent ascendancy of one who was the greatest bar to their constitutional concepts and to their political ambitions.

CHAPTER X

FRANCE AND THE GREAT POWERS AFTER LONDON

The circumstances of the collapse of the London conference posed once again for France the question of her relations with the Big Three and her inclusion in the work of peacemaking. In a broadcast immediately following the end of the conference, Secretary of State Byrnes warmly defended the right of France and China, as permanent members of the Security Council, to participate in the discussion of all peace settlements. Ernest Bevin apparently shared this view, and in a statement published on October 31 the British government demonstrated that the Anglo-American position on the right of the five members of the Council of Foreign Ministers to discuss all issues which were before it was, on the basis of the Potsdam decisions, beyond question. De Gaulle, of course, strongly reiterated France's firmness on the point in a press conference of October 12:

> In any case, insofar as France is concerned, she is to-day more than ever resolved to recognize and accept only those settlements in which she will have partici-pated in a direct manner. I am not sure that the former experiments which, to our taste, did not take sufficient

account of the French point of view, have been very happy. So much for a conference of "Three." Then there was a conference of "Five." For a conference of "Five" to develop and succeed there are many conditions necessary, but there is in any case one that concerns France. It is that all questions discussed by these conferences must be discussed by France with the others.[1]

But the United States, in particular, was eager to resume the work of peacemaking, and was prepared to make concessions to be able to do so. As a conciliatory gesture, the American government, together with the British, extended diplomatic recognition to Austria on October 20 and to Hungary on November 2, after each had promised to hold free elections at once —obviously a hint on the part of the Western powers of the terms on which they would also recognize the Rumanian and Bulgarian regimes. At the same time, Byrnes instructed Ambassador Harriman to make a direct approach to Stalin on Balkan problems and on the last proposal for the peace negotiations which the Americans had made at the London meeting—by which, in effect, they had offered to exclude France and China from discussion of the Balkan treaties in return for the holding of a general peace conference later to consider the drafts thus prepared by the restricted Council of Foreign Ministers.

As early as October 7 it was reported that Stalin had proposed a new meeting of representatives of the three Great Powers, either to find means to break the impasse created at London or to resume, without France and China, the substantive work which had been begun there. Again, a few days later, during Andrei Gromyko's brief visits to Washington and London, it appeared that efforts were underway to develop a three-power understanding on the procedural problem which had brought the London conference to an end and on the substantive issues dividing the three powers. The French were thus warned almost from the day the London conference ended that the Big Three might reach an understanding on terms involving a reversion to the formula of Yalta and Potsdam, and the exclusion of France. At the same time, the Anglo-American conversations which took place during Prime Minister Attlee's visit to Washington in mid-November ended, in *Le Monde*'s opinion, in the definitive appearance of an Anglo-Saxon bloc, nor were the French encouraged by reports that the two powers at Washington had agreed to make every attempt to restore the wartime entente with the U.S.S.R.—possibly on the wartime basis of three powers.[2] Definite rumors of a new three-power meeting were reported from Washington as early as November 13.

It was suggested in the preceding chapter that de Gaulle to some degree so strongly resisted Communist demands during the November political crisis because he wanted to continue to assure France of Anglo-American support in the three-power negotiations which were then obviously moving toward a solution of the existing impasse. At the same time he had no wish to alienate irrevocably the Soviet Union from France. It is therefore not surprising that in the ministerial declaration to the Constituent Assembly on November 23, de Gaulle again emphasized not only the necessity for France to be included in all Great Power discussions, but her role as a mediating link between the other powers.

> She [France] judges more firmly than ever that it is in the common interest for her to obtain this audience, and it is with this conviction, as well as with the will to protect her interests, that she could not consent to

anything that she has not approved, at the same time
and in the same way as the other great powers. Placed
where she is, in Europe, in Africa, in Asia, oriented
traditionally at the same time toward the West and toward the East, she can be and wants to be a link and,
under no condition, a pawn.[3]

Commenting on these words, *Le Monde* noted the close con-
cordance between such a foreign policy and the exigencies of
the domestic situation:

When he declares that France can be and wants to be
a link and under no condition a pawn, he is defining at
the same time national aspirations and the present possibilities of French policy. No one in France desires a
choice between the East and the West, a choice which
would aggravate certain internal and foreign dissensions.
Everyone would be happy, on the contrary, if our policy could help to appease quarrels.

But whatever the domestic merits of the government's foreign
policy, the journal had to admit that the international position
of France—sometimes excluded from the councils of the powers
as at Potsdam, sometimes included as at London, and often
called upon to subscribe to commitments in whose formulation
she had had no part—remained very unsatisfactory.[4]

The contacts among the three major powers aimed at breaking the London impasse reached their turning point on November 29, when Byrnes decided to implement for the first
time the machinery, established at Yalta and confirmed at Potsdam, providing for meetings of the three foreign ministers, and
proposed to Molotov that such a meeting be held in the Soviet

capital. This was accepted at once by the Russians, as well as by the British, but public announcement of the pending conference was made only on December 7.[5] On the same day Byrnes received the French and Chinese ambassadors separately, to assure them that such a meeting, which, he pointed out, was specifically provided for in the very protocol which had established the five-power Council of Foreign Ministers, would in no way derogate from the authority of the latter. But even though France was assured that Germany and other subjects of direct interest to her would not be considered at Moscow, and official Paris reportedly received the news "with interest and without emotion," the French government obviously strongly resented its new relegation to a second rank position. *Le Monde* correctly pointed out that the meetings of the three foreign ministers which had been provided for at Yalta had, in fact, never taken place, and that the return to the three-power formula was based only on the failure of the London conference, rather than on the existence of any problems with which the three were particularly concerned.[6] The very holding of such a meeting implied that the extent of French participation in world affairs, months after the end of the war, was still a matter which was to be decided by others, in the absence of France.

The public humiliation of the French government was profound, for it had often proclaimed that this state of affairs had passed, and had perhaps believed it at the time of the establishment of the Council of Foreign Ministers. Naturally, de Gaulle's position at home was not strengthened. The French were not ignorant of the cause of their exclusion. Though French relations with the United States and Great Britain were at best mediocre during this period because of disagreements over German policy, the Paris government had no doubt after the London conference that it was the Soviet Union which was blocking France's participation on an equal basis in Allied affairs. General Catroux noted that in December, 1945, "relations between the two allied countries became as glacial as the Moscovite winter" and that no attention whatsoever was paid in Moscow to the first anniversary of the Franco-Soviet pact. *Le Monde* no doubt fully expressed the official French attitude by noting in its commentary on the anniversary of the pact that the exclusion of France from the Moscow conference by the U.S.S.R. seemed hardly in accord with either the letter or the spirit of the treaty.[7]

Nevertheless, the French government neither aligned itself with the United States and Great Britain against the Soviet Union nor accepted Catroux's suggestion of trying to reduce Soviet hostility to France—engendered, he thought, by de Gaulle's talk of a Western bloc—by negotiating alliances with Poland and Yugoslavia.[8] Rather, it seemed determined to wrap itself ever more closely in its policy of balance and neutrality. In a broadcast of December 10, devoted to both domestic and foreign affairs, de Gaulle attempted to put the situation of France in the most advantageous light by stating:

> In the world as it is today, two very great powers remain, and we are exactly between them, the extreme point of Europe toward the West, the bridgehead of the West in Europe. One has only to look at the map to understand that, in this situation, our vital interest obliges us to hold ourselves strictly in balance. We claim, thus, to practice friendship insofar as it lies with us toward the East and toward the West, eyes open and hands free. This French policy may temporarily lead one or the other of the two very great powers, on the occasions when they clash, to agree at least to exclude

France. We regret these mishaps, for them, for us, and for the world. But we know that our balance corresponds to the balance of peace, and we are resolved not to depart from it, convinced that after various ups and downs it is on our attitude that the needle of the balance will be fixed, definitively and to the general advantage.[9]

De Gaulle spoke as if this policy were one which had been freely and deliberately chosen by the French government, on behalf of the cause of peace, in preference to all others. For him, indeed, this may have seemed to be the case, at least to the extent that it reflected the independent and national position which he held. It is difficult to see, however, what other policy could have been followed by a three-party government, or by a state which needed the concurrence of all three of the major powers in order to resume the coveted position in their midst which it had briefly held at London. The only alternative might have been to aspire to no significant role at all, that is, to have no policy.

The conference of the three foreign ministers opened in Moscow on December 16, and although France was absent the event was an important one for French policy. The first order of business concerned the writing of peace treaties with the former German satellites. The American delegation presented once again the plan it had proposed in the last days of the London conference, which in effect accepted the Soviet demand that only those states which had signed each armistice (plus France for the Italian treaty) would be able even to discuss the treaty with the relevant ex-enemy, but which also provided for a much wider peace conference which would later express its opinions on the draft treaties submitted to it. In addition, Byrnes now added a final provision, on the basis of talks Ambassador Harriman had had with Stalin in November, according to which the results of this peace conference were to be referred back to the authors of the original drafts, who would make the final decisions on them. By this complicated procedure, France (and China) would be excluded from both the preliminary and final work on the Balkan and Finnish treaties, and would be able to discuss their terms only in a general conference which would include, according to the American proposal, twenty-one states.

Molotov still wanted to confine the discussion of each treaty, even in the second or peace conference stage, only to those states which had actually waged war against each enemy. This was debated for several days, but in the end Stalin reversed Molotov's position and agreed to the American proposal. It was decided that the peace conferences should meet in Paris no later than May 1, 1946.

A new controversy was then opened by the Russians, who held that France and China should merely be informed of these decisions, rather than invited to adhere to them; they were finally both informed *and* invited to adhere. Byrnes, in particular, wanted to publish these results immediately, and the French and Chinese governments were at once informed of them. China's favorable reply was received on December 24. But since no answer had been obtained from Paris—which had been given a single day in which to reply—the conferees at Moscow decided to release the agreement with the statement that France and China had been invited to concur.[10] The agreement included these points:

1. Only those members of the Council of Foreign Ministers who signed each of the five satellite armistices, or who were considered by the Potsdam protocol as having done so, would

participate in elaborating the revelant treaties, though the council could ask other members to participate in questions directly concerning them. Thus, the Italian treaty would be drafted by Great Britain, the United States, the Soviet Union, and France; all of these powers except France would prepare the Hungarian, Rumanian, and Bulgarian treaties; and only Britain and the U.S.S.R. would participate in work on the Finnish treaty. The deputies of the foreign ministers were to resume work on the treaties in London, on the basis of agreements reached during the council's first session.

2. After this preliminary work had been completed, the Council of Foreign Ministers would call a conference to study the treaties thus elaborated. This conference would include, besides the five members of the council, Australia, Belgium, White Russia, Brazil, Greece, Holland, Denmark, Canada, New Zealand, Norway, Poland, the Ukraine, Czechoslovakia, Ethiopia, Yugoslavia, and South Africa. The conference would meet no later than May 1, 1946.

3. After the conference and the study of its recommendations, the states which signed each armistice (together with France for Italy), would draw up the final treaties.

4. These would be signed by the states represented at the conference which were at war with each of the relevant enemy states. The texts would be sent also to other members of the United Nations who had been at war with the enemy states.

5. The treaties would go into effect when ratified by the signers of the armistices (including France for Italy), as well as by the enemy states themselves.[11]

By this plan the Soviet Union had secured the substance of its wishes: the drafting both of the original treaties and of the final texts remained in as few hands as possible and, in particular, only three powers would work on the disputed Balkan treaties.

At the same time, the Americans had at least won a measure of public discussion of the treaties and, no doubt, hoped to be able to influence the Russians by the marshalling of international opinion at the conference.

But for the French this agreement of the Big Three was simply a defeat. Except for participation in the Italian treaty—promised them at Potsdam—it was a confirmation of their exclusion from a large area of European affairs in which they felt themselves entitled to participate. *Le Monde* observed with justified asperity that France, at least historically and geographically, had closer ties to Rumania than had Brazil or Ethiopia, yet she was to play no larger role than they in preparing the Rumanian peace treaty.[12] In fact, of course, France's influence on events in the Balkans was little greater than that of the most distant country—though it was also, in a sense, little less than that of the United States and the United Kingdom.

If it can be said that a Great Power is one which is considered as being entitled to participate on an equal basis in the consideration of all problems in the geographical area in which its status is agreed to be operative, including those problems that do not directly interest it, then the Big Three at Moscow, by excluding France from the Balkan discussions, implicitly decided that she was not even to be counted any longer as a European Great Power. French claims to being a world power had already more or less quietly disappeared, at least temporarily, with her practical absence from the Pacific war and Pacific affairs. Her presence as a permanent member of the Security Council and as an occupant of Germany and Austria was, in a sense, an exception to her general downgrading. With good reason, France could fear that her right to take part even in the German settlement remained more dependent on the convenience and interests of the three major occupying powers than on any enforceable or accepted right of her own to participate. Thus, in its summary of France's situation during 1945, *Le Monde* could write with justice:

It suffices to consider these phases of the diplomacy of the Big Three to see that the position of France was not always easy. Summoned, turned away, summoned again, thanked again, she had to ask herself what was her place. In the future organization of the world she is among the Five, at Berlin among the Four, but when the Three gather she is outside. Sometimes she can take initiatives, discuss on a footing of equality; sometimes they discuss, without her, her most important interests.[13]

It is not surprising, therefore, that the French government was very slow to frame a reply to the proposals made on December 22; refusal to comply with them seemed necessarily ruled out in advance, while acceptance meant abandonment of France's often repeated claim to equal participation in the settlement of European affairs. In the meantime, the Moscow conference turned to the consideration of other problems, of less direct interest to France. This stage witnessed a new round of sharp controversy on the composition of the Rumanian and Bulgarian governments. There were also discussions of atomic energy, the occupation of Japan, and the Iranian situation.[14] The scope of the conversations was reflected in the voluminous communiqué issued on December 27, which marked their conclusion. The substance of its main points was as follows:

1. A Far Eastern Commission, including the Big Five, Holland, Canada, Australia, New Zealand, India, and the Philippines was to supervise the occupation of Japan; each of the Big Five except France was given a veto in the Commission. An Allied

Council for Japan, composed of the supreme commander, one Russian and one Chinese member, and a fourth member representing Britain, Australia, New Zealand, and India was to maintain a closer but advisory contact with the occupation.

2. A Russian-American mixed commission was to prepare the way for a democratic regime in Korea. The United States, the Soviet Union, and Great Britain affirmed their non-interference in Chinese affairs.

3. The King of Rumania would be asked to name one representative and loyal member of the Liberal Party and of the National Peasant Party to the government, which was then to prepare free elections. A commission composed of Andrei Vyshinski and Ambassadors Harriman and Clark Kerr was to go to Bucharest to supervise this, after which the two Western powers would recognize the Rumanian government.

4. The Soviet government would advise the Bulgarian government to include two members of non-participating parties.

5. The three powers would recommend to the General Assembly of the United Nations that an atomic energy commission be established to consider elimination of atomic weapons and peaceful uses of nuclear energy. France, China, and Canada would be asked to co-sponsor this proposal.[15]

The French, of course, noted that in Far Eastern affairs they were relegated to the same position as New Zealand, Holland, and the Philippines, and feared that Indo-China might be discussed in their absence.[16] In addition, it was evident that the dispositions in regard to the Rumanian and Bulgarian governments confirmed in practice the French exclusion from Balkan affairs which had already been made clear in principle by the Moscow agreement on the peace treaties.

Despite these new blows French attention remained largely restricted to those decisions announced on December 24.

De Gaulle, who considered that the single day granted to the French government to prepare its reply to the announcement of December 24 constituted an affront to the dignity of the nation, insisted that the matter be taken up only at the regular cabinet meeting on the 28th. At that time Bidault favored immediate French acceptance of the Allied arrangements, and in this he was supported by the Communists, who were always meek before any decision in which the Soviet Union concurred. De Gaulle, however, was unwilling simply to acquiesce in the Moscow decisions and he received support from the Socialists and also from some of the M. R. P. ministers, who believed that the Moscow conference had been a victory of the U.S.S.R. over the Western powers and that France was therefore in a position to question the results. In the end, therefore, the cabinet decided in principle to seek a "clarification" from the three powers on certain points of their agreement.[17] On January 2, 1946, it formally approved the French reply, which was handed to Ambassador Caffery the next day and was made public on the 5th.[18] The French government stated that it welcomed the idea of a general peace conference and was ready to invite the participants to Paris. But on certain points it desired further information:

1. The future role of the Council of Foreign Ministers, which was to have been permanent, endowed with a secretariat, and charged with preparing the peace treaties, seemed uncertain. The French government wanted to know how the three powers envisaged its future work.

2. The Potsdam protocol had provided for the council to invite any other interested state to its deliberations on given points. The Moscow agreement appeared to limit this right only to other members of the council, thereby excluding, for example, Yugoslavia, Greece, and Ethiopia from any role in the

essential drafting stage of the Italian treaty. As for the French government itself and the Balkan treaties, it recalled the terms in which it had agreed to participate in the council: "It noted in this response that France is interested in all important questions concerning Europe or any region whatever of Europe."

3. The importance of the last point would depend on the functions of the peace conference. It is stated that the latter would examine the treaties and make recommendations on them, while the original drafters would make the final decisions on these recommendations. The French government expressed the hope that this literal interpretation did not correspond to the spirit of the system, for it desired as broad a discussion at the conference as possible and believed that the results of this discussion should be given the greatest weight.

4. The Moscow project made no provision for hearing at the conference the former enemy states themselves. The French government favored their being heard, and hoped that the three powers shared this desire. "It goes without saying that this does not constitute a precedent for the later discussion of the peace settlement with Germany, whose situation is completely different by reason of the clauses of its surrender."

5. The Moscow decisions indicated an important change in the plans for final drafting of the peace treaties. Whereas originally the council was to prepare drafts and submit them to the United Nations for final decisions, it appeared now that the original drafters were to make the final decisions. This posed even more sharply the role and powers of the proposed conference.[19]

In addition to this series of inquiries, the French government a few days later handed a note to the American ambassador by which it agreed to sponsor the proposal for an atomic energy commission. It also accepted the invitation to join the Far Eastern Commission. In the latter case, however, the government attempted to conceal its acceptance of its own effective exclusion from Pacific affairs by stating that if it should appear that French interests in the Far East (that is, Indo-China) were to come within the commission's competence, France, as a permanent member of the Security Council and a Pacific power, would claim the same veto within it which the United States, Great Britain, the Soviet Union, and China exercised—according to an ingenious formulation of the French note—because of their special relation to the Japanese surrender.[20]

The main interest of these documents, which were largely a face-saving device to avoid the appearance of unquestioning acceptance, lies in the French inquiries about the future role of the Council of Foreign Ministers, which they had hoped was permanently to supplant the Big Three and to exercise a general supervisory authority over all questions, and in the specific reassertion of France's interest in Balkan affairs. But it was clearly realized in Washington and London that Byrnes and Bevin had yielded on the latter question to the Russians and that it could not be reopened. It is hardly likely that this point was not equally clear in Paris or that the French commentary on the subject had not been more for the record and with an eye to later developments than with any real hope that France's wishes would be accepted.

The deputies of the five members of the Council of Foreign Ministers were to have resumed work on the satellite treaties in London on January 14, but France secured a delay until the three participants of the Moscow conference had answered the questions put to them by the French government. On that day Ambassador Caffery handed to Bidault the reply agreed upon by the Big Three. This, while it did not impair the substance of the Moscow agreements, reassured France of her right to present memoranda on all subjects discussed by the council, including, presumably, the Balkan treaties. The reply also promised that the former enemies, as well as all other interested states, would be consulted during all stages on each treaty, and stated that each participant in the peace conference would be free to present views which would be taken into consideration. In addition, it made clear that Moscow did not annul Potsdam and that the Council of Foreign Ministers remained unimpaired in its functions.[21] On the basis of this reply, which the French of necessity found acceptable despite its lack of real substance, Maurice Couve de Murville went to London on January 18 to participate in the work on the Italian treaty. The first session of the deputies took place on the same afternoon, when discussion of the Italian treaty was resumed at the point at which it had ceased in October.

During the same week a three-day debate on foreign policy took place in the Constituent Assembly which, though the participants were not aware of the fact, marked a summing-up of the achievements and standing of the de Gaulle government.[22] Speaking on the last comparable occasion, in November, 1944, Foreign Minister Bidault had presented the intentions and aspirations of the government; now, fourteen months later, he presented the case for the foreign policy which it had pursued. Apart from his discussion of Germany the principal problem which Bidault treated was one which had run through the whole of the earlier debate: France as a Great Power.[23] Despite the many disappointments of 1945, such as the Potsdam and Moscow conferences, the obvious weakness of France, and the continued ambiguity of her status in the world, Bidault defended the special position of the large powers—among whom he included France—and the relative exclusion of the small ones in terms of the "coefficient of power" which governed international responsibilities.

He restated the policy of the French government which had been evident at least since the San Francisco conference: "We do not intend either to play the superior to less strong nations nor to create and play on antagonisms between what are called small countries and the greater powers." France remained firmly on the side of the Great Powers—despite the doubt that they accepted her there. At the same time, Bidault could not have overlooked the latter problem, and he reaffirmed once more that France maintained her claims to being a world power and her intention "not to allow to be settled in our absence and without our participation the affairs of a world in which we have interests and a mission everywhere." French claims, he added, were not based only on the past, but on the realities of the present and the future. To those who questioned the practical results of this policy of grandeur (with some reason, since the French government had just sanctioned its own exclusion from Balkan and Far Eastern affairs), Bidault replied that it was only good sense. Though he did not amplify this, it seems clear he meant that any state would prefer to participate in the making of decisions concerning its welfare than not to participate, and that France, with considerable legal and other claims to participation, naturally was attempting, despite many obstacles and disappointments, to implement them.

The Communists, who had to justify the policies of the Soviet Union, found themselves in the position of agreeing with Bidault that France should not lead the smaller states against the Great Powers but should work for the concord of the latter. Florimond Bonte, the principal Communist speaker, went far beyond the foreign minister in proclaiming the need for harmony among the three major powers and denouncing those who sought to divide them and even those who complained against any of their actions (such as, presumably, the exclusion of

France!). But the complaisant acceptance by the Communists of the existing state of the world, including France's relegation to the second rank among the powers, was not shared by the other speakers, many of whom denounced the dictatorship of the Big Three. The most significant criticism of the government's policy came from the Socialists. Daniel Mayer insisted—in contradiction to Bidault—that physical power was not everything and that France was indeed a Great Power, but by other standards. She should neither push her way into the councils of the Big Three nor lead the small nations against them, but should pursue a policy of right and justice, which others would then follow. To build the world, he said, it was first necessary to build Europe by forming a federation of free peoples. Such a grouping would not constitute a bloc nor would it be directed economically against the United States nor politically against the Soviet Union. It should, on the contrary, pursue "a policy of rapprochement, of union, of synthesis between Soviet Russia and the United States of America. The economic and geographic situation of these states of the European West obliges them to do so, as does the safeguarding of peace itself." France should oppose the hegemony of a few powers, according to Mayer, even if tomorrow she was to be included among them. French security, he concluded, rested not on arms or frontiers but on the effectiveness of the international organization, and to perfect it the states must give up a part of their sovereignty.

In comparing this debate to that of November, 1944, it is striking that, on the latter occasion, representatives of practically every group had spoken of France as a link between East and West, while at the beginning of 1946 it fell mainly to the Socialists to reassert this theme, which, however, remained the burden of de Gaulle's statements and, according to him, of his policy as well. Neither the Communists nor Bidault and the

M. R. P. spoke in these terms. At the same time, the idea of France's neutrality between the two blocs was universally proclaimed. It was as if most of the French were less inclined to pretend to mediate the disputes of others and more disposed to assert their own interests and policies on those occasions when they were permitted to do so.

In this way the M. R. P. was separated both from the Communists, who accepted the relegation of France to the second rank, and the Socialists, who decried power politics altogether, repudiated the government's "policy of grandeur," and cast France in the role, first of peacemaker among the clashing powers, and then as the leader in the building of a stronger European and international community. The M. R. P., however, was in agreement with the Communists and much of the right in its German policy, but was again separated from the Socialists. The three principal parties of the majority were thus each divided from the others on important aspects of France's foreign policy, and two of them had basic differences with de Gaulle's views. The seeming community of views between the M. R. P. and the Communists on the German issue perhaps contributed something to the stability of the tripartite system by providing at least one bridge between those two parties. But this situation clearly foreshadowed some reorientation of French foreign policy in the event of a new government crisis and the withdrawal of de Gaulle's determined hand.

CHAPTER XI

GERMANY AFTER POTSDAM

Except for France's permanent struggle to secure the definitive establishment of a place among the Great Powers, her most important single problem with the Big Three during the last months of the de Gaulle government was the administration of Germany and its future under the Potsdam arrangements. The notes sent by the French government in August, 1945, to the three major Allies had made it clear that France was far from accepting all of the German policies laid down at Potsdam, and during his visit to Washington de Gaulle outlined his own German policy in considerable detail. But while France was preparing to lay her views on Germany before the first session of the Council of Foreign Ministers, the tendency toward uncoordinated developments in Germany, evident since the beginning of the occupation, continued.

In early September the Russians promulgated land reform throughout their zone, and on September 13 they announced the establishment of specialized agencies for economic and social affairs, each under a German director.[1] The French did not object to the decentralized control of Germany implied by this policy. But they did not overlook the fact that such actions, taken without consultation among the Allies, could only increase the breach between the three Western and the Soviet zones which had already begun to appear as early as May—a breach which might well end with each zone going its own way and with France thus being excluded from any role in much of the Rhineland and in the Ruhr. On the other hand, the French feared also that the Soviet action might lead to the early establishment of similar agencies for all of Germany. *Le Monde* therefore took occasion to restate the French position on these problems:

> As long as Germany possesses the Ruhr, which for a century has been her principal military arsenal, she will have the means to forge again a new war industry, and as long as she controls the Rhineland she will be able to use it as a springboard for new aggression against the west. Now the extensive amputations which the Reich has undergone in the east ensure that it will never accept of its free will the peace conditions imposed by the Allies. The "Drang nach Osten" will inevitably be succeeded, when Germany has recovered her economic and demographic forces, by a "Drang nach Westen."
>
> Cruel experiences for the nations of Western Europe have shown that the guarantees of a military control in a country resolved to rearm are illusory. The Rhineland, the Ruhr, and the regions bordering the Netherlands should be definitively withdrawn from German sovereignty. The Ruhr should be ruled by an international statute under the control of the Allies, and the lands of the left bank of the Rhine should be controlled by France, Belgium, and Holland.
>
> The fact that a central German government controlled by the Allies was to be installed in Berlin, in the

midst of the Soviet zone, would not be a guarantee of peace. The Russians, in the long run and by an inevitable trend, will have control over this organism and, consequently, over all Germany. A sharp line of demarcation should be drawn between the stated regions and the rest of Germany. It is at this price alone that Germanism will be prevented from again troubling the peace of the world.[2]

The French did not hesitate to argue in Washington, on the lines of this article, that a German government established at Berlin would soon fall into Soviet hands and, therefore, that the Western Allies would do well to wait before establishing the regime provided for at Potsdam.[3]

On the eve of the meeting of the Council of Foreign Ministers, the question of Germany was the one which most preoccupied the French. On August 24 General Catroux had again reminded Molotov of France's hope that Germany would be high on the agenda of the London meeting, only to be met with the chilling reply that German problems had been settled at Potsdam.[4] De Gaulle, in his interview to the London *Times* on September 10, spoke of an Anglo-French entente on the question of Germany as a *sine qua non* of a meaningful alliance between them—as if he wanted to be very sure that such an alliance, if it were ever signed, brought real advantages to French policy, which that with the Soviet Union had conspicuously failed to do. Since Potsdam, he said, had amputated Germany in the east, she would inevitably turn with greater force toward the west. It was therefore necessary to establish firm and effective security arrangements in the west, that is, in the Rhineland and the Ruhr. Of the Rhineland he stated: "The military and political security of those four countries [France, Belgium,

Holland, and Britain] requires that this territory be placed under their strategic and political control and be cut off once and for all from the body of the German state in such a way that its inhabitants should know that their future does not lie with Germany." As for the Ruhr, whose coal was as important to Italy, Switzerland, Holland, France, Luxembourg, and Belgium as to Germany herself, these states should control and distribute its production.

On September 14 the French delegates to the London conference filed a memorandum on Germany.[5] In this the French government recalled that in its notes of August 7 it had welcomed the Potsdam decisions which looked to the decentralization of political authority in Germany, but had expressed serious reservations as to the establishment of a central government, the reconstitution of political parties for the whole of Germany, and the creation of central administrative departments—the authority of whose state secretaries would extend to the entire country. Such measures, said the French memorandum, would inevitably prejudice the possible evolution of a truly decentralized and federal regime in the future Germany. Further, if no German territory except that administered by Poland beyond the Oder-Neisse were subtracted from the authority of the proposed central administration, it would appear that the frontiers of Germany had been definitively fixed, and the supposedly temporary arrangement would harden into a final settlement.

Now the Provisional Government has publicly indicated on various occasions the basic importance it attaches to the Rhenish-Westphalian region's being made incapable in the future of constituting Germany's arsenal, zone of passage, or point of departure to attack her western neighbors. It considers that the definitive

separation of this region, including the Ruhr, from Germany, indispensable for the protection of the French
frontier, constitutes in addition the essential condition
of the security of Europe and the world. It therefore
judges it necessary, if central German administrations
are to be established, that it be specified at the same time
that the Rhenish-Westphalian region will be subtracted
from their competence.

French concern that the premature establishment of a central
administration in Germany might discourage the growth of
federalism was thus very secondary to their fear that such an
administration would confirm the continued attachment of the
Rhineland and Ruhr to the German state. Therefore, they held
out the clear suggestion that they would bargain their consent
to the proposal of the three major Allies in return for the withdrawal of the stated areas from the control of the central administration—an arrangement which the French undoubtedly
believed would be permanent. The point of this proposed bargain was underscored in the last sentence of the memorandum:
"It [the French delegation] must declare . . . that the French
representative on the Berlin Interallied Control Committee will
not be authorized to subscribe to a measure prejudicing this fate
[that of the Rhineland and Ruhr] before the question posed
above may have been discussed by the five ministers and been
decided on by the Council."

After so clear a warning that France would not agree to the
implementation of the Potsdam accords—over which she held
a veto placed in her hands by the three powers themselves—
without a satisfactory settlement of the issues she had raised so
often in regard to western Germany, the major Allies would have
done well to initiate a serious discussion on this subject at the

London meeting. The French memorandum was, indeed, placed on the already lengthy conference agenda and was discussed on September 26 and 28. There appear also to have been private talks on Germany, at least between Bidault and Bevin, but the practical breakdown of the conference on September 22, during the discussion of the Balkan treaties, prevented a serious consideration of German affairs, and it was agreed only to pursue discussion of the subject through diplomatic channels.[6]

In the press conference he held on the day after the end of the conference, Bidault said of his principal memorandum on German affairs only that he was pleased that France had been given an opportunity to present her views on the question for the first time. But *Le Monde*, while sharing this satisfaction, recognized that in the circumstances in which the conference had broken up there was implicit danger to the French position not only on the Balkan treaties but perhaps on Germany as well: "we must wonder if the whole policy of Yalta and Potsdam is not going to be revised in the sense of Teheran, and if the failure at London will not lead to a new meeting of the Big Three from which we would again be excluded."[7] That is, though no action of France (or China) had obstructed the work of the council, it was all too possible that the Russians might insist henceforth on continuing their diplomatic struggle with the United States and Britain over the Balkans, and all other issues, in three-power rather than five-power meetings, and that the Western powers might accede to this demand at the expense of France.

While the London conference was in progress the German Control Council issued a series of general orders concerning the German economy and other subjects. The French were quick to note that reference was made in the documents embodying these decrees to "the frontiers of Germany as they have been fixed," and *Le Monde* drew the obvious point that the Allies had hitherto maintained that the German frontiers were not fixed. At the same time, it saw new evidence indicating that other measures taken separately by each occupant—such as the division of the American zone into three states—might well solidify into a permanent settlement.[8] The French of course had no objection to "provisional" arrangements which might become permanent if they were in accord with French policies, and the division of the American zone was well received in Paris: "This policy of our Allies tending to detach from Berlin the German 'lands' and to re-enforce their regionalist tendencies is in perfect agreement, declares an authorized French source, with the views of the Republic regarding the fate of Germany."[9] But, in the face of these events, there was considerable uncertainty in France about the government's policy toward Germany, and already some public complaint that it was ineffective.

As if to answer these charges, as well as to win popular support in the French occupation zone in Germany for the policies being followed, de Gaulle, on October 2, began a speaking tour of the zone. Taken in conjunction with de Gaulle's interview of September 10, his speeches in Germany show that the hitherto unsuccessful French policy of separating the Rhineland and Ruhr from Germany was being redefined in terms of the establishment of a Western European framework into which these territories could eventually be fitted. In thus holding out the hand of France to the Germans—a remarkable gesture for a French leader so soon after the end of the war—de Gaulle was not abandoning the separatist policy which, indeed, the French government continued to press during the remaining few months of his tenure. He was, however, adding a new dimension to it by offering the Germans, or at least some of them, the prospect of a future beyond defeat and occupation. To him this future may have meant no more than that a more or less satellite German state or states would be ranged at France's side in a Western European grouping whose combined strength would enable Paris to play an equal role with the major Allies in European and world affairs. But the relating of the Franco-German problem to a broader Western European framework has had a longer life than the French policy which originally gave rise to it.

While the French government continued to develop its German policy more or less in a vacuum, for lack of a forum of Allied consultation in which to discuss it, the Control Council was attempting to apply the Potsdam directives. A series of laws was agreed to and issued dealing with, among other things, denazification, demilitarization, reorganization of the German judiciary, the trials of lesser war criminals, and control of the property of the I. G. Farbenindustrie.[10] But the establishment of common economic institutions for the four zones as provided for at Potsdam proved finally to be impossible because of French opposition. As early as August 10, General Koenig had formally made known to his colleagues on the Control Council that Allied discussion on certain points, such as the establishment of central administrations, would be necessary before he would be able to participate in the policies they proposed. On September 22 General Koeltz, the French member of the Coordinating Committee, first implemented this French policy by vetoing the establishment of a central transport administration.[11] On October 1, in a declaration to the Control Council, General Koenig once again stated that intergovernmental discussions were an indispensable prerequisite to French agreement on these matters. He added:

... whatever limitations might be put on the role which the proposed central administrations would have to play, the very principle of their creation prejudices the status of the regions in question.

The discussion opened at London not having yet concluded, I am obliged, in conformity to the instructions which I have received from my government, to ask that there be a suspension in the study of the two projects for creation of central administrations which have been submitted to the Council today. I could only, in fact, in the present state of things, reject these projects.[12]

In this way, and on repeated specific occasions throughout the remainder of 1945, the French formally prevented the control organs from implementing the Potsdam decision to establish a central German administration.

The reaction in Great Britain and the United States was extremely unfavorable to France. But Le Monde, which asserted that the bases of the French position and of Allied cooperation in Germany had been established by the four-power agreement of June 5 and not at Potsdam, strongly developed the French case against the establishment of central administrations, which would confirm the existing frontiers and a unitary German state before formal Allied decisions had been taken on these subjects. However, the journal clearly repeated France's interest in a compromise between the French and Big Three positions on the linked problems of German frontiers and a centralized administration: "France is not hostile, as has been claimed, to the creation of central administrations. She subordinates this measure to the fixing of frontiers. She judges that the two problems are intimately linked: an indisputable fact, since an administration cannot be made to function without knowing exactly in what area it is to operate."[13]

Unfortunately for the French, they were dealing from a basically weak power position. Since only a fraction of the area they wanted to subtract from Germany was in their own zone of occupation, they could win their point only through agreement with the other Allies. Since the latter, for reasons of their own, declined a straightforward discussion of the problem, the French made full use of the one weapon they held—the veto placed in their hands at Potsdam—to try to wring an important concession from the Big Three in return for permitting them to organize Germany (except for the Rhineland and the Ruhr) as they pleased. The French probably did not overvalue their one card; they simply had no other to play. It is not unlikely, in fact, that the French government feared that the three other Allies might attempt, as rumor reported, to exclude France from the German occupation, for it was the French government, rather than the other three, which most urgently pressed for a general discussion of the broad aspects of the German question and a negotiated settlement among the four occupants. When, despite the pressure which they had applied by their vetoes at Berlin, this clear effort to bargain led to nothing, they then fell back on bilateral conversations with each of the Big Three.

Thus, as early as mid-October, detailed conversations on the French memorandum on Germany took place between the British government and Ambassador Massigli, who was joined by a group of special representatives, including Maurice Couve de Murville and Hervé Alphand. The French proposals, as presented to the British on this occasion, were as follows: (1) the Ruhr would be placed under a permanent international administration; (2) the Ruhr state would be as small as possible, including about five million inhabitants; (3) the Ruhr industries would be administered by international councils and their profits would be used for reparations, or to assist the new German state; (4) factories in the Ruhr not necessary to the international economy would be suppressed; and (5) production from the factories and mines would be distributed among the nations having the greatest need for them, including Germany. Once more it was clearly added that, "If the Ruhr should come out from under the control of Berlin, the question of a central administration for the rest of Germany would lose much of its importance," that is, the French would lift their veto on a central administration.[14]

There was considerable speculation in both London and Paris during this period on the possibility of an Anglo-French alliance, and the French, who continued to insist that some kind of agreement about Germany was essential for such an understanding, attempted to convince the British, evidently on the basis of the experience of the London conference, that a concerted policy would permit both France and Britain to play a greater role at future Allied meetings than either could do alone. In an address on October 26, Bevin spoke sympathetically of France's fear of a united Germany, and he stressed that Germany must not be able to use the Ruhr and the Rhineland to begin a new war. He remained vague, however, on the means by which this was to be prevented. It appears, indeed, that there were no concrete results from this confrontation of views, for French sources minimized the scope of the discussions by describing them as a mere presentation of French policy, and denied that any political or diplomatic negotiations had been carried on.

Approaches had been made through diplomatic channels to both the United States and the Soviet Union for talks similar to those held with the British, but neither government had responded before the London discussions ended in the last week of October. The French, however, could foresee that neither the British nor the Americans would welcome the Russians into the control of the Ruhr, particularly while Silesia remained an exclusive Russian preserve. The Soviet reiteration to Washington and London at the beginning of November of their wish, already expressed at Potsdam, to participate in the administration of the Ruhr, did little to strengthen the French case in those capitals. At the same time the French also realized that even the Russians, who were courting the German people and their political parties, might hesitate to endorse the drastic revision of Germany's western frontier which France proposed. Despite these gloomy prospects, however, the French government clung to its German policy and persevered, in default of a four-power negotiation, in presenting it to each of its allies in turn.

On November 9, in the midst of the political crisis in France, Couve de Murville went to Washington to present the French proposals on Germany to the American government in the same way that he had presented them in London two weeks earlier. His first discussions, with Assistant Secretary of State Dunn, on November 13, concerned not the French plan for the Rhineland and the Ruhr but the more prosaic topic of the 25 percent reduction which the interallied coal agency had just made in the allocation of German coal to France. This initial emphasis was prophetic. Constant negotiation went on at Washington and London on this subject from November onward and, since the Ruhr coal which was so essential to the recovery of the French economy was physically in the control of the British, the economic problem of obtaining a secure supply of Ruhr coal from those who controlled it tended to assume increasing political significance, after de Gaulle left office, in the formation of French policy.

Most of Couve's mission, nevertheless, was devoted to the problem of the Ruhr and Rhineland, for which he proposed that: (1) the Rhineland be detached from the German Reich and made a sovereign state; (2) the Allies occupy strategic points in this new state; and (3) the industrial basin of the Ruhr be internationalized. He emphasized once again that no solution to the question of a central administration was possible until this problem had been settled.[15] On his return to Paris, Couve stated, as after the London conversations, that his mission had been one only of information and that he hoped he had been able to explain to the American government and people that France would not oppose the establishment of a central administration in Germany whose authority would not include the Ruhr and the Rhineland. He refrained from speculating on the decision of the American government.

The French were at last able to round out the series of bilateral discussions of their proposals for Germany in talks between Molotov and Ambassador Catroux and Hervé Alphand, which began in Moscow on December 12.[16] The French plan as presented in Moscow, and no doubt tailored to the presumed wishes of the hearers, included these points: (1) there would be a political detachment of the Ruhr and not mere international control of it; (2) the Ruhr would be at the service not only of the western states bordering it but of all the Allies; and (3) nothing would be changed in existing reparations arrangements (that is, the U.S.S.R. would continue to draw reparations from the Ruhr). In answer to questions from Molotov the French representatives argued that, although the United States and the British had not yet given their definite reactions to these proposals, the best way to bring them around would be to confront them with a common Franco-Soviet position—a clear attempt to revive in a specific case the general policy of Franco-Soviet "pre-emptive" coordination that de Gaulle had failed to get Russian support for just a year earlier. The French stated, however, that the status of the Ruhr would be fixed by all four of the occupying powers (though Belgium and the Netherlands, they said, might later have some voice in the government of the area—an idea that Molotov did not seem to find attractive).

Molotov gave no indication of his reaction to this plan after his first interview with Catroux and Alphand (though of course it had been before the Russians as before the other major Allies also since Bidault had submitted his memorandum on Germany to the London conference). At the second meeting, on December 22, Molotov said only that the project required further study and that he was concerned to know the views of the British. The Soviet foreign minister was unmoved either by Catroux's observation that each power seemed to be waiting for the others or by his sharp comment that the Soviet Union knew how to act with despatch when its own interests so required. Catroux could only conclude that the Soviet government did not yet want to commit itself on Germany. If this at least left the door open to the French plan, it nevertheless seemed clear that an early decision could not be expected—with all that this implied for the increasing consolidation of the existing German frontiers within the occupation framework.

While this sterile series of talks continued, the crisis between France and its three allies, created by the French veto of a central German administration, had reached a dramatic climax by mid-December and had begun to subside. Negotiations had continued at Berlin in the early days of November in an attempt to find some arrangement by which a central administration could be established with French concurrence. No progress was made, however, since the Big Three were unwilling to meet the indispensable French condition, and rumors spread that plans were being worked out to circumvent the French veto. It was suggested that, though the Control Council itself could take no action, the separate commanders-in-chief were able to contract interzonal agreements with each other, and that on this basis a central administration could be established over all zones but the French.

Rumors and hints of this kind failed to move the French. By early December it was clear that official American opinion had hardened in support of a German central administration. On December 5 Secretary of State Byrnes said that the United States was ready to establish trizonal financial and transportation administrations which would exclude the French zone if the French government chose not to participate. He said that he had so informed the French during the recent discussions in Washington.[17] It is not clear what the Russian attitude to this proposal was, but at this point the British government drew back from the American plan and announced, on December 8, that it wanted to maintain four-power control of Germany.[18]

The result of this still obscure chain of events was that France thus obtained at least a reprieve in the development of the German situation as attention shifted to the conference of the three foreign ministers, which opened in Moscow on December 16. Since Germany was formally excluded from the agenda because of the absence of France, the worldwide disagreements of the three powers could not be disguised by a spurious unity of policy against France on German problems. Neither the American nor particularly the British delegation could well disregard the fact, again underlined at Moscow, that the divisions between them and the Soviet Union were far more profound than those which separated them from France and that, in their worldwide competition, of which Germany was only one theater, their antagonist was not France but the Soviet Union.

It is therefore not surprising that less was heard of trizonal administration of Germany after the Moscow conference than before it. Indicating that such plans had been deferred, if not abandoned, the American government decided unilaterally to transfer direct administration of its zone to German civilians by early 1946, and a few days later it was reported that the British were developing similar plans, though no date had been fixed for their implementation. More important, the United States and Britain, with renewed hope of being able to establish a central German administration with France since they could not agree to do so without her, began at last to explore the possibility of offering the French a plan providing for the economic though not the political internationalization of the Ruhr while deferring any decision on the French proposals for the Rhineland.

The future was, in fact, to develop on these lines, but in late 1945 de Gaulle probably had come to the conclusion that the Big Three would not be able to unite against France in Germany and would eventually have to come to terms with her. He therefore remained firmly committed to political as well as economic internationalization of the Ruhr for, as *Le Monde*, stated: "It is observed . . . at Paris that the economic internationalization of the Ruhr is entirely in line with the French projects. The maintenance of German sovereignty over this region nevertheless continues to be considered unacceptable. As long as German officials send orders to Cologne or Essen, it is much to be feared that the measures of economic internationalization will remain illusory." Again, on the 21st, *Le Monde* urged: "Only monetary and customs frontiers between the

Ruhr and Germany would assure an effective control. It is then necessary to envisage a permanent military occupation which will permit imposing Allied decisions and making them respected. . . ."[19] These views were pressed on Byrnes and Bevin by Ambassador Catroux in Moscow, without definite result. But in any case the issue increasingly became one for negotiation between France and the two Western Allies, if not of four-power discussion, and the possibility of a trizonal arrangement excluding France seems by the end of 1945 to have been abandoned. Meanwhile, unilateral developments continued. The British, on December 21, confiscated without compensation the heavy industry and coal mines of the Ruhr. Four days later, the French military government followed this example by proclaiming the sequestration of the mines of the Saar, which was carried out on January 3, 1946.

By the beginning of 1946 the French government had presented its plans for the Ruhr and the Rhineland to each of the Big Three in turn, without notable results. But the urgency with which the United States and Great Britain had attempted to establish an all-German administration during the last months of 1945 was disappearing, and though the Moscow conference made detailed provision for the resumption of negotiations on the satellite peace treaties, nothing was done to expedite discussion either of the German occupation or of the final settlement. International attention, which had been focused during much of December on the Moscow conference, shifted in January, not to Germany, but to preparations for the first meeting of the United Nations General Assembly, which convened on January 10 in London. The three major powers continued to study the French proposals on the Ruhr and Rhineland, and it was reported on January 11 that Couve de Murville would begin negotiations on the subject with the foreign ministers of Great

Britain, the United States, the Soviet Union, and China, perhaps during the General Assembly session. Some discussion of the subject seems to have taken place during the week of January 13 but there were no serious negotiations before the resignation of General de Gaulle on January 20.

During the debate on foreign policy which was held in the Constituent Assembly on January 15, 16, and 17, German problems were discussed at some length.[20] In the speech concluding the debate Bidault said that since the three major Allies had decided by their action at Potsdam in regard to the Polish-German frontier that the peace would be a "hard" one, there was no reason why the same policy should not be followed in the West also: ". . . on pain of suicide we cannot accept, at the edge of our threatened territory, that any centralized German power whatever be established. I see no reason why the decision of our Allies, the Soviet Union and Poland, as regards the German menace, is not valid also, in a form whose rigor may be less but whose goals are identical, at our doors."

Making only this general reference to the often repeated French plans for the Rhineland, Bidault put particular emphasis on the Ruhr, which, he insisted, should be treated as a political entity independent of Germany and placed under an international regime which would be political as well as economic— a comment which constituted an answer (and perhaps a bargaining counter) to recent suggestions that the Western Allies might accept some form of international economic control of the Ruhr but without any special political regime. The states most directly interested in the Ruhr, Bidault said, should participate in choosing its governing personnel; other interested powers would participate in its control in some other manner. The population would be permitted to select local administrations and in time might take part in the government of the entire

Ruhr area. The mines and most important industries of the latter would be managed "in the international interest" by "enterprises of international public utility."

In addition, and for the first time in a parliamentary address, Bidault spoke of a special regime for the Saar. Its mines, he said, should pass to France and, as a corollary to this, the territory itself should be included in the French customs and monetary frontiers and French forces should be stationed permanently there to guarantee this regime. This detailed discussion of the Ruhr and particularly of the Saar, apart from the Rhineland, indicates that the foreign minister was already sceptical of the possibility of acceptance of the French plan for the Rhineland, if not for the Ruhr as well, by the Allies who held most of the territory in question. He was preparing to secure at least minimal economic satisfaction by open or disguised annexation of the Saar, which was in French hands. The policy of a special French regime in the Saar had not been officially presented prior to this debate in January, 1946, and although it matured only later in that year, its foundations probably lie in the period of the serious and apparently unsuccessful presentation of the French policy for the Ruhr and Rhineland to the other occupying powers. The increasing importance which the Saar was assuming in French calculations was indicated by the frequent references to it in other speeches made during the debate, and the unanimous demand for a special regime there which would bind the territory closely to France.[21]

The main interest of the debate, apart from these signs of changing policy in Bidault's speech, lay in the statements of the party positions on Germany made by the successive orators. While the M. R. P. members of the assembly who discussed Germany naturally supported the policies of the government, it was remarkable that the main Communist spokesman, Florimond Bonte, who of course agreed with the rather indefinite public Soviet position on the subject, and conservative traditional nationalists, such as Louis Marin and Jules Ramarony, used a strikingly similar vocabulary and tone in their advocacy of the same policy or, indeed, even more rigorous treatment of Germany than the government was pursuing. In contrast to the entente on this subject of the extremes of the chamber, and to the more measured attachment of the M. R. P. to the same position, all of the Socialist speakers openly took exception to the annexation, open or disguised, of German territory, or the dismemberment of that country, and advocated instead control of German industry and re-education of the German people. This division among the parties was thus the same as it had been during the foreign policy debate of November, 1944, and the discussion in the spring of 1945 which preceded the San Francisco conference. On both occasions the Socialists also stood apart from the nationalistic position adopted by both the Communists and the right, among others.

The importance of this division among the political parties, and even the new emphases contained in Bidault's exposition of the government's policy, remained muted while de Gaulle kept control of French foreign policy. But it was already clear by early 1946 that the deterioration of the relations between East and West, in which the future of Germany was a key factor, could not fail in due course to force a change in France's German policy. The assembly debate reflected the long-held positions of the parties rather than these developments, but Bidault was surely not alone in concluding that de Gaulle's persistence in seeking the political detachment of the Rhineland and the Ruhr was less and less likely to be successful.

CHAPTER XII

THE END OF THE DE GAULLE GOVERNMENT

The long political crisis of November, 1945, had ended to the general satisfaction in the sense that a government, headed by de Gaulle and including all of the major parties, had finally been formed and accepted by the Constituent Assembly. But it was clear both to de Gaulle and to the parties that his position was basically far weaker, now that he faced an elected assembly, than it had been earlier. It was obvious also that the issues underlying the crisis had only been pushed beneath the surface rather than solved. The conflict between de Gaulle's concept of the presidential office and the principle (supported by the Communists and others) of an omnipotent assembly, despite the apparent mandate given to de Gaulle by the results of the second question of the referendum, would certainly break out again in the drafting of the new constitution—the primary task of the assembly. The desire of the Communists to govern with only the Socialists as partners—or at most in a revived Popular Front—was also not ended by their temporary setback; nor was the dilemma of the Socialists, who did not want to break with either the Communists or the M. R. P. and who dreaded the day when such a choice might become inevitable. The

M. R. P., for its part, had loyally supported de Gaulle in the crisis but undoubtedly foresaw a new crisis when it might be forced to abandon him or to permit the Communists and Socialists to take power alone. In addition, the three principal parties were also divided on important issues of foreign policy. Finally, the eyes of all parties were fixed on the new elections which would be held no later than June, so that pre-electoral calculations entered into play even before the government was established in November.

The forty-two-member Constitutional Commission which had been established by the assembly provided the principal forum for political activity and rivalry during December. Though the M. R. P. and the Socialists voted together against the Communists on a number of issues, the latter two parties tended to a closer and closer rapprochement in the commission by voting not to give any substantial power to the proposed second house of the legislature, the Council of the Republic, and, most significantly, to adopt provisions by which the future National Assembly rather than the president of the Republic would name the premier, and the President himself would be ineligible for re-election.[1] In addition to these blows to de Gaulle's constitutional desires, the prestige and position of his government were being undermined on several other fronts during December. France's exclusion from the Moscow conference cast a serious shadow on de Gaulle's foreign policy. At home, the threatened strike of public employees in mid-December; the premature ending of bread rationing on November 1 and its reimposition on December 28; and the devaluation of the franc on December 26, all helped to create an atmosphere of malaise and crisis.[2]

The Communist-Socialist rapprochement was glaringly illustrated in the assembly on January 1, 1946, during consideration of the military budget, for which the government had requested

125 billion francs. The Socialists suddenly moved that this be reduced by 20 percent, and the Communists, who feared being outmaneuvered on a popular political issue, at once supported the motion, although the government's figure was at first defended by Charles Tillon, the Communist minister of armaments. The merits of so large a military budget were no doubt questionable at a moment when economic reconstruction seemed to many to be France's paramount task, but those who attacked it were well aware of the importance of the army to de Gaulle and his foreign policy. The question was therefore more political than strictly budgetary or economic, and Vincent Auriol strongly protested this action by his own Socialist colleagues which seemed to call into question the very life of the government. In the afternoon, de Gaulle himself appeared and strongly supported the original figure. In addition, he took the occasion to denounce a system of government by assembly which could thus lightly attempt to overturn the government's considered wishes. The Socialists for a time remained adamant and the Communists stood beside them, but in the end a compromise reduction of 5 percent was accepted by all sides and the military budget was passed, after which the assembly adjourned until January 15.[3]

The debate gave de Gaulle clear warning that behind the façade of unanimous agreement in the cabinet the parties which the ministers represented did not feel themselves committed to support the government's measures when there was political advantage to be gained by deserting it. Each party was pursuing its own policies and attempting to enjoy at the same time the benefits of participation in and opposition to the government. In addition, the Socialist-Communist entente, already re-initiated on the constitutional issue, had been manifested in the assembly in a way which asserted the intention of both parties to put into immediate practice as well as into the constitution their opposition to an independent executive. It can hardly be doubted that de Gaulle, at least from the first day of 1946, had serious doubts as to both his ability to lead the type of government for which he had seemed to lay the base in the October referendum and the November crisis and the possibility of establishing such a system in the new constitution, in which the Communists and Socialists were emptying the presidency—to which everyone expected him to be elected—of all political content. These problems were surely uppermost in his mind when on January 4 he left for a short vacation at Antibes.

During the next weeks the parties continued their round of political activity against a background of increasing popular discontent with the economic situation, the food crisis, and, in general, with those governing the country.[4] The M. R. P., meeting on January 12 to consider what was described as the current political crisis, announced its opposition to the "government by assembly" toward which the Communists and Socialists were moving and stated that if this were incorporated in the constitution the M. R. P. would oppose its ratification. It was thus in an extremely strained political atmosphere that de Gaulle returned to Paris on January 14.

When the Communist-Socialist entente committee met on January 18, it was clear that relations between the two parties were continuing to improve, including their cooperation in the Constitutional Commission—as the M. R. P. declaration had evidenced. The Socialists rejected the idea of drawing up a common constitutional text with the Communists, but their fear of being driven into an anti-Communist camp was such that they had practically ruled out the possibility of opposing the Communists on the constitution, despite the M. R. P. warning. They therefore apparently agreed with the Communists that the constitution should provide for a fully sovereign assembly—and an honorary president. The next day Jacques Duclos explained that although the Communists had not been able to establish a two-party government with the Socialists in November, the changed attitude of the Socialists now gave reason to believe that a new government formula—that is, a two-party coalition—could well be envisaged, though perhaps only after the next elections.[5]

On Saturday, January 19, de Gaulle informed the cabinet that a special meeting would be held at noon on the following day. He there announced his irrevocable decision to resign the presidency.[6] "The ministers seemed more saddened than surprised. Not one of them uttered a word, either to ask me to reconsider my decision or even to say that he regretted it. After having said goodby, I returned to my home. . . ."[7]

In the letter of resignation he sent to assembly president Gouin, de Gaulle said that he had intended to resign after the elections but had remained in office during the period of transition. That period had now ended; France was no longer in a state of alarm; life had been resumed; abroad, despite certain doubts, her independence was firmly established; she held the Rhine and was in the first rank of the international organization. As a consequence, de Gaulle stated that his work had been accomplished.[8] The inaccuracy in almost every respect of this picture of the condition of France and the inadequacy of the reasons advanced by de Gaulle to account for his abrupt resignation convinced no one, but the exact occasion for it was—and remains—somewhat uncertain. It was already clear from the debate of January 1 as well as from the work of the Constitutional Commission that the Socialists and Communists were coalescing against both his government and his ideas of an independent executive. In his statement to the assembly on that day de Gaulle said that he was probably speaking there for the last time, and he says in his memoirs that he had concluded, on leaving the debate, that he would resign, in order to leave "morally intact."[9] But at Antibes, on January 9, he had stated in reply to a question from a journalist that he might go to London to participate in the work of the United Nations.[10] Unless this was a maneuver of deception, it indicates that he had not at that time reached the decision to resign, or at any rate fixed the date to do so. Perhaps the results of the meeting of the Communist-Socialist entente committee on the 18th and the conclusions drawn from that meeting by Duclos on the following morning finally convinced de Gaulle that he could remain in office only as the captive of the Communist-Socialist majority in the Assembly—for him an intolerable situation.[11]

Possibly he hoped, on the basis of his success in November, that the M. R. P. would remain faithful to him and thereby force the Socialists, with or without the Communists, to re-elect him on his own terms, which this time would include an agreement on the constitution. More probably he expected the M. R. P. to follow him into opposition and to form the nucleus of the group which he would lead against the Communist-Socialist constitution, as a prelude to his own return to power. In either case these expectations were disappointed at once, when it became clear that the parties would make no attempt to re-elect de Gaulle and that the M. R. P. would remain in the majority. But it cannot be doubted that de Gaulle was convinced that the parties could not long maintain themselves without him and that he would eventually return to office as, once again, the indispensable arbiter among quarreling factions and the supreme custodian of France's interests before the world.

CHAPTER XIII

THE BALANCE SHEET AND LEGACY OF De GAULLE'S FOREIGN POLICY

The catastrophe which overwhelmed France in the spring of 1940 suddenly revealed to the French people and to the world the full extent and results of the inadequacy of the nation's military establishment, the decline of its diplomatic position which had been in progress at least since 1925, and the industrial and demographic weakness which had made France of second rank to Germany on the continent since 1870. The very swiftness with which the artificial hegemony established by France in the peace treaties of 1919 had crumbled away posed the question of the country's place in the twentieth century with brutal urgency. But even before the military defeat, this problem had been understood by many Frenchmen and, in particular, by those who in their varying manners during the 1930's resigned themselves to France's loss of the independence of initiative and action which define a Great Power. The positions they had adopted during the last years of peace foreshadowed the attitudes which many assumed after the defeat. Apart from the mere opportunists and adventurers, the appeasers of the 1930's who became the Vichyites of the 1940's accepted the inevitability of German ascendancy in Europe and concluded that it would be better for France to play the role of a brilliant second within the New Order than to resist it in vain; better, as one of them wrote, to exert the civilizing influence of Athens on the German "Rome" than to be bypassed by history.[1] But even many of the anti-Munich men despaired of France's continuing to play a truly independent role in Europe. For them, too, she was doomed to the second rank, but it was democratic Britain in whose wake they chose to follow.

In disagreement with both of these groups were traditional nationalists for whom the formal political independence of France was meaningless without real independence as a Great Power. Charles de Gaulle was not alone in holding this view in 1940, though the number who did so was small. But by the play of circumstances it was he, from his position as a junior minister, who not only refused both the capitulation and the role of a British auxiliary but moved to implement his ideas by the creation of Free France. His actions expressed his reflexive nationalism, but the form his undertaking assumed was guided by the basic conviction that France could not exist as herself without the grandeur of a role of the first rank. He saw that she could not even maintain internal harmony against the "ferments of dispersion" of her people without holding such a rank and participating in "vast enterprises" on the basis of it. These views defined the rationale of Free France, whose aim was to restore France not only as an independent nation but as a Great Power; after the war they were the basis both of de Gaulle's foreign policy and of the domestic policies which in large part grew out of them.

The Allies on whom Free France was dependent were far from accepting or even clearly grasping this essential aspect of de Gaulle's policy, and the endless irritations which poisoned his relations with Great Britain and the United States during the war derived from their refusal to concede the equality of position on which de Gaulle, in glaring contradiction to his material resources, insisted. To Britain and the United States, France had been defeated and thereby eliminated, perhaps permanently, from their councils. For de Gaulle, on the other hand, the French defeat was only a temporary incident in a war which had begun in 1914 and in which France was and remained a major participant. The stubbornness with which de Gaulle promoted this view did not improve his relations with the Allies, but it had at least two consequences of the first importance. First, his attitude toward the Allies was one of the factors which won for him the allegiance of the French resistance and made possible his triumph at Algiers and the eventual establishment of his government in France itself. It seems probable, from the circumstances of the French resistance, that if there had been no generally accepted French authority to assume power after the liberation, and the Allies had instead set up a military government or a group of prewar politicians, the eventual beneficiaries of the French popular reaction to such an imposed regime would have been the Communists. De Gaulle's presence in July, 1944, deprived them of an opportunity to exploit an insurrectionary situation, and during his seventeen months of more or less personal government the other political organizations were able to gather sufficient strength and resolution to contain the Communist drive for power. This is not to say that France, occupied as it was by Allied armies, would necessarily in de Gaulle's absence have become a Communist state. But, nevertheless, his wartime policy and attitude in this respect clearly served both France and what was soon to become the Western cause.

At the same time, it is inconceivable that France would have been accepted, as early as October, 1944, as a permanent member of the United Nations Security Council, with all which this implied about her rank in the world, if there had been no wartime French organization pressing the claims of France as the Gaullists pressed them. It is possible that the British desire for a bulwark in Western Europe against Soviet expansionism would in time have helped to raise France to a significant position. But it is difficult to see how this could have taken place as soon as it did without the wartime existence and activity of the Free French; their skillful propaganda made France's re-emergence seem more normal and natural than the crushing defeat of 1940 and her material position after the war might have indicated.

De Gaulle thus established orderly government in France and won at least formal if not effective recognition of her Great Power status. These achievements, directly rooted in his wartime action, were, as it turned out, the most important he would obtain before leaving office in early 1946. An increasing frustration and sadness fall across his seventeen month rule in France.

The principal problem in foreign policy before the Provisional French Government after the liberation was to perfect its still nominal position as a Great Power and implement it in regard to the German settlement and otherwise. The question whether liberated France was wise to seek to resume her Great Power status was in fact irrelevant by the autumn of 1944, for it had already been conceded in form by the Allies themselves. The question, indeed, can hardly be asked at all in the sense that France had a real option either to seek or refuse to seek such a role. The war had seen the establishment of a Great Power directory, and it seemed increasingly clear that the Great Powers would dominate the peace as well. The only choices before the French, therefore, were to attempt to join the Great Powers or to cultivate their garden and leave decision-making to others. Few states would accept the latter alternative if the former seemed open; and the Great Powers themselves, by the autumn of 1944, had already opened it so far to France as to make practically inevitable her determination to secure full and final admission to their ranks.

One corollary of this was that the French government, despite its exclusion from Yalta, Potsdam, and Moscow, was obliged to maintain its claims with a stubbornness which, following its own wartime experience, it hoped would finally achieve the desired result. The incessant official talk of French equality of rights and greatness—the famous "policy of grandeur"—was irritating to many outside France who saw only her material weakness. But de Gaulle knew better than his critics the value of constantly reiterated propaganda, which had already won him so much and had given him a base from which to demand more in a way which the Allies, having gone thus far, could not, and finally did not, deny. Despite the failure of the de Gaulle regime—marked by its exclusion from the Moscow conference—to achieve its primary foreign policy goal, the claims pressed by it during 1945 contributed directly to the inclusion of France among the powers at the conference of foreign ministers in April, 1946, and, indeed, to the presence thereafter of France among the Big Four, including the summit meetings of 1955 and 1960.

France's decision to base her policy on recovery of her Great Power position made the often proposed suggestion that she lead the smaller, excluded states against the directory of the major powers highly unrealistic, since success in her most important goal—already half-achieved—depended in the end on the goodwill or acquiescence of the Great Powers. If the French government had indeed seriously considered playing such a role—as its proposed amendments to the Dumbarton Oaks draft suggest—it definitely abandoned the idea when it was invited to join the four host powers in the substantive work of the San Francisco conference. Though this inclusion was soon seen to be less permanent than the French had hoped, they remained firm thereafter in their policy of identifying themselves in principle with the major powers and of accepting in practice what was granted to them, while pressing for more.

As a third consequence of its decision to continue the wartime effort to restore France to her formal pre-war rank—and in fact to an independence which she had not fully exercised since the 1920's—the Gaullist regime inevitably tried to justify its claims to Great Power status. Military and economic strength were obviously lacking in 1944 and 1945, and historical claims, while of some value to France, were hardly adequate. There thus emerged before the end of 1944 the idea that the mission of France was to serve as a bridge among the Great Powers, linked to all and committed to none. Such a policy had several advantages for the French government. It held out the hope to each of the powers that France would offer it support in its contests with the others, thereby strengthening her claim to admission to their councils; it permitted her at the same time to clothe herself in the role of peacemaker; and, finally, it responded perfectly to the exigencies of a domestic political coalition which ran from the Communists through the nationalist right. The date of the origin of this policy—late 1944—suggests that its roots lay more in foreign than domestic politics, but it was entirely suitable to domestic problems as they developed during 1945. Whatever inclination the Catholic M. R. P. and the Socialists may have felt for the West (particularly, in the case of the Socialists, after the Labour victory in Great Britain), de Gaulle himself, after his bitter wartime experiences with the Western powers, was probably no more drawn to them politically than to the U.S.S.R. itself. His first major act of foreign policy had been to conclude a treaty with the Soviet Union in order to liberate himself diplomatically from dependence on the Americans and British and raise France's value in their eyes, and his independent nationalism did not admit of French dependence on any power. It is notable also that, whatever degree of wishful thinking lay behind the French assumption of disunion among the major Allies, the basing of France's policy of "neutrality" and "balance" on this assumption indicated a considerable degree of prescience and realism among the French policymakers at a time when such ideas were far indeed from being common in the United States or even in Great Britain.

De Gaulle's achievement in making possible France's restoration to her Great Power status so soon after the disaster of 1940, and thereby reviving as far as was possible French self-confidence and national pride after the defeat and the ugly blot of Vichy, seems to this writer to outweigh, in appraising the significance of his work, the errors or miscalculations which he made. Yet there were a number of such errors in both domestic and foreign policy. At home, the most basic of these was in the area of fiscal and economic policy, in which he had no real interest at all. A second, perhaps, was his unwillingness to share power with the parties and his withdrawal from office in 1946. A case can be made (more persuasive since 1958 than earlier) to the effect that he did well—for himself and for France—by refusing to "play politics" and rejecting the parties, their constitution, and their system. Would the type of regime he wanted to establish in 1946, and did in fact establish in 1958, have provided the broad constitutional synthesis which has been so painfully lacking in France, more adequately than the system set up by the parties in the constitution of the Fourth Republic? Might a compromise between them have made possible a regime more satisfactory than either of the others? But was such a compromise possible in 1946?

In the conduct of foreign affairs, de Gaulle's most disastrous mistake was in the Levant. The crisis in the Levant was caused by the French refusal to accept the liquidation of their colonial position, which the defeat and the circumstances of the reoccupation of the area in 1941 had made inevitable. By attempting to secure, against the wishes of the local population, a position similar to that enjoyed by the British in Iraq, the French government found itself obliged to attempt to hold Syria and Lebanon by force, at a moment when its material power in the area was inadequate to the task and its political and moral positions were even more vulnerable. Though French complaints against British intrigue may have been largely justified, and the British military intervention in itself was singularly brutal, it was too late by 1945 to undo the damage done to the French position throughout the mandate, and particularly since 1940. The attempt to remedy the situation by the methods of 1925 bequeathed an evil example which the Fourth Republic followed with few exceptions in dealing with colonial problems and, indeed, finally perished of—to de Gaulle's own advantage, ironically—in 1958.

A second, though less clear-cut or avoidable error was made in Germany, where the French policy of forming separate states in the Ruhr and the Rhineland was remarkably similar to that of 1919. The French were on logical ground in one sense in protesting the acceptance by the Western Allies of unilateral Soviet actions in eastern Germany and the denial of similar security measures to France. But in this case the French did not follow through on their own predictions of Great Power discord, which implied a struggle in Germany for the allegiance of the German people—already begun, at least by the Russians, in the summer of 1945. Their predictions also implied a Western policy which, sooner rather than later, would seek to make Germany economically viable, not only, as at first, to relieve the burden on the Western Allies but to win the support of the German population for the West. This factor was not explicit in the policy of Washington and London by the end of 1945, but it was implicit, as has been said, in the French analysis of the international situation, and it doomed French policy in Germany to disappointment.

At the same time, the French attitude had one consequence whose importance is evident but whose exact significance is difficult to judge. By vetoing the establishment of a central German administration at a moment when the three other occupying powers, for varying reasons, had agreed to set one up, the French in effect ensured the division of Germany, although such a result was neither foreseen nor explicitly desired by them. But it is unclear what would have followed their acceptance of the plan pressed on them. They themselves believed apparently that an all-German government or administration established at Berlin would soon fall under Soviet domination. If this would have been the case, then the French unknowingly saved Europe and the Western world from an initial defeat in the East-West contest from which neither might have recovered. On the other hand, a coalition German government at Berlin, even including Communists, might conceivably have evolved in the direction of that at Vienna and ended with a unified and democratic or non-Communist regime, albeit perhaps neutralized, between East and West. But this is a historical "might-have-been" without a clear answer, and French policy in 1945 had no such considerations in mind.

Consideration of de Gaulle's policy toward Germany, apparently so anachronistic and unsuccessful at first glance, brings us, however, to a complex of ideas which have underlain much of French foreign policy since 1945. In addition to demanding the separation of the Ruhr and the Rhineland from Germany, the de Gaulle government proposed that these areas be included in some kind of Western European organization which would include France, the Low Countries, and perhaps Great Britain. De Gaulle, who spoke of Western Europe as a natural unit, no doubt saw France as the leader of such a group—to him, perhaps, the idea was only camouflage for French hegemony in Western Europe and a concomitant strengthening of France's claims to Great Power status. Others who looked forward to a European grouping which could serve as a link and balance between East and West believed that France, in her weakened condition, would have to share leadership in it with Great Britain. But in both cases the "idea of Europe" as it first appeared in 1945 merged with a second idea, also well developed by nearly all French political groups in 1944-1945, of France as a balancing, independent force between East and West. Both concepts were closely tied at their origin to the idea of independence from the super-powers.

De Gaulle himself accomplished nothing on this line during his tenure of power. But the ideas put forward by him and others in 1945 continued to animate French foreign policy, and finally became concrete, after Britain's decision in 1950 to hold aloof from the continent, in the attempt to build an integrated Western Europe on a Franco-German basis. In other hands the idea of Western European unity has assumed forms which de Gaulle, the first major French leader to express the idea, has repudiated. In particular, he has always rejected the notion of derogations of national sovereignty to the advantage of "supra-national" structures. But for his successors, as for himself, the policy of Western European unity, however variously defined, can hardly be understood without considering its relationship, in various combinations and forms, to the three goals that de Gaulle pursued with such tenacity: the independence of France, its function as a link or balance between East and West, and above all its restoration by whatever means to its rank and status as a Great Power.

SELECTED BIBLIOGRAPHY

Aron, Robert. *Histoire de la Libération de France.* Paris: Librairie Arthème Fayard, 1959.

Balfour, Michael, and John Mair. *Four-Power Control in Germany and Austria, 1945–1946.* Survey of International Affairs, 1939–1946. London: Oxford University Press, 1956.

Bieber, Konrad F. *L'Allemagne Vue Par les Ecrivains de la Résistance Française.* Geneva: Librairie E. Droz, 1954.

Byrnes, James F. *Speaking Frankly.* New York: Harper & Brothers, 1947.

Catroux, Georges. *J'ai vu tomber le Rideau de Fer.* Paris: Hachette, 1952.

Churchill, Winston S. *The Second World War.* 6 vols. Boston: Houghton Mifflin, 1948–1953.

Clay, Lucius D. *Decision in Germany.* New York: Doubleday, 1950.

Craig, Gordon A., and Felix Gilbert (eds.). *The Diplomats, 1919–1939.* Princeton: Princeton University Press, 1953.

De Gaulle, Charles. *Discours et Messages 1940–1946.* Paris: Editions Berger-Levrault, 1946.

————. *Mémoires de Guerre.* Vol. I: *L'Appel, 1940–1942.* Vol. II: *L'Unité, 1942–1944.* Vol. III: *Le Salut, 1944–1946.* Paris: Librairie Plon, 1954–1959.

————. *The Army of the Future.* Philadelphia: J. B. Lippincott, 1941.

De Lattre de Tassigny, Jean. *Histoire de la Premiere Armée Française*. Paris: Librairie Plon, 1949.

Documents Français Relatifs à l'Allemagne. Paris: Imprimerie Nationale, 1947.

Documents of the United Nations Conference on International Organization: San Francisco, 1945. 12 vols. London and New York: United Nations Information Organizations, 1945.

Eden, Anthony. *The Reckoning*. Boston: Houghton Mifflin, 1965.

Elgey, Georgette. *La République des Illusions 1945–1951*. Paris: Fayard, 1965.

Les Entretiens de Gaulle-Staline. Paris: Recherches internationales à la lumière du marxisme, 1959.

Feis, Herbert. *Between War and Peace: The Potsdam Conference*. Princeton: Princeton University Press, 1960.

———. *Churchill, Roosevelt, Stalin*. Princeton: Princeton University Press, 1957.

Foreign Relations of the United States: Diplomatic Papers: The Conferences at Malta and Yalta, 1945. Washington, D.C.: U.S. Government Printing Office, 1955.

Foreign Relations of the United States: Diplomatic Papers: The Conference of Berlin (The Potsdam Conference), 1945. 2 vols. Washington, D.C.: U.S. Government Printing Office, 1960.

Foreign Relations of the United States: Diplomatic Papers: The Conferences at Cairo and Teheran, 1943. Washington, D.C.: U.S. Government Printing Office, 1961.

Foreign Relations of the United States: Diplomatic Papers, 1943. Vol. II: *Europe*. Washington, D.C.: U.S. Government Printing Office, 1964.

Foreign Relations of the United States: Diplomatic Papers, 1944.

Vol. III: *The British Commonwealth and Europe*. Washington, D.C.: U.S. Government Printing Office, 1965.

Funk, Arthur Layton. *Charles de Gaulle: The Crucial Years, 1943–1944*. Norman, Okla.: University of Oklahoma Press, 1959.

Grosser, Alfred. *La IVe République et sa politique étrangère*. Paris: Librairie Armand Colin, 1961.

Journal Officiel de la République Française. Débats de l'Assemblée Consultative Provisoire. November–December, 1944; February–March, 1945; June, 1945.

Journal Officiel de la République Française. Débats de l'Assemblée Nationale Constituante. November, 1945; January, 1946.

Kirk, George. *The Middle East in the War*. Survey of International Affairs, 1939–1946. London: Oxford University Press, 1952.

Lipschits, Isaac. *La Politique de la France au Levant, 1939–1941*. Paris: Editions A. Pedone, 1963.

McNeill, William Hardy. *America, Britain and Russia: Their Cooperation and Conflict, 1941–1946*. Survey of International Affairs, 1939–1946. London: Oxford University Press, 1953.

Michel, Henri, and Mirkine-Guetzevitch, Boris. *Les Idées Politiques et Sociales de la Résistance*. Paris: Presses Universitaires de France, 1954.

Le Monde (Paris). December 10, 1944–January 22, 1946.

Mosely, Philip E. "Dismemberment of Germany," *Foreign Affairs*, 28 (April, 1950), 486–498.

―――. "The Occupation of Germany: New Light on How the Zones Were Drawn," *Foreign Affairs*, 28 (July, 1950), 580–604.

Murphy, Robert. *Diplomat Among Warriors*. New York: Doubleday, 1964.

Ruhm von Oppen, Beate (ed.). *Documents on Germany under Occupation, 1945-1954.* Royal Institute of International Affairs. London: Oxford University Press, 1955.

Russell, Ruth B. *A History of the United Nations Charter.* Washington, D.C.: Brookings Institution, 1958.

Selected Documents on Germany and the Question of Berlin, 1944-1961. Command 1552. London: Her Majesty's Stationery Office, 1961.

Sherwood, Robert E. *Roosevelt and Hopkins.* 2 vols. Revised ed. New York: Harper & Brothers, 1950.

Siegfried, André, Roger Seydoux, and Edouard Bonnefous (eds.). *L'Année Politique, 1944-1945.* Paris: Editions Le Grand Siècle, 1946.

Stettinius, Edward R. *Roosevelt and the Russians.* Edited by Walter Johnson. New York: Doubleday, 1949.

Toynbee, Arnold (ed.). *Hitler's Europe.* Survey of International Affairs, 1939-1946. London: Oxford University Press, 1954.

Truman, Harry S. *Year of Decisions.* New York: Doubleday, 1955.

Viorst, Milton. *Hostile Allies.* New York: Macmillan, 1965.

White, Dorothy Shipley. *Seeds of Discord.* Syracuse: Syracuse University Press, 1964.

Willis, F. Roy. *The French in Germany, 1945-1949.* Stanford: Stanford University Press, 1962.

NOTES

PREFACE

1. See Arthur Layton Funk, *Charles de Gaulle: The Crucial Years, 1943–1944* (Norman, Okla., 1959); Dorothy Shipley White, *Seeds of Discord: De Gaulle, Free France and the Allies* (Syracuse, N. Y., 1964); and Milton Viorst, *Hostile Allies: FDR and Charles de Gaulle* (New York, 1965).

CHAPTER I: Introduction: The Decay of French Foreign Policy

1. Jules Cambon, "The Permanent Bases of French Foreign Policy," *Foreign Affairs*, 8 (January, 1930), 173–185.
2. Richard A. Challener, "The French Foreign Office: The Era of Philippe Berthelot," *The Diplomats, 1919–1939*, ed. Gordon A. Craig and Felix Gilbert (Princeton, 1953), pp. 49–85.
3. Irving M. Gibson, "The Maginot Line," *Journal of Modern History*, 17 (June, 1945), 130–146.
4. Elizabeth R. Cameron, "Alexis Saint-Léger Léger," *The Diplomats*, pp. 378–405.
5. D. W. Brogan, "The Problem of *Union Sacrée* in France," *International Affairs*, 20 (January, 1944), 103–108.

CHAPTER II: Free France and the Resistance

1. De Gaulle later said that "we had to make, in the night, at least three acts of faith." These were: that Britain would fight on, that the United States and the Soviet Union would eventually enter the war, and that the French people would not accept the defeat (Charles de Gaulle, *Mémoires de Guerre*, I: *L'Appel, 1940–1942* [Paris, 1954], p. 674). Translations of French texts are my own unless otherwise noted.

2. *Ibid.*, p. 1.

3. These (and subsequent) quotations from *Vers L'Armée de Métier* are from the American edition of the book, *The Army of the Future* (Philadelphia, 1941), pp. 15–18, 22.

4. *Ibid.*, pp. 30–31.

5. *Ibid.*, p. 82.

6. *Ibid.*, p. 37. Because of the special defensive needs of France, because of her numerical inferiority to her most probable opponent, and because he believed that the day of the nation in arms had gone by, de Gaulle advocated a highly mechanized, highly mobile professional army. Events were to confirm at least half of his forecast: mechanization and mobility were, in fact, to be the keys to the Second World War. But warfare, far from being carried on by small professional armies, was to involve a much greater degree of national mobilization and more nearly unlimited objectives than before.

7. *L'Appel*, p. 69. Writing privately in 1942 of the possibility that the Free French might have played a purely military role, de Gaulle said: "It is this which the imperialists of Washington and London and the good apostles of Vichy both recommended to us. It would have meant a few more French corpses on the fields of battle without doing anything for France" (*ibid.*, p. 609).

8. As a further argument to the same end he elaborated the theory of the "Thirty Years' War," according to which the war which began in 1914 was still in progress and the contributions made by France in the first act of the drama (1914–1918), as well as the second, should weigh heavily in the final settlement (*ibid.*, pp. 478, 566, 631, 673). De Gaulle explained this position eloquently in a letter to Roosevelt, October 26, 1942 (Charles de Gaulle, *Mémoires de Guerre*, II: *L'Unité, 1942–1944* [Paris, 1956], pp. 381–385).

9. *L'Appel*, p. 67.

10. At the moment of the French surrender, he says, "Mr. Churchill appeared imperturbable, full of resilience . . . already seized, and perhaps not without an obscure satisfaction, by the terrible and magnificent perspective of an England left alone in her island which he himself would have to lead through trial toward salvation" (*ibid.*, p. 54).

11. *Ibid.*, p. 70. When Eden said to de Gaulle in May, 1943, that he had caused the British more trouble than all the other European allies, de Gaulle said, "I do not doubt it. France is a great power" (*L'Unité*, p. 102).

12. Churchill was aware of this motive of de Gaulle's actions (Winston S. Churchill, *Their Finest Hour* [Boston, 1949], p. 509).

13. *L'Appel*, pp. 111, 209.

14. *Ibid.*, pp. 38–39.

15. One of those whom de Gaulle cites in his memoirs as having refused his call was Jean Monnet. The two of them had worked, with

others, in preparing the project for Franco-British union which Churchill had offered to the French cabinet before France surrendered. But Monnet wrote de Gaulle to say that, while he too wanted to carry on the struggle, he thought that a committee formed in London would appear in France to be too dependent on the British (*ibid.*, p. 83). Their paths would cross again, in Algiers three years later, with interesting results.

16. *Ibid.*, pp. 71–73, 74, 79. Arnold Toynbee (ed.), *Hitler's Europe* (London, 1954), p. 439, says 6,000.

17. *L'Appel*, pp. 274, 278–283; *France No. 2 (1940)*, Command 6220 (London, 1940), pp. 2–9; and Winifred N. Hadsel, "Struggle for a New France," *Foreign Policy Reports*, 20 (1944–1945), 101.

18. See, among many examples, de Gaulle's telegrams of May 17, August 9, and September 22, 1941 (*L'Appel*, pp. 409–411, 476–477, and 481–482).

19. *Ibid.*, pp. 194, 545, 506. But for an example of de Gaulle's flexibility, see below, note 25.

20. De Gaulle welcomed the entry of the Soviet Union and the United States into the war because, among other reasons, it "meant for England in her turn the heavy burdens of an alliance with colossi . . ." (*ibid.*, p. 198).

21. Though Churchill, in an open letter to de Gaulle accompanying the agreement of August 7, 1940, had said that the British government was resolved to assure the "full restoration of the independence and greatness of France," he specified in a secret letter that this pledge was not intended as a rigorous guarantee of the French frontiers (*ibid.*, pp. 282–283). See also, *ibid.*, pp. 80, 90, 99, 123, 139–141.

22. *Ibid.*, pp. 145–180; *L'Unité*, pp. 15–33.

23. See, for example, his broadcast of July 8, 1940 (*ibid.*, pp. 275–277).

24. De Gaulle was aware of this early. See his telegram of May 31, 1941 (*ibid.*, pp. 412–413). This development strengthened his determination to restore France to her proper status: "If France fails to play her traditional role as leader of the old continent, this effacement of England, which in spite of her insularity is closely linked to it, was a poor augury for the way in which the affairs of Europe would finally be settled" (*L'Unité*, pp. 3–4).

25. *L'Appel*, p. 181. It is interesting to note the line of argument which de Gaulle used to counter this American policy. On December 27, 1941, he ordered his representative in Cairo to point out to William Bullitt that (1) the American policy of trying to "neutralize" France's overseas possessions by agreement with Vichy tended to destroy the unity of the French Empire and of France and to jeopardize "the very future of our country as a great power"; (2) France must play a Great Power role if it was to provide "an indispensable factor of equilibrium" with the U.S.S.R. in Europe; (3) the discontent of the French people if faced by

the dismemberment of their possessions and Allied refusal to let them participate in the war could only profit "the elements which will try to exploit, for domestic political ends, the successes of the Soviet armies" (*ibid.*, pp. 501–503).

De Gaulle no doubt believed much of this—the importance of there being a prestigious French authority ready to assume power when France was liberated was constantly in his thoughts—but it also indicates that he had worked out very early a policy of promoting France's power claims by showing to each principal ally how a restored France would support its own purposes. In this case de Gaulle assumed, perhaps prematurely, that the American government was already concerned with the postwar shape of Europe and was interested in blocking Soviet expansion. Bullitt, in any case, avoided these grand considerations and confined the discussion to St. Pierre and the Antilles (*ibid.*, pp. 507–508). De Gaulle again pressed this argument in a letter to Roosevelt of October 26, 1942 (*L'Unité*, pp. 381–385). See also his conversation with Archbishop Spellman, March, 1943 (*ibid.*, p. 95). Rebuking Churchill for the deal made with Darlan in November, 1942, de Gaulle said that if the French people thought that the Anglo-Saxons wanted Darlan to be their liberator, the real winner would be Stalin (*ibid.*, p. 404).

26. *L'Appel*, pp. 602–603.

27. Toynbee (ed.), *Hitler's Europe*, pp. 361–363, 463–465; William Hardy McNeill, *America, Britain and Russia: Their Cooperation and Conflict, 1941–1946* (London, 1953), pp. 96–97; and Douglas G. Anglin, *The St. Pierre and Miquelon Affaire of 1941* (Toronto, 1966).

28. *L'Unité*, pp. 360–361.

29. Anthony Eden, *The Reckoning* (Boston, 1965), p. 400.

30. De Gaulle denounced this "sort of new Vichy . . . being reconstituted in North Africa under the thumb of the United States" (*L'Unité*, pp. 399, 406–407). But he correctly foresaw that ". . . in a short time the vomiting will begin and . . . we will appear as the only clean and effective organization" (*ibid.*, p. 396). Churchill, too, seems to have thought that neither Darlan nor Giraud had any long political future (*ibid.*, p. 405). Darlan's assassin, Fernand Bonnier de la Chapelle, "had made himself the instrument of the exasperated anger of the turbulent spirits around him, but behind which, perhaps, there stirred a policy intended to liquidate a 'temporary expedient' after having used it" (*ibid.*, p. 67).

31. Henri Michel, *Histoire de la Résistance* (Paris, 1950); Gabriel A. Almond, "The Resistance and the Political Parties of Western Europe," *Political Science Quarterly*, 63 (March, 1947), 27–39.

32. *L'Unité*, p. 254.

33. Henri Michel and Boris Mirkine-Guetzevitch, *Les Idées Politiques et Sociales de la Résistance* (Paris, 1954).

34. When naming the Socialist and labor leader Adrien Tixier to

be his principal representative in Washington, de Gaulle wrote (in a telegram to René Pleven of September 23, 1941) that "the social problem is the great problem for tomorrow" (*L'Appel*, p. 482; see also pp. 529–533, 632, and 678–680).

35. In two meetings held in early 1944 between a Chatham House group and a number of French officials, scholars, and diplomats, the French advocated a policy for Germany which was very similar to that of much of the resistance, rejecting radical dismemberment and emphasizing control of German industry, both as a security measure and as a prelude to the ultimate organization of all Western European industry under a single international body (T. E. Utley, "French Views on the German Problem," *International Affairs*, 20 (April 1944), 243–249). On the broader subject of the attitude of the resistance toward Germany and the Germans, see Konrad F. Bieber, *L'Allemagne Vue par les Ecrivains de la Résistance Française* (Geneva, 1954).

36. Michel, *Histoire de la Résistance*, pp. 47–48; *L'Unité*, pp. 101, 491–493. After Moulin's capture by the Germans and death in June, de Gaulle had trouble finding a successor sufficiently loyal to him, acceptable to the resistance groups, and yet not associated with any one of them. In September he named Emile Bollaert as his representative in France, but he was soon captured. In March, 1944, he named Alexandre Parodi. The C. N. R., meanwhile, elected Georges Bidault as its head, thus dividing the double function held by Moulin (*ibid.*, pp. 163–166).

37. De Gaulle summarizes his differences with Giraud mordantly in *L'Unité*, pp. 10–11.

38. The resistance denounced the Darlan deal and supported de Gaulle from the beginning of the North African affair. In mid-May, 1943, at the most critical moment of the de Gaulle-Giraud negotiations, the newly established National Resistance Council declared that de Gaulle was the sole chief of the resistance and demanded that he head any provisional government that might be formed. *Ibid.*, pp. 101, 407–408, 475.

39. In a conversation with Sumner Welles on November 12, 1942, André Philip, speaking for de Gaulle, contrasted Giraud's position— "a French general who holds no power from a French authority and who depends exclusively on American military authority"—and that of the Free French, who "had received the adherence of the French internal resistance organizations, which are the only authentic expression of resisting France and which alone are qualified to speak in the name of the people of France" (*ibid.*, p. 400). De Gaulle contemptuously stated his view of what Giraud represented in a private message of May 2, 1943: ". . . the whole affair is being played, not between us and Giraud, who is nothing, but between us and the government of the United States" (*ibid.*, p. 469).

40. "In sum, according to the memoire signed by General Giraud, things would develop as if France, as a state, no longer existed, at least up to the victory. This was exactly the thesis of Roosevelt" (*ibid.*, pp. 97–98).

41. *Ibid.*, pp. 109, 488–490.

42. *Ibid.*, pp. 108, 505–506; *Foreign Relations of the United States: Diplomatic Papers, 1943*, II: *Europe* (Washington, 1964), pp. 156–157, 163–165. Cited hereafter as *Europe*. Of the five members of the original committee, General Georges Catroux, Jean Massigli, and André Philip had been with de Gaulle in London; General Alphonse Georges and Jean Monnet entered as Giraud men. A few days later René Pleven, André Diethelm, and Adrien Tixier were named to the committee by de Gaulle; René Mayer, Jules Abadie, and Maurice Couve de Murville were named by Giraud. Henri Bonnet was named as belonging to neither side but turned out to be a Gaullist (*L'Unité*, pp. 112–113).

Giraud clearly showed his lack of political sophistication in agreeing to the enlargement of the committee, which gave de Gaulle control. He explained to Robert Murphy, General Eisenhower's political adviser, that he had thought the original seven-man group would retain full authority and that Jean Monnet, who advised him to sign the decrees enlarging it, had "betrayed" him. Murphy judged that Monnet had come to agree with de Gaulle that French rights must be "more aggressively asserted in respect of the Allies" (*Europe*, pp. 152–153). See also Robert Murphy, *Diplomat Among Warriors* (New York, 1964), pp. 178–182, for Monnet's key role in bringing about de Gaulle's success.

43. *L'Appel*, pp. 26, 70, 231–232; *L'Unité*, p. 2; *Europe*, pp. 187, 191. See also, above, n. 25.

44. The decree establishing the single president and the responsibility of the commander-in-chief to the C. F. L. N. had been adopted—with Giraud's reluctant concurrence—on October 3 (*L'Unité*, pp. 533–534, 537, 547–548).

45. *Europe*, pp. 152–153, 164, 170, 172–173.

46. In November, 1943, Andrei Vyshinski told de Gaulle that it was the Soviet Union that had taken the initiative for the inclusion of France on the Mediterranean Commission (renamed the Advisory Council for Italy) and that Stalin had said that no European question could be settled without France (*L'Unité*, p. 605). Yet in the same month at Teheran, Stalin and Molotov spoke in most unfavorable terms about both France and the Free French (*Foreign Relations of the United States: Diplomatic Papers: The Conferences at Cairo and Teheran, 1943* [Washington, D.C., 1961], pp. 484–485, 509–510, 514, 568–569, cited hereafter as *The Conferences at Cairo and Teheran*; see also 845–847). Edward Benes commented on his own observation of this cool Russian attitude to de Gaulle in January, 1944 (*L'Unité*, p. 616). De Gaulle, speaking to the Soviet representative in Algiers on April 28, complained

of the difference between Soviet words, in the recognition formula, and Soviet action—or non-action—in regard to French interests (*ibid.*, pp. 634–635).

47. *Europe*, pp. 166–167; *Keesing's Contemporary Archives*, September 4–11, 1943, p. 5971.

48. *The Conferences at Cairo and Teheran*, pp. 310, 345, 485, 872–873; Murphy, *Diplomat Among Warriors*, p. 168; Eden, *The Reckoning*, p. 438; McNeill, *America, Britain and Russia*, p. 320; Herbert Feis, *Churchill, Roosevelt, Stalin* (Princeton, 1957), p. 317. Thus, Roosevelt's emissary in Dakar, Rear-Admiral William A. Glassford, telegraphing the State Department for further instructions in November, 1943, wrote that: "It was intimated to me in no uncertain terms [when he assumed his duties] that Dakar itself should be taken over eventually by the United Nations to be administered by the United States, as a delegate of the United Nations. The French were to move to St. Louis, about one hundred miles to the northward on the coast" (*Europe*, pp. 192–193).

49. Eden, *The Reckoning*, p. 432; *The Conferences at Cairo and Teheran*, p. 256.

50. Eden, *The Reckoning*, pp. 461–462. Roosevelt, at Teheran, indicated that American troops would withdraw from Europe soon after the war (*The Conferences at Cairo and Teheran*, p. 531).

51. Winston S. Churchill, *Closing the Ring* (Boston, 1951), pp. 177–179; *Europe*, p. 171.

52. *The Times* (London), August 27, 1943, p. 3.

53. *Europe*, p. 185.

54. De Gaulle no doubt believed during this period that American hostility to him had never been greater. See, for example, the message sent to him by his representatives in Canada, reporting that Canadian missions throughout the world found their American colleagues "emotional and irrational" on the subject of de Gaulle and the Free French (*L'Unité*, p. 496), and the report from Washington quoting James Dunn of the State Department as saying that the British and American governments could not cooperate in any way whatever with a man so notoriously anti-English and anti-American (*ibid.*, p. 505). De Gaulle believed that, in late August, 1943, "the American and British conspirators," having despaired of Giraud, were trying to bring President Lebrun to North Africa to set against himself (*ibid.*, p. 162). De Gaulle's understanding of the American attitude was by no means inaccurate. Roosevelt repeatedly declared himself "fed up" with de Gaulle, and on at least three occasions in 1943 (in May, June, and December) indicated that the Allies should break with or depose the general (*Europe*, pp. 111–112, 155–157, 196). Churchill seemed ready to agree in May but was deterred by his cabinet (Eden, *The Reckoning*, pp. 447–449). Eden characterized the American attitude to de Gaulle at this time as "hatred" (*ibid.*, p. 457).

55. *L'Unité*, pp. 560–568.

56. *Ibid.*, p. 566.

57. The alert Soviet government inquired of the French representative in Moscow what de Gaulle had in mind in speaking of a grouping of Western European states. It was informed that the committee had no specific project in mind and was engaged in no such negotiations (*ibid.*, pp. 621–622).

58. *Ibid.*, pp. 261–262, 135. Had France been included, wrote de Gaulle, the "fact that . . . an American general was in charge of the North, an English general of the South, might certainly have made us nostalgic for the past but would not have disturbed us as to the present and future. But the Anglo-Saxons never consented to treat us as true allies. They never consulted us, government to government, on any of their arrangements" (*ibid.*, pp. 259–260).

59. Roosevelt indicated on several occasions that he favored a military occupation (*Europe*, pp. 111, 156–157). Eden quoted Admiral Leahy, Roosevelt's personal chief of staff, as having said that Pétain was the most reliable person to whom the Allies should look for help in rallying the French people after the invasion (Eden, *The Reckoning*, p. 519).

60. Anthony Eden shared de Gaulle's opinion on this point (*ibid.*, p. 431).

61. *L'Unité*, pp. 211–227, 606–608, 620, 636–637, 639; McNeill, *America, Britain and Russia*, pp. 420, 426; Feis, *Churchill, Roosevelt, Stalin*, pp. 318–321; Robert Aron, *Histoire de la Libération de France* (Paris, 1959), pp. 62–75.

CHAPTER III: Liberation and War: July–December, 1944

1. *Foreign Relations of the United States: Diplomatic Papers, 1944*, III: *The British Commonwealth and Europe* (Washington, 1965), p. 715. Cited hereafter as *The British Commonwealth and Europe*.

2. *Ibid.*, pp. 716–721.

3. *L'Unité*, pp. 236–241.

4. *Ibid.*, p. 243; *The British Commonwealth and Europe*, pp. 723–724; McNeill, *America, Britain and Russia*, pp. 426–427; Feis, *Churchill, Roosevelt, Stalin*, pp. 321–322.

5. *The Times* (London), August 26, 1944, p. 4.

6. *Department of State Bulletin*, 11 (August 27, 1944), 204–205.

7. *L'Unité*, pp. 277–284, 289–322, 664–666, 670–674; de Gaulle, *Mémoires de Guerre*, III: *Le Salut, 1944–1946* (Paris, 1959), pp. 23–27. De Gaulle was particularly anxious to obtain Paris in order to frustrate power drives by the Communists and by Vichyites or leaders of the Third Republic who might seek—with American support, in de Gaulle's opinion—the re-establishment of a "legal" regime based on the former

parliament. He was eager, in general, that the French confirm their revival as a Great Power and their role in the alliance by taking as large a part in the fighting as possible. He welcomed the prolongation of the war into 1945 because of the opportunities thus given France to fight. The French were able to occupy a considerable area of southwest Germany, seize small areas on the Italian frontier which de Gaulle wanted to annex, and fight against the Japanese in Indochina where, "knowing the ill-will of the Allies, especially the Americans, toward our position in the Far East, I held it to be essential that the conflict not end without our having become, there also, belligerents." De Gaulle was right about the American attitude toward restoring French rule in Indochina. See *Le Salut*, pp. 139, 152–156, 160–163, 163–167; and *The British Commonwealth and Europe*, pp. 769–784.

8. The personal relationship between de Gaulle and Bidault seems to have been very bad and the General's contempt for his minister hardly disguised. See Georgette Elgey, *La République des Illusions, 1945–1951* (Paris, 1965), pp. 39–41, 76.

9. John E. Sawyer, "The Reestablishment of the Republic in France: The de Gaulle Era, 1944–1945," *Political Science Quarterly*, 62 (September 1947), 354–380; André Siegfried, Roger Seydoux, and Edouard Bonnefous, *L'Année Politique 1944–1945* (Paris, 1946), p. 14; *Le Salut*, pp. 9–10.

10. Sawyer, "The Reestablishment of the Republic in France," p. 362. De Gaulle gives Thorez credit for thus rendering "service to the public interest" (*Le Salut*, p. 101). When Thorez died in July 1964, de Gaulle issued this statement: "For my part, I do not forget that at a decisive moment for France president Maurice Thorez—whatever his actions may have been before and after—contributed, in answer to my call and as a member of my government, to the maintenance of national unity" (*Le Monde*, July 15, 1964, p. 4).

11. *The British Commonwealth and Europe*, pp. 733–748.

12. *Le Salut*, p. 312.

13. *Keesing's Contemporary Archives*, October 7–14, 1944, p. 6740.

14. *Le Salut*, pp. 336–344, 403–406.

15. *Keesing's Contemporary Archives*, November 11–18, 1944, pp. 6807–6808.

16. *Le Salut*, pp. 49–54, 350–359; Winston S. Churchill, *Triumph and Tragedy* (Boston, 1953), pp. 249–253. In fact the British tended to favor equipping the French in order to have their support in holding down Germany when the Americans left Europe and pressed this policy on the United States, with little success (*ibid.*, pp. 252–253; *Foreign Relations of the United States: Diplomatic Papers: The Conferences at Malta and Yalta, 1945* [Washington, 1955], pp. 283, 286–287, cited hereafter as *The Conference at Malta and Yalta*).

17. *Le Salut*, pp. 52–54.

18. *L'Unité*, p. 224; *Le Salut*, p. 54. According to Churchill, he stated this choice in much more limited and immediate terms (Churchill, *Closing the Ring*, pp. 628–630), but Eden confirms de Gaulle's version (Eden, *The Reckoning*, p. 526).

19. Great Britain, 5 *Parliamentary Debates* (Commons), CDIV, 1798–1800.

20. Siegfried, *L'Année Politique*, p. 65. The Russian government told the French in September that it had always favored French inclusion but had been opposed by the British and Americans. In November the Russians said that they wanted France to participate in all the work of the commission, while the British wanted the French confined to German questions. *Le Salut*, pp. 314–315, 362, 363.

21. *Journal Officiel de la République Française, Débats de l'Assemblée Consultative Provisoire* (November-December, 1944), pp. 309–333.

22. De Gaulle explicitly referred to rivalry between the United States and the Soviet Union in his talks with Churchill in November. He claims, indeed, to have welcomed it because of the "exceptional chances of action" it offered to France (*Le Salut*, pp. 52, 179).

23. See, for example, Churchill, *Triumph and Tragedy*, pp. 252–253, and *The Conferences at Malta and Yalta*, p. 286.

24. "It was agreed that I would go, with Georges Bidault, to pass a week in the Soviet capital. We could thus mutually inform each other of the manner in which each party conceived the future peace settlement. Perhaps it would be possible to renew in some way the Franco-Russian solidarity which, misunderstood and betrayed as it had often been, was nevertheless in conformity with the natural order of things, as much vis-à-vis the German danger as the attempts of Anglo-Saxon hegemony. I had in mind even the project of a pact, by virtue of which France and Russia would pledge themselves to act in common if one day Germany again became menacing. This dangerous possibility would no doubt not eventuate soon. But the conclusion of a Franco-Russian treaty would aid us immediately to open out into the area of the European settlement" (*Le Salut*, pp. 54–55).

25. *Ibid.*, pp. 60–79, 364–381; *Les Entretiens de Gaulle-Staline* (Paris, 1959), pp. 43–69.

26. Roosevelt informed both Churchill and Stalin that he thought a simple Franco-Soviet pact preferable to a tripartite treaty because the former would appear to be less of a competitor to the proposed world security organization (*The Conferences at Malta and Yalta*, pp. 288–290, 291).

27. He had, he wrote later, no illusions that France could prevent the execution of Soviet designs in Poland, and he foresaw that the British and Americans would not do so either. "But, however slight the influence of France's attitude for the present, it could be important later that she took that attitude at that moment. The future lasts a long time.

Anything can come to pass one day, even this: that an act in conformity with honor and honesty might turn out to be good politics." He did, however, agree to send an officer to Lublin, though without explicit agreement with the committee and on the understanding that this would not be announced until December 28 (*Le Salut*, pp. 73, 77).

28. *Ibid.*, pp. 381–383.

29. *Les Documents politiques, diplomatiques et financiers; Section Diplomatique* (Paris, 1945), pp. 4–5.

30. *Le Monde*, December 19; and *Journal Officiel, Débats* (November-December, 1944), p. 484.

31. *Journal Officiel, Débats* (November-December, 1944), pp. 579–581, 583, 595–596.

CHAPTER IV: War and Victory: January–April, 1945

1. De Gaulle, in his memoirs, reprints the analyses made to him by Mendès-France and Pleven (*Le Salut*, pp. 426–436, 440–448).

2. For the discussion of economic and financial policy in the Consultative Assembly, see *Journal Officiel, Débats* (February-March, 1945), pp. 902–918, 955–967.

3. *Le Salut*, pp. 98–99.

4. On December 27, 1944, de Gaulle said that "many who were serving at Vichy believed that they were serving their country in their own way. It was possible to have different conceptions of serving one's country" (Charles A. Micaud, "The Launching of the Fourth French Republic," *Journal of Politics*, 8 [August 1946], 294).

5. In the debate of March 29–30, Jacques Duclos's intervention was lengthy, but, while mildly critical of Pleven's "timidity," it was notable mainly for an attack on the "trusts"—and for its specific repudiation of the measures proposed by the Socialists (*Journal Officiel, Débats* [March 1945], pp. 956–961).

6. *Le Monde*, April 13, 1945, p. 2.

7. *Ibid.*, December 28, 1944, p. 1; and Siegfried, *L'Année Politique*, p. 99. Churchill was in no hurry to conclude such a treaty (Churchill, *Triumph and Tragedy*, p. 261).

8. De Gaulle, *Le Salut*, pp. 52, 68, 507–508.

9. Charles de Gaulle, *Discours et Messages 1940–1946* (Paris, 1946), p. 546.

10. *Le Monde*, January 12, 1945, p. 1; January 14, p. 2; January 19, p. 1.

11. *Le Salut*, pp. 81, 387–388; *The Conferences at Malta and Yalta*, pp. 16–17, 291. The British, however, favored inviting de Gaulle to participate in at least part of the conference (*ibid.*, pp. 285, 290).

12. *Le Salut*, pp. 81–84, 389–392; and Robert E. Sherwood, *Roosevelt and Hopkins* (revised ed.; New York, 1950), pp. 847–848.

13. *Le Monde*, February 7, 1945, pp. 1–2; *Le Salut*, pp. 387–388.

14. *The Conferences at Malta and Yalta*, p. 499; Edward R. Stettinius, *Roosevelt and the Russians*, ed. Walter Johnson (New York, 1949), pp. 37, 63. The American government had already reached this decision prior to the Malta meeting, and the French had by then approved, in the European Advisory Commission, the substance of the Allied arrangements for the surrender, zonal division, and occupation machinery for Germany—on condition that they be included on an equal basis with the Big Three (*The Conferences at Malta and Yalta*, pp. 297, 293). See also chap. vii below.

15. *The Conferences at Malta and Yalta*, pp. 573, 616–619, 628–630; Stettinius, *Roosevelt and the Russians*, pp. 100–102; James F. Byrnes, *Speaking Frankly* (New York, 1947), p. 24.

16. Sherwood, *Roosevelt and Hopkins*, p. 858.

17. *The Conferences at Malta and Yalta*, pp. 701–702, 706, 710–711, 718–719, 899–900, 908, 913; Sherwood, *Roosevelt and Hopkins*, pp. 858–859; Byrnes, *Speaking Frankly*, p. 25; *Stettinius, Roosevelt and the Russians*, pp. 123–139, 162–171, 262.

18. *The Conferences at Malta and Yalta*, pp. 700–701, 874, 879, 899–900, 908; Stettinius, *Roosevelt and the Russians*, pp. 254, 261. In the discussion of reparations, Stalin, arguing for allocation of the major part to the Big Three, pointed out that France then had eight divisions in the field, while the Yugoslavs had twelve and the Lublin Poles had thirteen (*ibid.*, p. 623).

19. *Le Monde*, March 3, 1945, p. 1.

20. *Ibid.*, February 14, 1945, p. 1.

21. *The Conferences at Malta and Yalta*, p. 948; *Le Salut*, pp. 87, 395–397. De Gaulle wrote in his memoirs that Yalta itself had shown that France could no longer be deprived of her proper rank and role (*ibid.*, p. 90).

22. *Ibid.*, pp. 87–89, 398; Sherwood, *Roosevelt and Hopkins*, pp. 859, 861.

23. *Le Salut*, pp. 87–88.

24. If so, he was soon undeceived, at least in part. He records in his memoirs his bitterness at seeing many politicians—"living in a world rather distant from the motives of higher interest and national dignity which I obeyed"—criticize his action. "The leaders were inclined, in general, to find the foreigner right, provided he was rich and strong, and to blame, on the French side, whatever seemed resolute . . . I had to realize that the idea I had of the rank and rights of France was hardly shared by many of those who guided opinion" (*ibid.*, pp. 89–90).

25. *Ibid.*, pp. 399–400.

26. *Le Monde*, February 21, 1945, p. 1.

27. See below, chap. vii.

28. *Le Salut*, pp. 131–132, 152–153, 155–156, 167–172.

29. *Ibid.*, p. 490.

30. For the French campaign in Germany, see Jean de Lattre de Tassigny, *Histoire de la Première Armée Française* (Paris, 1949), pp. 478–582.

31. Harry S. Truman, *Year of Decisions* (New York, 1955), pp. 237–239; de Lattre, *Histoire de la Première Armée Française*, pp. 567–571. De Gaulle passes over this dispute very tersely in his memoirs, writing only that France evacuated Stuttgart in exchange for taking over Saarbrucken, Trier, Coblenz, and other cities in the French zone (*Le Salut*, p. 207).

32. De Gaulle's dim view of France's relations with the Allies at this time—and probably not only at this time—is reflected in a curious passage of his memoirs (*Le Salut*, pp. 175–176). Writing of the last weeks of the war and of Germany's disintegration in defeat, he says:

> Himmler had delivered to me semi-officially a memorandum which reveals trickery under distress. "It is agreed! You have won!" recognizes the document. "When we know where you started, General de Gaulle, we must tip our hat to you. . . . But now what are you going to do? Put yourself in the hands of the Anglo-Saxons? They will treat you as a satellite and make you lose your honor. Join the Soviets? They will put France under their law and liquidate you yourself. . . . In truth, the only road which can lead your people to grandeur and independence is that of an entente with conquered Germany. Proclaim it at once! Enter into contract without delay with the men in the Reich who still have power and want to lead their country in a new direction. . . . They are ready. They ask it of you. . . . If you overcome the spirit of vengeance, if you grasp the occasion that history offers to you today, you will be the greatest man of all time."
>
> Leaving aside the flattery with which this message, from the brink of the tomb, was decorated on my behalf, *there is, no doubt, some truth in the outline which it sketches*. But the tempter at bay, being what he is, receives no answer from me, nor from the governments of London and Washington. Besides, he has nothing to offer. . . . (Italics added.)

33. George Catroux, *J'ai vu tomber le Rideau de Fer* (Paris, 1952), pp. 41, 50, 63–68.

34. *Le Monde*, February 20, 1945, p. 1; March 22, p. 1; March 25–26, p. 2.

35. *Ibid.*, April 27, 1945, p. 2.

36. *Ibid.*, May 8, 1945, p. 1.

CHAPTER V: The Founding of the United Nations

1. *The Conferences at Cairo and Teheran*, pp. 530–531.
2. The United States apparently understood this phrase to refer to the *de jure* recognition of the French government (*The Conferences at Malta and Yalta*, p. 793).
3. *Le Monde*, December 31, 1944–January 1, 1945, p. 1. De Gaulle and Bidault had stressed this point in their talks with Stalin in December (*Le Salut*, p. 374).
4. *Ibid.*, pp. 400–401; *Le Monde*, February 17, 1945, p. 1.
5. *Documents of the United Nations Conference on International Organization, San Francisco, 1945* (London, 1945), I, 1.
6. Full text of the French proposals in *ibid.*, IV, 522–533.
7. In his press conference of April 21, 1944, at Algiers, de Gaulle had said that the future world security organization must have "tribunal, procedure and secular arm" (*L'Unité*, p. 629).
8. *Documents of the United Nations Conference*, III, chap. viii, sec. C, 2.
9. *Le Monde*, February 11–12, 1945, p. 1; March 7, 1945, p. 1.
10. *Journal Officiel, Débats* (March, 1945), pp. 772–786.
11. *Le Monde*, March 31, 1945, p. 8. A complete list of the French delegation is in *Documents of the United Nations Conference*, I, 24–26.
12. *Le Monde*, March 14, 1945, p. 1.
13. *Ibid.*, May 4, 1945, p. 1.
14. *Ibid.*
15. *Documents of the United Nations Conference*, I, 471–478.
16. *Ibid.*, XI, 294.
17. This was included in Article 23 of the United Nations Charter that provided that: "The General Assembly shall elect six other Members of the United Nations to be non-permanent members of the Security Council, due regard being specially paid, in the first instance to the contribution of Members of the United Nations to the maintenance of international peace and security and to the other purposes of the Organization, and also to equitable geographical distribution."
18. *Documents of the United Nations Conference*, I, 667–670.
19. *Le Monde*, June 27, 1945, p. 1.
20. *Ibid.*, June 28, 1945, pp. 1, 8; Jacques Gascuel, "La Charte des Nations Unies," *Revue Politique et Parlementaire*, 185 (October, 1945), 114–139.
21. *Le Salut*, p. 201.
22. *Le Monde*, May 11, 1945, p. 1.
23. Jean Chevalier, "La Conférence de San-Francisco," *Esprit*, 13 (June 1, 1945), 139–148; Jean-Jacques Mayoux, "San-Francisco, Histoire et Leçons d'une Conférence," *Politique Étrangère*, 10 (October, 1945), 141–160.

CHAPTER VI: Anglo-French Relations and the Crisis
in the Levant

1. See Isaac Lipschits, *La Politique de la France au Levant, 1939–1941* (Paris, 1963), which gives a detailed account of Vichy rule in Syria and Lebanon and of the British-Free French takeover; see also *L'Appel*, pp. 145–180.

2. *L'Unité*, p. 22.

3. Lipschits, *La Politique de la France au Levant*, pp. 157–169, 220–225.

4. Georges Catroux, *Dans La Bataille de Mediterranée* (Paris, 1949), p. 137.

5. *Ibid.*, p. 171; *L'Appel*, pp. 455–456.

6. *Ibid.*, p. 459.

7. Churchill said that "in so far as any European countries have influence in Syria, that of France will be preeminent," but he added that "Syria shall be handed back to the Syrians, who will assume at the earliest possible moment their independent sovereign rights" and "there is no question of France maintaining the same position which she exercised in Syria before the war . . ." (5 *Parliamentary Debates* [Commons], CCCLXXIV, 76). In a telegram of May 3 to his officials in London de Gaulle raised the juridical point whether a unilateral termination of the mandates was consistent with obligations to the League of Nations (more was to be heard of this later) and argued that "it is impossible in the midst of battle to overthrow the nature of authority" in the Levant. His insistence on "a transition in the transmission of powers" confirms that he did not view Catroux's proclamation of Syrian and Lebanese independence as terminating French control of those countries (*L'Appel*, pp. 412–413, 430–431).

8. *Ibid.*, pp. 201–202.

9. There would be no serious divergence between France and the two states, said *Le Monde* in its issue dated January 31, 1945, "if third parties do not come to envenom things wantonly" (p. 1). Some British observers conceded the accuracy of this French judgment ("Middle Eastern Dilemma," *The Economist*, 148 [February 17, 1945], 205–206). The British government consistently denied such allegations.

10. *Le Monde*, January 26, 1945, pp. 1–2.

11. *Ibid.*, February 3, 1945, p. 4.

12. *Ibid.*, February 10, 1945, p. 2; February 11–12, p. 1. Churchill claimed in his memoirs (*Triumph and Tragedy*, p. 562) and in the House of Commons on June 5 (5 *Parliamentary Debates* [Commons], CDXII, 689) that he persuaded Syria and Lebanon to pursue these negotiations.

13. *Ibid.*, CDVIII, 1290. "Finally, at the market of Yalta, Churchill had obtained from Roosevelt and Stalin a free hand at Damascus and

Beyrouth" (*Le Salut*, p. 185).

14. On June 15, Bidault stated in the Consultative Assembly that, though General Catroux had only promised rather than proclaimed the independence of Syria and Lebanon on June 8, 1941, and that, therefore, the mandates continued to exist legally, France did not hold this technical position but recognized the independence of the states by securing their invitation to the San Francisco conference (*Journal Officiel, Débats*, June 1945, p. 1114).

15. *Le Salut*, pp. 185, 512–513.

16. *Le Monde*, May 25, 1945, p. 1.

17. *Ibid.*, May 30, 1945, p. 4.

18. *Le Salut*, p. 186.

19. *Le Monde*, May 23, 1945, p. 1.

20. *Le Salut*, pp. 186–187, 510–513. For Churchill's account of the crisis, see Churchill, *Triumph and Tragedy*, pp. 561–566, and his remarks in the House of Commons on June 5, in 5 *Parliamentary Debates* [Commons], CDXI, 689–695.

21. See Churchill's account in the House of Commons on June 5, cited above, and also the remarks of Anthony Eden, cols. 40–41, 193–194, 320–322, 378–380, 491.

22. This assertion was made by de Gaulle in his press conference on June 2, and was repeated by Bidault to the cabinet on June 5. General Beynet, on June 10, said that the situation in Syria had been re-established by May 31. General Oliva Roget, on June 7, said that Damascus was securely in French control by June 1. On June 12, Sir Edward Grigg, the British minister resident in the Middle East, specifically denied that order had been restored before the British intervened, asserting that fighting continued throughout the night of May 31. Churchill on June 5 also said that fighting was still in progress on the morning of May 31. (*Le Monde*, June 15, 1945, pp. 3–4; June 6, p. 4; June 9, p. 1; June 12, p. 1; June 13, p. 1.)

23. *Ibid.*, June 2, 1945, p. 1.

24. *Le Salut*, pp. 190–191.

25. French communiqué of June 1 and de Gaulle's press conference of June 2 in *Le Monde*, June 3–4, 1945, p. 1, and June 5, pp. 3–4.

26. *Ibid.*, June 2, 1945, p. 1; June 3–4, p. 1; *Le Salut*, pp. 517–518; Truman, *Year of Decisions*, p. 243; *Foreign Relations of the United States: Diplomatic Papers: The Conference of Berlin (The Potsdam Conference), 1945* (2 vols.; Washington, 1960), I, 959 (cited hereafter as *The Conference of Berlin*).

27. *Le Salut*, p. 191; *Le Monde*, June 2, 1945, pp. 1, 4. De Gaulle did not answer this second British note (*Le Salut*, p. 194).

28. *Le Monde*, June 2, 1945, p. 1.

29. *Ibid.*, June 5, 1945, pp. 3–4.

30. *Le Salut*, p. 198.

31. *Le Monde,* June 13, 1945, p. 1.
32. *Journal Officiel, Débats,* June 1945, pp. 1114–1130, 1134–1150.
33. *Le Monde,* June 27, 1945, p. 1.
34. *Ibid.,* July 5, 1945, p. 4, and July 11, p. 1.
35. *Ibid.,* July 10, 1945, p. 1.
36. *Ibid.,* July 26, 1945, p. 4.
37. *The Conference of Berlin,* II, 246–247, 306–308, 314–316, 317–319, 1399–1400.
38. *Le Salut,* p. 194.

CHAPTER VII: Germany and the Potsdam Conference

1. For the work of the European Advisory Commission, see Philip E. Mosely, "The Occupation of Germany: New Light on How the Zones Were Drawn," *Foreign Affairs,* 28 (July 1950), 580–604.
2. *Selected Documents on Germany and the Question of Berlin 1944–1961,* Command 1552 (London, 1961), pp. 27–33.
3. Feis, *Churchill, Roosevelt, Stalin,* pp. 221–223; *The Conferences at Cairo and Teheran,* pp. 594–595, 600–604.
4. The failure of the three-power committee on German dismemberment to accomplish anything removed one of the most dangerous threats to French participation in the German settlement made at the Yalta conference. It became clear after the committee's first meeting on March 7 that the three governments were not as zealous as they had seemed to be at Yalta to go ahead with plans for dismembering Germany. On March 26 the Russians made known that they considered dismemberment only one of several possible policies that might be applied to Germany. The American government also instructed Ambassador Winant to adopt an attitude of "study and postponement of final decision." On May 8 Stalin declared that the Soviet Union "does not intend to dismember or destroy Germany." The Yalta decision in principle to proceed with dismemberment had thus been dropped by the time of the German surrender. The French unofficially learned of the existence of the secret committee on April 11 and were assured by the American government that it was pressing Moscow to admit France as a member. The Russians never agreed and France never joined the committee, but by then the matter was of no importance. For a detailed account of this subject, see Philip E. Mosely, "Dismemberment of Germany," *Foreign Affairs,* 28 (April 1950), 486–498.
5. *Conference of Berlin,* I, 592; *Le Salut,* pp. 336–344. The idea was an old one with him. In a telegram of August 25, 1941, to his associates in London, de Gaulle urged "the greatest prudence" in regard to the article of the Atlantic Charter by which the signatories renounced territorial aggrandizements: "Without speaking of the Rhine at present, we must

keep (*nous ménager*) the possibility of extending our position in the Rhineland in the event of a collapse of the Reich. Because, in this case, being given the material and moral destruction [which will have] begun in the Rhineland, unforeseen things might happen" (*L'Appel*, p. 478). See also de Gaulle, *L'Unité*, p. 618. According to his memoirs, de Gaulle wished to dissolve the central German state: if "each of the states belonging to the German body could exist by itself, govern itself as it chose, take care of its own interests, there would be a good chance that the federal grouping might not try to subjugate its neighbors" (*Le Salut*, pp. 46–47).

6. *Keesing's Contemporary Archives*, November 11–18, 1944, pp. 6807–6808.

7. *Le Salut*, pp. 68, 365, 377.

8. Stalin, on March 20, 1945, listened to General Catroux's presentation of French plans for Germany but said only that the U.S.S.R. was keeping a free hand on the subject (Catroux, *J'ai vu tomber le Rideau de Fer*, pp. 66–67).

9. *Le Monde*, January 26, 1945, pp. 1–2.

10. *Ibid.*, February 2, 1945, p. 1; February 4–5, 1945, p. 1.

11. *Ibid.*, February 7, 1945, pp. 1–2.

12. *The Conferences at Malta and Yalta*, pp. 299–300; Stettinius, *Roosevelt and the Russians*, p. 56; Sherwood, *Roosevelt and Hopkins*, pp. 847–848; *Le Salut*, pp. 389–392.

13. *Le Monde*, February 18–19, 1945, p. 2.

14. *The Conference of Berlin*, I, 592–595; Truman, *Year of Decisions*, p. 102.

15. *Selected Documents on Germany*, pp. 35–36.

16. Beate Ruhm von Oppen (ed.), *Documents on Germany under Occupation, 1945–1954* (London, 1955), pp. 29–37.

17. *Le Salut*, pp. 503–504.

18. These negotiations are discussed in Mosely, "The Occupation of Germany," 599–602. For a description of the French zone, see F. Roy Willis, *The French in Germany, 1945–1949* (Stanford, California, 1962), pp. 96–108.

19. *Le Monde*, July 4, 1945, p. 1; July 7, 1945, p. 1; July 8–9, 1945, p. 2. The European Advisory Commission was not able formally to assign a zone to France until July 26. For the text of the agreement establishing the French zones in Germany and Berlin, see *Selected Documents on Germany*, pp. 45–48. The delay arose because the Russians, citing the Yalta precedent for the establishment of the French occupation zone entirely out of the territory assigned previously to the United States and Great Britain, insisted that the same procedure be followed in Berlin. The Americans and British finally yielded (*Conference of Berlin*, I, 597–604; II, 1001–1006). Mosely suggests that they did so because, by late July, the Russians had made clear that the western occu-

pants would have to supply their own zones in Berlin with food and fuel. They therefore did not want more of Berlin on their hands (Mosely, "The Occupation of Germany," 601–602). The first meeting of the Control Council was on July 30. A full account of the organization and problems of the French occupation will be found in Willis, *The French in Germany*.

20. *The Conference of Berlin*, I, 512, 517.

21. Stalin told Hopkins that the Western attempt to include France on the Reparations Commission was an insult and an attempt to humiliate the Soviet Union (*ibid.*, pp. 32, 36; Byrnes, *Speaking Frankly*, p. 61).

22. Catroux, *J'ai vu tomber le Rideau de Fer*, pp. 50, 65–66.

23. *Le Monde*, July 1–2, 1945, p. 1; July 7, 1945, p. 1.

24. One attempt was made during Bidault's visit to Washington in mid-May; a second was Ambassador Bonnet's demarche to the State Department on June 25 (*The Conference of Berlin*, I, 128–129). Parallel representations were probably made to the other two powers. De Gaulle, however, claims in his memoirs that he had little reason to go to Potsdam because the loss of Eastern Europe to the Soviet Union, which he would have fought at Teheran and Yalta, was by then irreversible (*Le Salut*, pp. 202–203). But, as de Gaulle knew, much business of greater importance to France than the Balkans would be transacted at Potsdam.

25. See, for example, Churchill's conversation with Davies, *The Conference of Berlin*, I, 64–78.

26. Catroux, if not his government also, blamed the Russians for France's exclusion. Catroux, *J'ai vu tomber le Rideau de Fer*, pp. 92–93, 97–98.

27. *Le Salut*, pp. 180–184; Truman, *Year of Decisions*, pp. 15, 239–242; Herbert Feis, *Between War and Peace: The Potsdam Conference* (Princeton, 1960), pp. 128–132.

28. Truman, *Year of Decisions*, p. 242.

29. *Ibid.*, pp. 240–241.

30. *The Conference of Berlin*, I, 16–18.

31. *Le Monde*, May 26, 1945, p. 4.

32. *The Conference of Berlin*, I, 147–148.

33. *Ibid.*, I, 285, 295–296.

34. *Ibid.*, II, 52–59, 66–70, 101–102, 158, 167, 281, 612–613, 614, 615; Byrnes, *Speaking Frankly*, pp. 69–72.

35. *The Conference of Berlin*, II, 510–541.

36. *Ibid.*, I, 50; II, 183–184, 482, 521–522, 535–536, 569–570, 580, 1000–1001, 1503–1504.

37. *Le Monde*, August 4, 1945, p. 1.

38. *The Conference of Berlin*, II, 1549–1550; *Le Monde*, August 5–6, 1945, p. 3.

39. *The Conference of Berlin*, II, 1543–1547.

40. *Documents Français Relatifs à l'Allemagne* (Paris, 1947), pp. 7–11; *The Conference of Berlin*, II, 1551–1555.

41. Bidault told Ambassador Caffery that the French "were much concerned about the article referring to the possibility of setting up a central government for Germany for they take it to mean that it is the intention of the Soviet government to Sovietize all Germany as rapidly as they can do so" (*ibid.*, II, 1548–1549). But the French certainly had other objections as well, notably to the implicit acceptance of existing German frontiers (after amputation in the east) as definitive.

CHAPTER VIII: French Diplomacy after Potsdam

1. *The Conference of Berlin*, II, 129; Truman, *Year of Decisions*, pp. 359, 379.

2. *Le Salut*, pp. 209–214, 550–555.

3. *The Conference of Berlin*, II, 1557–1564.

4. *Le Monde*, August 26–27, 1945, p. 4; August 28, 1945, p. 4.

5. Subsequent to the establishment of the French protectorate over most of Morocco in 1912, the powers, by a series of agreements (treaty of November 27, 1912; convention of December 18, 1923, as modified in 1924, 1928, and 1935) set up an international administration for the city and environs of Tangier. The area was governed by (1) a representative of the Sultan of Morocco, the Mendoub, who directly administered the native population, presided over the Legislative Assembly, and promulgated the laws voted by it and approved by the president of the Control Committee; (2) a Legislative Assembly, consisting of four Frenchmen, four Spaniards, three British subjects, three Italians (after 1928), one Belgian, one Dutchman, and one Portuguese, named by their respective consuls in Tangier (an American seat was also established but never filled), and six Moslems and three Jews named by the Mendoub; (3) a Control Committee, consisting of the consuls of the signatories of the Act of Algeciras of 1906. The actual administration of the territory was carried on by four foreign officers: a French president, a Spaniard charged with health and public assistance, a British director of finance, and an Italian director of justice. The gendarmerie was commanded by a Spaniard.

6. *Le Monde*, June 14, 1945, p. 1.

7. *The Conference of Berlin*, I, 988–993, 1008; II, 285–286, 1411, 1496; *Le Monde*, July 13, 1945, p. 1.

8. *Le Monde*, August 25, 1945, p. 1.

9. *Ibid.*, September 6, 1945, p. 1; October 13, 1945, p. 1.

10. "The French Reaction," *The Economist*, 149 (August 25, 1945), 256; "Seeking Allies for France," *ibid.*, (September 1, 1945), 298.

11. *Le Monde*, September 6, 1945, p. 8.

12. *The Times* (London), September 10, 1945, p. 4.

13. *Le Salut*, pp. 369–370.

14. *Ibid.*, pp. 179–180.

15. On September 19 de Gaulle tried out this idea on T. V. Soong. After pointing out that the Soviet Union and the United States were both massive powers, he developed the advantages of a Western European grouping—including also most of Africa—especially in the economic sphere (*ibid.*, pp. 566–567).

16. *Le Monde*, July 31, 1945, pp. 1–2.

17. *Ibid.*, September 8, 1945, p. 1.

18. *Le Salut*, pp. 219–221; *Le Monde*, October 4, 1945, pp. 1, 8; October 6, p. 1; October 7–8, p. 1.

19. On February 24, 1944, de Gaulle had written to his foreign minister, René Massigli, of a "strategic and economic federation" among France, Belgium, the Netherlands, Luxembourg and, perhaps, Great Britain, with which a detached Rhineland might be linked (*L'Unité*, p. 618).

20. *Le Salut*, p. 222.

21. *Le Monde*, October 13, 1945, p. 1.

22. *Ibid.*, October 14–15, 1945, p. 3.

23. The French may have foreseen this Soviet hostility to the "Western bloc" and tried to disarm it in advance. An editorial appearing in *Le Monde* of July 1–2, 1945, on the occasion of the cession by Czechoslovakia to the U.S.S.R. of the Sub-Carpathian Ukraine praised the emergence of an "Eastern bloc" in these terms:

> A Slavic bloc of imposing dimensions is being formed under our eyes. Russia, the Ukraine, White Russia, Poland, Czechoslovakia, the Slavs of the Balkans, are henceforth more or less grouped under the aegis of Moscow.
>
> France enjoys much active sympathy among the Slavic peoples. . . . Moreover, no territorial or other difference opposes her to the Slavic world.
>
> At this moment when the Greater Ukraine is being formed, she salutes this historic event without reservation.
>
> As the friend of all the Slavs, she can only rejoice at their fraternal union.

This may, of course, have been no more than an attempt to disassociate France from the objections which the United States and Great Britain were formulating against Soviet policy in Eastern Europe and thereby to win greater support for French claims and policies than had been forthcoming. It may also be, however, that this editorial was a premonitory hint that the policy of the "Western bloc" was being thought about in Paris and that those doing the thinking hoped to head off Soviet (and French Communist) objections by comparing it to the U.S.S.R.'s own policies in the East.

24. *Documents Français*, pp. 13–15.

25. The proposed rectifications included notably the annexation of the towns of Brigue and Tende and of a small area in the region of Bardonnechia to improve the military defense of the valleys of Maurienne and Briancon and to provide the population of the latter city with an outlet to the Paris-Modane-Turin railroad (*Le Monde*, September 15, 1945, p. 8).

26. The French also wanted the restoration by Italy of a naval tonnage equivalent to that seized by her in December, 1942, at Toulon and Bizerte; limitation on the level of Italy's military establishment; and the complete demilitarization of Tripoli, Sardinia, Pantalleria, Lampadusa, and Piedmont and the Ligurian coast (*ibid*).

27. In his memoirs de Gaulle frequently castigates the "Anglo-Saxons" for having sacrificed Eastern Europe to the Soviet Union at Teheran, Yalta, and Potsdam (*Le Salut*, p. 217). But he did not urge this against the Soviet Union in 1945.

28. On August 24, Molotov had told Catroux that he accepted this formula (Catroux, *J'ai vu tomber le Rideau de Fer*, p. 107).

29. *Le Monde*, September 18, 1945, p. 4.

30. *Ibid.*, September 19, 1945, p. 1.

31. Byrnes, *Speaking Frankly*, p. 102.

32. Catroux, *J'ai vu tomber le Rideau de Fer*, pp. 113–116.

33. Byrnes, *Speaking Frankly*, p. 103.

34. *Le Monde*, September 25, 1945, p. 8; September 26, 1945, pp. 1, 4.

35. Truman, *Year of Decisions*, pp. 516–518; Byrnes, *Speaking Frankly*, p. 103.

36. Catroux, *J'ai vu tomber le Rideau de Fer*, pp. 120–122.

37. Byrnes, *Speaking Frankly*, p. 103.

38. *Department of State Bulletin*, 13 (October 7, 1945), 513; *Le Monde*, October 5, 1945, p. 1.

39. *Le Monde*, October 5, 1945, p. 1.

40. General Catroux, noting the violent hostility of the Soviet press during mid-September not only to the policy of a "Western bloc" but also to de Gaulle's government as such, believed that this policy triggered the Soviet action at London (Catroux, *J'ai vu tomber le Rideau de Fer*, pp. 109–111).

CHAPTER IX: Challenge and Reprieve at Home: The Political Crisis of November, 1945

1. *Le Salut*, pp. 255–257; Siegfried, *L'Année Politique*, pp. 248–251.

2. *Le Monde*, July 11, 1945, pp. 1–2.

3. See de Gaulle's speech of September 4, 1945 (*Le Salut*, pp. 599–602).

4. *L'Appel*, pp. 66–67.
5. *Le Salut*, p. 587.
6. Siegfried, *L'Année Politique*, p. 254.
7. *Ibid.*, p. 493.
8. For the November political crisis, see Elgey, *La République des Illusions*, pp. 60–73.
9. *Le Monde*, November 6, 1945, p. 3. In this, of course, the Communist Party shared the view of the Soviet government, which strongly opposed de Gaulle's initiatives toward a regrouping of Western Europe.
10. *Ibid.*, November 8, 1945, p. 4.
11. *Ibid.*, November 6, 1945, p. 3.
12. *Ibid.*, November 14, 1945, p. 1.
13. For his account of the crisis, see *Le Salut*, pp. 273–276.
14. *Le Monde*, November 17, 1945, p. 1.
15. *Ibid.*, p. 3.
16. *Le Salut*, pp. 627–628.
17. *Journal Officiel, Débats*, November 19, 1945, pp. 72–80.
18. *Le Monde*, November 22, 1945, p. 1. The ministers of state were assigned these functions at the first cabinet meeting: Auriol, relations with the assembly; Gay, German and Austrian affairs; Jacquinot, North Africa and Alsace-Lorraine; Thorez, administrative reform (*ibid.*, November 24, 1945, p. 3).

CHAPTER X: France and the Great Powers after London

1. *Le Monde*, October 14–15, 1945, p. 3.
2. *Ibid.*, November 17, 1945, p. 1.
3. *Journal Officiel, Débats, Assemblée Nationale Constituante*, November 23, 1945, p. 120.
4. *Le Monde*, November 25–26, 1945, p. 1.
5. Byrnes, *Speaking Frankly*, p. 109.
6. *Le Monde*, December 9–10, 1945, pp. 1, 4.
7. Catroux, *J'ai vu tomber le Rideau de Fer*, pp. 136, 139; *Le Monde*, December 11, 1945, p. 1.
8. Catroux, *J'ai vu tomber le Rideau de Fer*, pp. 147–149.
9. *Le Monde*, December 12, 1945, p. 1.
10. Byrnes, *Speaking Frankly*, pp. 111–115; Catroux, *J'ai vu tomber le Rideau de Fer*, pp. 131–135.
11. *Department of State Bulletin*, 13 (December 30, 1945), 1027–1028.
12. *Le Monde*, December 26, 1945, p. 1.
13. *Ibid.*, January 1, 1946, p. 1.
14. Byrnes, *Speaking Frankly*, pp. 115–122.
15. *Department of State Bulletin*, 13 (December 30, 1945), 1027–1032.
16. *Le Monde*, December 30–31, 1945, p. 1.

17. Bidault's support for a more conciliatory tone toward the Allies appears to have been the first occasion on which he openly disagreed with de Gaulle on a major matter of foreign policy, or at least the first that was recorded. Was he preparing for the future? But some considered that this episode was only the latest of a series and spoke of de Gaulle's "chronic disagreement with Georges Bidault on the tone to take in relations with the Big Three" (François Goguel, "Le Véritable Dilemme," *Esprit*, 14 (February 1, 1946), 332–336). See also, above, chap. iii, n. 8.

18. The note of the three powers had been communicated to the French government by the American ambassador in the name of Secretary Byrnes, who was then acting as president of the conference.

19. *Le Monde*, January 6–7, 1946, p. 1.

20. *Ibid.*, January 8, 1946, p. 1.

21. *Ibid.*, January 16, 1946, p. 1; January 19, 1946, p. 1.

22. *Journal Officiel, Débats, Assemblée Nationale Constituante*, January 15–17, 1946, pp. 2–18, 33–64, 73–107.

23. The portion of the debate dealing with Germany is discussed in chap. xi.

CHAPTER XI: Germany after Potsdam

1. Ruhm von Oppen, *Documents on Germany under Occupation*, pp. 59–66.

2. *Le Monde*, September 4, 1945, p. 1.

3. Byrnes, *Speaking Frankly*, p. 170; see also, above, chap. vii, n. 41.

4. Catroux, *J'ai vu tomber le Rideau de Fer*, p. 106.

5. *Documents français*, pp. 13–15.

6. Catroux, *J'ai vu tomber le Rideau de Fer*, pp. 120–122; *Department of State Bulletin*, 13 (October 14, 1945), 566–567; *Le Monde*, September 21, 1945, p. 4; and Byrnes, *Speaking Frankly*, p. 170.

7. *Le Monde*, October 4, 1945, p. 1; October 5, 1945, p. 1.

8. *Ibid.*, September 27, 1945, p. 2; September 29, 1945, p. 1.

9. *Ibid.*, October 2, 1945, pp. 1–2.

10. Lucius D. Clay, *Decision in Germany* (New York, 1950), p. 107; Ruhm von Oppen, *Documents on Germany under Occupation*, pp. 68–82, 83–86, 88–92, 97–107.

11. Clay, *Decision in Germany*, pp. 109–111.

12. *Documents français*, p. 16.

13. *Le Monde*, October 17, 1945, p. 1.

14. *Ibid.*, October 30, 1945, p. 1.

15. *Ibid.*, November 23, 1945, p. 1.

16. Catroux, *J'ai vu tomber le Rideau de Fer*, pp. 139–144.

17. *New York Times*, December 6, 1945, pp. 1, 5.

18. *The Times* (London), December 10, 1945, p. 2.
19. *Le Monde*, December 21, 1945, p. 1; December 22, 1945, p. 1.
20. See chap. x, n. 22.
21. In his press conference on October 12, de Gaulle had been specifically asked his view on the Saar. His answer dealt only with the general problems of the Rhineland and the Ruhr, without direct reference to the Saar itself (*Le Monde*, October 14-15, 1945, p. 3).

CHAPTER XII: The End of the de Gaulle Government

1. Siegfried, *L'Année Politique*, pp. 360-365.
2. *Ibid.*, pp. 373-380, 385-397.
3. *Le Salut*, pp. 278-280; *Le Monde*, January 3, 1946, pp. 1, 3; Raoul Dumaine, "Le Mois Parlementaire," *Le Monde Français*, 2 (February 1946), 316-319; Elgey, *La République des Illusions*, pp. 77-81.
4. *Le Monde*, January 15, 1946, p. 3. For a complete account of the economic and fiscal crisis which the de Gaulle government bequeathed to its successor, see the investiture speech of the next president, Félix Gouin, in *Journal Officiel, Débats, Assemblée Nationale Constituante*, January 29, 1946, pp. 107-111.
5. *Le Monde*, January 20-21, 1946, p. 4.
6. *Ibid.*, January 22, 1946, p. 1.
7. *Le Salut*, p. 285.
8. *Le Salut*, pp. 645-646.
9. *Le Salut*, pp. 273, 280-281.
10. *Le Monde*, January 11, 1946, p. 2.
11. He states in his memoirs that he fixed the date of his resignation a week in advance and informed certain ministers and others in the interval (*Le Salut*, p. 284). See also Elgey, *La République des Illusions*, pp. 81-94.

CHAPTER XIII: The Balance Sheet and Legacy of de Gaulle's Foreign Policy

1. Drieu La Rochelle, quoted in Raymond Aron, *L'Âge des Empires et l'Avenir de la France* (Paris, 1945), pp. 237-238.

INDEX